Persimmon Wind

Persimmon Wind

Persimmon Wind

A Martial Artist's Journey in Japan

Dave Lowry

Koryu Books
Berkeley Heights, New Jersey

Published by Koryu Books
P.O. Box 86
Berkeley Heights, NJ 07922-0086
http://koryu.com/
fax: 1-212-208-4366; toll-free tel: 1-888-665-6798

First hardcover edition 2005, newly edited and corrected.
First published in 1998 by Tuttle Publishing.

Book and jacket design by Koryu Books.
Frontispiece calligraphy by the author.
Printed in the United States of America.

Publisher's Cataloging-in-Publication Data

Lowry, Dave, 1956–
    Persimmon Wind / by Dave Lowry. — New ed.
    p. cm.
    ISBN-13 978-1-890536-10-7
    ISBN-10 1-890536-10-5
    1. Martial Arts. 2. Non-fiction. 3. Philosophy.
1. Title.
HD38.2.S353 2005   658.4'09—dc22
                              LCCN 2005925307

This is for the late
Masao Fujiwara

I knew it was coming—
and yet the melancholy
I was prepared for
still cuts to my heart
when I hear the breath of autumn's wind.

> *Keiun (ca. 1330–70)*

Contents

Foreword

I've known Dave Lowry for over ten years now and yet it was only last year, when he came to Hawaii, that we finally met. Odd?

Perhaps. Our friendship, which has deepened and ripened over the years, has been long distance, and we have gleaned each other's thoughts through long rambling letters, he and I. And I have come to respect Dave as a martial artist and as a human being on a very straight and humble path.

We first met when he wrote me after an article of mine had appeared in a martial arts publication. He had a host of questions for me. Those questions were about the martial arts I was studying at that time, but they also told me a lot about Dave. Obviously, he knew more of martial arts—in particular the *koryu* (older martial arts schools of Japan created before 1860)—than the average American *budoka*.

I answered his questions as best I could and, as part of my reply, had questions of my own. Yes, I had read his excellent book, *Autumn Lightning,* and marveled at his ability to capture the mood and spirit of the koryu. As a fellow writer, I was also impressed by his writing. He had a definite and sensitive style, a way of setting prose down that ranked him with the best authors writing about the contemporary Asian-American experience. Who was this guy? How did a haole from the Midwest learn so much about older Japanese traditions? Where did he develop a knowledge of customs, rituals, and meanings that most Japanese-Americans (and most young native Japanese, I should add), caught between two very different cultures, have long since lost?

Thus developed a long and mutually rewarding correspondence. Each letter between us was full of questions. In performing a *temae* (tea ceremony form), Dave noticed something about a certain movement. Would I clarify its meaning? Certainly. But by the way, I would write back, what did his style of swordsmanship, the Shinkage-ryu, say about the meaning of the character of *kage* in their name, a term laden with philosophical implications for all martial artists?

We wrote, and gradually and inevitably there crept into our correspondence details about our personal lives and our opinions about things other than the martial arts. He avidly followed my lengthy stay in Japan. We wrote to each other not only of the bonding experiences of budo, but also of the universal human experiences of our love, our disappointments, joys, triumphs, and happiness.

The everyday world is always with each of us. We have to pay our bills, maintain our family ties, bond with friends and lovers, get up and go to work. Yet in the cracks and crannies of our lives are the things that make life worthwhile: the satori-like enlightenment one is hit with looking at a newborn baby, the sudden and unexpected brush with a spiritual "otherness" while wielding a brush or a *bokken* during practice, the taste of a bitter cup of tea whisked by a beautiful woman. Those moments lead us along the path, the *michi* or *do* of becoming a human being. Each of us, in our own way, walks a path. Some of us are farther along than others, some of us have stumbled and lost our way in the forest. Some have taken a simple and straightforward path, others have to take a long, grueling, and little-traveled road.

Dave has taken the particularly difficult path to enlightenment of the *bugeisha*, the martial artist. Many others stumble along this way because they are cognizant only of the *bu* element of the word "bugeisha." They know their study is of the martial, the arts of war and conflict. But a true bugeisha is also a person (*sha*) trying to transform the arts of battle (bu) into a study of beauty and universal truths, or *gei*. Very few martial artists, even in Japan, grow mature enough at such an early age to attain this realization. The flash and color of tournaments, of fleeting notoriety, of stardom and glamour, capture them and lead them too far astray.

And yet, one of the deepest techniques of the koryu was not of winning a tournament or a battle. Passed along from master to disciple was the short phrase: *setsuninto, katsujinken*. "A sword that kills, a sword that gives life." Dave was confronted with this Zen-like koan because centuries ago, a master of the Yagyu Shinkage-ryu, Yagyu Tajima-no-Kami Munenori, wanted to know the great Zen master Takuan's opinion about the true goal of martial arts.

A small-minded martial artist, even if his technique was excellent, would only be aware of the martial arts as a tool for personal gain. The *bugei*, the warrior arts, would then be only a sword that kills other people, a mere method for destruction. And if he saw beyond that, this martial artist would only perceive these arts as a vehicle for petty fame and ego-satisfaction — or worse, for unscrupulously making ill-gotten money.

The true bugeisha knew the real meaning of setsuninto, katsujinken. The sword that kills does not destroy other human beings. It is the sword of justice, the sword of light. The sword slays the darkness of our souls, giving new life to the bugeisha. How is this sword tempered, honed, and wielded? By unceasing diligence, in the practice hall and in one's daily life — most especially in one's daily life, for it is there that the real battles of the soul are fought, and defeat and victory are decided. The martial arts then become an integral part of the bugeisha's life, as he opens himself up to all that the world and society throws at him.

In *Autumn Lightning*, Dave took us on his first steps along his own path of the bugeisha. In this present book, he leads on from where the first account ends, taking us further along his path to Japan, to a meeting with his martial arts teacher, and on a journey into the depths of his spirit. It is a beautiful account, one that fulfills the promise of his first book and one that is, in the end, bittersweet, *sabishii*. The path of the bugeisha is not only a rocky road, it is a lonely one. A teacher may set you on the path. But the bugeisha must walk the path, dependent only on himself and the mercy of God. This is Dave's own account of his continuing growth as he walks along the way of the bugeisha, which is but another trail that leads to becoming a true human being. I wrote that I know Dave Lowry very well, in spite of having only recently met him in person. But like you, the reader, I feel that through his writings, I have been lucky enough to have touched a bit of his spirit.

Wayne Muromoto
Honolulu, Hawaii, 1998

Acknowledgments

The list of individuals who gave me their friendship and assistance, in Japan and later, in writing this would be daunting to number. I can only hope they will know how grateful I am to them all. I would be remiss in not extending a special thanks to some. To the Yoshikawas in Tokyo. In Suwa, to all the Fujiwara and Nagata: Etsuji and Michiko, Mitsuo, Hiromi, Akiko, and Tomoko. To Mayor Kasahara there, and Tsuchida-san, Aruga-san, and Chino-san. To all the folks at the seventh bend in the road below Takamado-san who tolerated me so graciously. To Wayne Muromoto, colleague and *brah*. And as always, to my *kanai*.

To all of them, *kore wa kata jikinai yo*.

1
Nara... Rain

*T*he mists of early October come lightly onto Nara at night. They fall so finely in this southern part of the main island of Japan that they seem to hang like a vapor, nearly weightless in the soft air. The mists of Nara in autumn are more like a fog than a rain proper. Still, it was precipitation, and wet and real enough to dampen my hair and my cotton shirt. The drizzle beaded on the waterproofed fabric of my backpack and ran off in thin rivulets that dripped in a nearly steady stream whenever I stood motionless for a moment or two. I half-hoped the soaking I was receiving might make of me a more pathetic and pitiable sight. I was, after all, committing a crime. The premises were closed to visitors at that hour. If I was apprehended, my plan was to plead ignorance and trust to a thoroughly forlorn appearance to solicit some mercy.

It was already dark, early in the evening.

According to the city map I had of Nara, I could cut off at least three blocks of my hike from the train station to the inn where I had a room reserved. All I had to do was to cross the grounds of a temple instead of following the street and taking the long way around them. So rather than following the directions the innkeeper had given me over the phone when I called him at the station, I ducked through a narrow passage in the head-high stone wall I'd been walking beside and sneaked into the deserted precincts of Kofukuji Temple. Against a wet background of night sky, the sharp rectangular shapes of the temple buildings loomed, their wide batwing roofs stretched out protectively. My footsteps crunched on the crushed gravel path.

I was trespassing, but I rationalized that this, after all, was not the first intrusion into these grounds. In the twelfth century, during the epic struggles between the great families of the Taira and Minamoto, the main temple of Kofukuji and its compound had all been put to the torch, a victim of the first of many civil wars to control Japan. The crackling flames and spark showers that had once illuminated the night at Kofukuji were long gone, cold and quenched, and where the main hall of the temple once stood, its recreation had been erected. The main hall, the octagonal Nanendo, had miraculously survived the fire. To its north, the powerful Fujiwara clan eventually rebuilt its twin, Hokuendo. Over the centuries there were other subsidiary temples consecrated at Kofukuji, gardens constructed there, and to promote the efficacious flux of male and female forces that generated their own powers within the earth below, pagoda towers modeled after those in China were added to the temple complex.

In the vestibule of one of Kofukuji's pagodas stood guard the wooden incarnations of the Junijusho, the twelve Celestial Generals whose martial spirits had policed Kofukuji since the Heian age almost fifteen hundred years before. In books on Japanese art, I had seen photographs of these statue generals with their furious grins and muscular postures full of menace. I hurried on my way. I might be able to talk myself out of an encounter with a priest questioning my presence there after hours—not so some medieval wraith hell-bent on revenge against a defiler of this sacred patch of Nara soil.

As it turned out, neither clergy nor vengeful deity accosted me as I cut across the temple grounds. Perhaps it was too drizzly for either to be about. I veered a couple of times and sent myself in one circle and up two blind alleys before I finally came across the main gate. Crossing out onto Noboriojidori, I had it almost to myself. The broad avenue was silent and nearly empty. The headlights of a taxi swept past, and then a girl whose thick braids swung back and forth rhythmically as she pedaled by on her bicycle. She glanced back at me, looked again a few pushes of the pedals later, then she stamped her bike to a halt and waited for me to catch up to her.

"You are lost!" It was a simple observation. Not a question. A statement of fact.

"Is this Nara?" I asked as innocently as I could.

"Yes, yes, this is the city of Nara." Her laughter was a bubble of brightness in the gloom of the rainy night as she sensed I was teasing. Then it popped, her face suddenly serious as the thought occurred, apparently, that I might not be. I too, grew up in a place with lots of tourists. I knew, as she must have, how mind-bogglingly lost they can get themselves.

"Nara is where you want to be, isn't it?"

"Yep," I said, allaying her fears. "I'm looking for the Tamaru Inn. Do you know where that is?"

Her twin damp braids bobbed affirmatively. She jutted her chin down the street and gave me directions. Then, as I started off as she had pointed, she began pushing her bike alongside me. Like many people I'd already met in Japan, it was obvious she didn't trust a foreigner to follow simple directions, even though they were no more complex than making a left turn a few blocks away and continuing down that street, perfectly straight, until it led to the inn, six minutes away. Nara was founded upon the same city planning principles that were used in China to build the Tang Dynasty capital of Chang-an. It was a logical, neatly ordered gridwork of intersections, all situated in an auspicious place as Imperial court geomancers dictated, in the Yamato basin of south central Japan. It hasn't changed. Losing one's way there requires the kind of serious dedication I'd exerted earlier in taking the shortcut through the temple precincts.

My guide's name, she told me, was Miyoko. One more year of study stood between her and graduation from a university in Nara. Pushing her bicycle beside her, she kept up a steady monologue of information about herself. I'd judged her to be about fourteen. She was actually seven years older and she insisted upon showing me her student ID to prove me wrong. I was still not accustomed to women in their early twenties looking, as they often did in Japan, as if puberty was as yet some distance away for them. Miyoko-san escorted me right up to the front of the Tamaru Inn where Nakanishi-san, the innkeeper and owner, stood beneath an umbrella, keeping a watch down the street for me. Like Miyoko-san, he knew all foreigners suffered from congenital *hoko onchi*, "direction deafness."

"Good evening sir!" Miyoko-san greeted the innkeeper with earnest enthusiasm. "This is my friend, Dave-san. Please take good care of him." She bowed. "Please have a pleasant stay in Nara," she said to me, bowing once again in my direction this time.

Nakanishi-san watched Miyoko pedal off into the shadows. Heartily, he said in English, "I think you must have good taste, Dave-san!"

"Oh no," I started to protest. "I just met her a few minutes ago."

"It's past time for dinner to be served in the inn," Nakanishi-san interrupted, "but will you come have a bite to eat with me?" Not much, he insisted. Just some fish and pickled vegetables his wife was preparing. But he hoped, he added, it would be enough to take care of my "good taste."

My host settled himself on the tatami in front of a low table in his quarters and motioned for me to join him. His wife slid open a door and silently delivered trays of grilled trout, chilled slices of *shiro-uri* melon pickled in a pungent paste of sake dregs, shiitake mushrooms, and bowls of rice.

"I'm sorry to say," Nakanishi-san told me as we ate, "that my English is not very good. But I have a keen interest in improving it. I have quite gotten out of practice speaking it since my days at the university." He asked me to please correct him whenever I caught an error in pronunciation or grammar.

"Well, in the arena of syntax, you need to review the difference between the words 'taste' and 'hunger'," I explained, and I explained too, the momentary chagrin he caused me by confusing the two when I arrived at the inn with Miyoko-san.

"When you said I had good taste, I thought you meant my preferences in women. You meant to say that you thought I had a good appetite, that I was hungry. For food."

"If you say so," Nakanishi-san replied. "But isn't taste always about appetites in one way or another?"

It was a good point.

My innkeeper host at Tamaru had taken a degree in business administration when he graduated from Takushoku University, one of the premier schools in Japan. But he passed up a career in the business world that would have taken him to Tokyo or another of the country's commercial centers. He returned to Nara and took his turn at managing the inn that had been in the Nakanishi family for several generations. I noticed on the bookshelves behind where he sat were several titles printed in Sanskrit.

"My real passion," Nakanishi-san confided in me, "is studying the sutras." Numerous Buddhist sects were founded in Nara. My host had made his way through the doctrinal texts of many of them, pursuing his study so intently that he'd learned Sanskrit to read them in their original form. Nakanishi-san was squat and completely bald. He wore the plain black cotton trousers and blouse of a Buddhist priest, giving him the mien of a scholarly old temple abbot. He drained off a thimble cup of sake and cut loose with a resonant burp, then peered at me over his gold, wire-framed glasses.

Eructation—burping—is one of the less serious dilemmas faced by the serious Western visitor to Japan. True, he can for the most part avoid this issue of etiquette by dining at crowded restaurants where ambient noises around him will mask his culturally ingrained reluctance to peal out with a healthy burp. But when he finds himself in a private home where he knows with some certainty that the cook is in the next room listening through the shoji for auditory proof of her culinary skills—well, that's another matter entirely. One the particulars of which Miss Manners has never been prevailed upon to render judgment, I'm willing to bet. I praised the food artistry of *shun* that had gone into its presentation. Shun refers to that which is "appropriate to the season." *Shunmono* are foods that reflect the time of year they are best enjoyed. Strawberries in mid-winter lack a sensitivity to shun. The trout and pickled vegetables we ate, the way they were served, even the plates we ate from, all were thoughtfully appropriate to this period of autumn. I was egotistical enough to enjoy demonstrating this knowledge that I'd been taught during my time with my *sensei,* and hopeful that my comments would be taken as evidence I really did appreciate the meal.

But I did not burp. Just as I chose not to refer to my wife, when she came up in conversation in Japan, as a "stupid spouse" or "my old mountain goat," or any other of the standard appellations that even the most loving and devoted Japanese family man will use when mentioning his wife. Some habits of culture defy cross-pollination. Some manners do not translate. It can be a difficult line for us to walk, those of us who are not Japanese but who have, in significant ways, been affected by Japanese civilization. I was to experience it over and over my first time in Japan, to see parts of myself that my teacher had molded that fit me in this country in places where I had never fit so easily in my own. Yet there were other moments when my Western nature surfaced, just as unselfconsciously. Best to be yourself, my teacher's wife had told me more than once. There are few sights more pathetic than the Westerner in Japan who is unhappy with himself, the "Japanophile" who has tried desperately to discard his own heritage in favor of adopting a foreign one. Poor souls, they are enthusiastic, often perfecting the language skills and even the mannerisms of Japan. Yet adrift from their own cultural moorings, Kaoru had warned me, these types inevitably "find" a Japan that is really more a reflection of their own needs. In the end they fit no better into the Japanese ways than they did into those of the West.

(George Orwell called this malaise "transferred nationalism." His essay on the subject, "Notes on Nationalism," should be required therapeutic—or cautionary—reading for all those who have fallen uncritically in love with Japan or with the Orient in general.) I found myself thinking about this and I was startled when Nakanishi-san broke the silence.

"You're only staying in Nara this one night?" he asked.

"I'm leaving tomorrow, yes."

He sighed. "The typical tourist spends one day in Nara. That's what the Tourist Organization tells us. Then he goes hurrying off to Kyoto. One cannot see Nara in a day. Not even in a year."

"I'll be coming back to Nara," I assured him. "But I'm going to stay just outside the city, staying with my teacher." The word I used was not sensei, the common one used for a teacher in Japanese and the one I would normally have used. Instead, I said *danna-sama*. In current usage, it is a slang reference used by women to refer sarcastically to their husbands, for it means, literally, "my master." Nakanishi-san looked puzzled. So I explained. I had apprenticed, when I was still a schoolboy, in the classical martial art of swordsmanship and strategy under a Japanese adept of these arts who had been living and working for a time in the United States.

"You mean kendo?" Nakanishi-san asked. It was a misunderstanding I encountered so frequently in Japan I'd learned to anticipate it. Most of the time I just nodded and let it go at that. When I said "swordsmanship," Nakanishi-san assumed I meant the modern combat sport of kendo. Most Westerners have seen it on TV or in movies and some have trained in it; kendo is a sport with enthusiasts worldwide now. Exponents strap on padded armor and fence with staves of split bamboo, trying to score points by striking selected targets. Kendo is a popular sport in Japan; in schools, along with judo, it is offered to children and so the majority of Japanese have some experience with it. Kendo, though, like judo and karatedo, are *gendai budo*, modern martial ways. While kendo was inspired by the feudal arts of the sword, it did not come into being until the age of the classical warrior in Japan was nearly over. The method of the sword I had learned was not a sport and it was certainly not one known to the average Japanese. My teacher was from a *koryu*, an "old school" of the samurai's combat arts. The koryu, the martial skills that were actually implemented on the battlefield during the medieval period in Japan, are traditions that reach back many generations in that nation. Their roots are powerfully interwoven with the most venerable of Japan's cultural properties. Like the Noh drama, the tea ceremony, and many of Japan's folk arts, the koryu are carried on in unbroken lineages by those devoted to them. They are not practical, no more so than the pottery or the baskets made by hand in many parts of backcountry Japan. Instead, these ancient martial arts, their practical applications long a thing of the past, embody spiritual and cultural values that are, to their exponents, inexpressibly wonderful and worthy.

"And so you've come all this way to see your teacher again?"

"To see him and to visit and pray at the graves of other masters of our lineage..." I shrugged. I felt awkward. I did not really care to talk about this and in the time since I had arrived in Japan I had avoided the topic as much as possible. It all sounded more dramatic than to me, it actually was. Other students of the arts and crafts of Japan had learned and trained under Japanese teachers in the u.s. They had been taught sword-polishing, or folk dance, or the playing of Japanese instruments like the *taiko* drum or the thirteen-stringed koto. Of their numbers, some of those students had eventually found themselves coming to Japan to see where their arts began, to learn more. It was not that unusual for a foreigner to come to Japan to study an art of some kind.

Others had come and still were, even though Japan was an expensive place to visit. "But the koryu; those are different," Nakanishi-san agreed with me. "The warrior arts of the samurai are the *kokoro kagami* of Japan." They are, he said, "the mirror of its soul."

His wife served us cups of tea and then the Sanskrit-reading innkeeper showed me the way to my room. He checked to see that my futon mattress and comforter had been laid out on the tatami by the maid. Nakanishi-san showed me that opening the shoji screens in my room gave me a view over the tops of the trees around the inn. I could see the twin spires of black slate-tiled temple roofs a couple of blocks away.

"Todaiji," he pointed out. "Its center hall there is the largest wooden structure in the world." The hall of the Todai temple housed a statue of the Buddha sixteen meters tall, one of his huge palms lifted placidly in a sign meant to symbolize the Buddha's ability to relieve men of their quotidian worries.

"Tell me, if you don't mind doing so," Nakanishi-san said as we looked out together over the rooftops of Todaiji, "what do you suppose your master will think of you after all this time? Do you think he will be happy with what you have made of your life so far?"

I did not have an answer.

Later, I stretched out on my futon and watched the lights that were sprinkled and twinkling on the slopes of the Asakura Mountains, which surround Nara to the west. It was so quiet I could hear Nakanishi-san in his apartments chanting prayers, sitting no doubt, in front of his family altar as he fingered the knots of his Buddhist rosary. When I had last seen my sensei, I was still in college. He and his wife had returned to Japan after his work assignment was ended in the u.s. I'd declined an invitation to join them. I'd stayed, graduated from the university. I was married and, becoming a writer, I'd acquired something like a profession. But I was too, my master's student, one of only two he'd ever taught and the only non-Japanese. He and his wife and others connected to the traditional arts of Japan had invested an enormous amount in me. They made sacrifices on my behalf that I did not begin to appreciate until after they had left to return to Japan. Just as the scholar's true education does not get underway until after he's left school, my understanding of my teacher, my sensei, did not begin to develop until we were separated and I was alone to ponder the many lessons he had instilled.

Kodomo tame ni is an expression used often by Japanese parents: "for the sake of the children." It was kodomo tame ni that motivated those early Japanese immigrants to wrestle twelve-hour days out of the red dirt of the pineapple and sugarcane fields of Hawaii, not for themselves but for the future of their offspring. For largely the same reason, for the sake of the children, many Japanese-Americans allowed the outrages of the relocation camps during World War ii. They believed that surrendering their rights as citizens, their property, was the best hope they had of making a better future for the next generation. In ways that were different but no less exacting, the teacher makes sacrifices for the disciple. Sensei had taken me under his care, taught me patiently. What would he think of the results so far?

Nakanishi-san's prayers trailed off and a different kind of incantation took up the slack. It had stopped raining. When it did, the insects of the night took up their chorus. The dull, raspy screech of crickets outside my room sounded tired, the final coda of a summer's symphony being finished. I listened to these sounds of an autumnal evening in Nara and thought of things long ago.

"Are you sure you want to get off here?" The bus driver took my five hundred yen note and made change slowly, watching to be certain this was the stop I wanted. Clearly, he was reluctant to leave off a foreigner in such a remote place. His concern was understandable. Across the road there was an auto body repair shop and alongside it, a neat and tidy little shack housing a business that sold cylinders of natural gas. Aside from these businesses, there were no other signs of civilization. Only steep hills layered with bamboo and dark evergreen sugi cedars. A slender asphalt lane that was dusted and drifted with amber pine needles branched off the main road and twisted its way over the crest of a hill.

"Yes," I said. "I think this is the place."

It was not exactly the place, I knew. But it was as near as the bus line could get me.

"Well, listen," the driver said solicitously, "the next bus will be along here in two hours. Bus #220."

An old man leaned forward in his seat behind the driver. "It'll take you right back to Nara, right back indeed to the station where you left," he said. And he smacked his cane tip on the floor of the bus for emphasis. Both he and the few other passengers aboard looked doubtful I would really want to step off the bus we'd taken out from Nara into the woodsy backwaters of this remote corner of the prefecture.

"It's okay," I said. My fare clanked through the slot. I jumped heavily from the doorstep, weighed down by the luggage of my pack and a plastic bag of *yakigashi* sweet bean cakes. I set off down the spur road—or rather up it, since I was going in the direction where it fetched itself over a sharp incline and wandered off between two hills. The sun was warm. The air was light and dry and fragrant with the smell of mountain forests. The geography, the mountains and the foliage, except for the bamboo, all looked as though I was in the middle of the Catskills, somewhere in Sullivan County. Sunlight threw freckles on the feathery leaves of the bamboo that grew luxuriously along the roadway, creating patterns of green that waved and danced when the breeze moved them. Emboldened by the warmth, or perhaps in recognition of it soon passing, a grasshopper sprang up now and then, and whirred noisily away from me. The ditch by the road was filled with bright water. If anyone was around, they did not show themselves, and aside from my footsteps, I heard nothing but the sounds that belonged there.

The average farm field in Japan, I had read somewhere, is just a bit larger than the average suburban lot in Ohio. The fields I hiked past on this road were not that big. They were odd-shaped lots of brown stubble, all that remained of the rice crop for that year, and they were stuck in anywhere that was flat enough for them to be cultivated. Some were literally no larger than my living room. In a few of these miniature fields, tan sheaves of grain stalks were draped over pole racks to dry in the sun. The ground beneath was rich black, marled soil still sodden from having been under water for most of the growing season. I wondered who owned this ground or who worked it. A dozen steps later I thought I had my answer. They were probably the responsibility, I decided, of whoever lived in the two farmhouses that stood behind a copse of pines, back from the road a way and covered with straw thatched roofs. They looked as if they were posing for the artist Hokusai to come along and make sketches for one of his woodblock prints.

Past the farmhouses and around another bend, the road rose up again. On the hill was a clutch of homes, five or six of them built close together in an open spot in the forest. They were secluded, perched right on the side of the hill at various heights. All had the distinctive tiled roofs that had, in nearly all of Japan, long ago replaced the kind of thatch work I'd just seen on the farmhouses. They looked as though they had been there a long time, however. From the lines of the architecture of most of them, and from the air of permanence that came from the way they sat, I guessed they had been constructed back when the then-Emperor Hirohito's grandfather had occupied the Imperial throne, around the turn of the twentieth century. Most of them had stonework banks that came down the hillside right to the edge of the road, to prevent them from sliding off their foundations. They were surrounded by gated walls of stone or sturdy cedar plank fencing, with vents cut into the gates for the postman to make his deliveries. Engraved in metal or painted in black ink on faded posts were the names of the residents. I had to climb up to the entrance to each house to read each one and decipher it: Okawara, Suzuki, Ito.

Finally, I found a sign to match the name I was looking for. To gain entry, one went through the gate. These are customarily locked only at night and most times, in quiet country places like this, not at all. The visitor could walk through the gate and up a path to the door to be formally received. I walked around to the side of the house's protective wall, beneath the branches of an arthritic old persimmon tree. In the rear was a shed with rakes and bundles of dried bamboo poles leaning against it. A fruit tree dominated one corner. At the other were three pines, ancient and twisted, with their boughs still being trained. Bamboo rods were tied to the undersides of the branches, directing their growth and shape.

The fruit tree was a *nashi*; it's something like a pear. A dish of nashi, yellow-green and swollen to nearly ripe, had been left on the doorstep. In from the fields, a clunky pair of wooden clogs were resting beside them, their woven cloth thongs frayed and faded, their teeth blunted and worn and mud-stained. They were well-used and plain; country-style footgear that were distant hillbilly cousins of the dainty lacquered clogs worn by the geisha in Kyoto.

I stepped over the nashi and the clogs to kick off my own shoes. I shoved the outer *fusuma* shutters back along their tracks, then pushed the paper panels of shoji the same direction. My pack slid off my shoulders and thumped to the tatami. Lunch was just about to be served inside. Chiyoko sat on the floor at the table, legs tucked beneath her, nibbling a wedge of apple from a skewer. Her face was the kind that was called *urizanegao* in old-fashioned Japanese, round as a melon seed. Her eyes were black and luminous behind her glasses. Her Aunt Kaoru, my sensei's wife, stood behind her in the doorway that led to the kitchen, a dishcloth in one hand. With the other she had been adjusting the knob on the radio to turn up the noon broadcast of the news from a station in Nara. Sitting at the table directly across from me, his newspaper folded in front of him, was Sensei. It was three months more than twelve years, and half a world away, since I had seen him.

I bowed. *"Kimashita yo,"* I said. Then, "I'm home."

No one moved for a long moment. Then Chiyoko's somber face tilted open with a softening about her mouth that could have been the shadow of a smile. Kaoru dropped her hand away from the radio. She blinked. Sensei folded his arms across his chest.

"Yokoso," he said. "Welcome home."

I dropped to my knees and scooted up to the table across from him. Kaoru leaned over to pinch my face and then she rubbed it. "You need to shave," she said. Then she blinked again and this time the blinking did not hold back the tears. I tried too, and failed and there were suddenly hot, salty puddles that pooled in my eyes and washed the room into a blur.

Home.

2
Echoes of the Past

$\mathcal{T}$he moon, a scallop of bone, was the only illumination when I woke. Sleep had been meandering in its coming. When it did, it was viscous and fitful for me. As I said, there are artists of every persuasion, craft, folk, fine, and in my case, martial, whose dream it is to go to Japan to study with the masters there. But for a long time I was not among them. My dreams had been vague and tattered on the night before leaving and in their background was a constant noise, faint, nearly indistinguishable…

> *the hollow clopping clack of seasoned wood, like the staccato rhythm of the narrator at the Noh theater, clapping together his blocks of kaya to keep time…*

I do not care much to travel. I am left unsettled by interruptions in the routine of my daily life and activities. Practice with the sword at the dojo, writing, friends, and familiar places. I recoil especially from the isolation that sets in once a journey has gone beyond mere contemplation and has reached the final stages of planning, a process I find far worse than the loneliness of travel itself. My wife will go to her school to teach this morning, come home to our house, continue on with the ordered existence of our lives. Yet already she has drawn away into her own seclusion, her soul sealing itself off from its connection to mine in anticipation of enduring the separation to come. It is a survival mechanism of the spirit, I suppose. And so, as much to get it over with as anything else, I am up and driving with her through suburbs still asleep outside St. Louis, on the way to the airport there. On the way to Japan to…

the clickety-clack of the bokuto, the wooden practice swords used in training, struck together over and over, a metronome of combat, life and death...

The house on the quiet street where Sensei and his wife had lived during their stay in America was always filled with Japanese students from the nearby university, it seemed to me at the time. Other expatriates came through almost constantly, either on their way to or just back from Japan. It was a place of many a time warmly remembered, where I did a great deal of growing up. With Sensei's departure, I lost what was to me a second family of sorts. I missed the Friday night *maze-koze* suppers when the household stripped the refrigerator and cupboards of leftovers from the week before and assembled maze-koze—"a little of this, a little of that"—meals that were likely to pair cold fried chicken with fragrant miso soup, or chestnuts and rice along with potato salad. I missed the oak-slatted tub Sensei and I had built upstairs at his house. I missed the sense of belonging. I longed too, for my teacher's advice and instruction, the lessons in the dojo there, Sensei's *bokuto* a whistling blur, the steel blade, when he used it, an arc of light—always, as the term "sensei" itself means, a "guide who has gone before" for me.

The decision to go to Japan finally was one made with the same unhurried deliberation as had been my choice, years earlier, not to go. "Come back to Japan with us," Sensei had urged. His wife and others pushed me to do the same. I had not, after weighing the advantages and their opposites. In the intervening years since my teacher had left to return to Japan I had gone my own way. I had continued my training in the more modern martial ways, karatedo and aikido. By myself, I practiced the movements of the classical arts of the warrior that Sensei had taught me.

There was no one else in the U.S. who was involved in the particular discipline in which I'd been trained.

For me, Japan was an alternative in my life upon which I consciously turned my back. It was a decision made more palatable to some degree, by a lot of what I had heard and read about modern Japan. "Tokyo is New York City on a massive overdose of amphetamines," I was told by a journalist who had worked in both places. The mental pictures he drew of Japan for me were reinforced by scenes I saw on television: frantic throngs shopping for bargains in Shinjuku, whooshing "bullet trains," smog, and ferroconcrete buildings. I hadn't any eagerness to be-bop in Harajuku parks with the gyrating kids in poodle skirts and motorcycle tough-guy leather jackets, recreating their bizarre notion of the American fifties each weekend. I was not excited about queuing up for a plastic platter of the Colonel's Extra Crispy served under the shadow of Fuji-san. The Japan I cared about was a long time gone, I was convinced. Gone too, most conveniently for me, were any obligations I might have had to anyone or anything there.

I created a Japan for myself that made me comfortable with it and so I made myself comfortable with the distance between myself and my teacher as well. Seasons passed into years and there was nothing at all from within that made me want to close the separation that had grown...

> but the softly insistent clatter, like the rustling racket of
> a pipestem grove of green bamboo against the wind of a
> coming storm...

I visited infrequently now the town where I had spent my childhood and apprenticed with Sensei. It had been years since I had some reason to walk the length of the quiet street where he had lived. When on a spring day, I finally did, I wasn't sure why. Perhaps it was simply to see if every tilt and crack of the sidewalk was as it had been when the path was part of my daily routine. Whatever the reason, I was soon standing in front of the old house where Sensei and his wife had lived. Kaoru's iris beds were still there, pale green knives poking out of dirt that was still in clumps half-frozen from winter. The house itself was one of those steep-hipped examples of the Queen Anne style of the American Midwest. Its details, ornamented gables and spindlework, had been popular in the first decade of the century, manufactured back East and shipped by railroad to towns in Iowa and Kansas and Missouri. Standing out on the sidewalk—I had no idea who was living there now—I craned my neck and I could see inside the front windows. The great wide dining room that I'd always pictured as having held family reunions and Thanksgiving feasts when the house was young had been converted by my sensei into a small dojo for our use. Now it was converted once again. It was a spacious sitting room, full of hanging baskets of plants and a wicker sofa and chairs and shelves of books. The little Shinto shrine that had once sat on a shelf was gone, of course. I wondered if any of the kami spirits that had inhabited it were still around.

Months after walking by the house on the quiet street, near the middle of an autumn, my wife and I drove out into the countryside near my hometown, to Riverdale. When I was a student, my teacher and I had taken the same road many times. We drove it before dawn and parked beside the river. We were there for the waterfall at the abandoned mill dam there, to sit nearly naked beneath a narrow split in the dam that sluiced a cascade of icy water over us. This was a part of *misogi*, Sensei had taught me, a Shinto-inspired purification of body and spirit. The dam had been left in ruins years before. Its millhouse was a crumbling relic when we did misogi there, its gear-toothed iron spindle rusted and broken off at the axle and left spiked up from the depths of the mill pool. Now, though, a restoration program was underway. A new millhouse was being framed out beside it. Riverdale, an informational sign told us, was on its way to becoming a park, an historical site, the first and now sole surviving mill in the county. When Sensei and I had done misogi there, we'd never been disturbed by much more traffic than an occasional lone fisherman working the river for bass and perch. Now gravel for a parking lot had been poured into a mound for spreading and I was not sure I would have recognized the old place at all, save for the mossy stone dam and the rushing roar of water over it…

> *and the resonant whack, whack, whacking, like the "deer scarer" in Japanese garden streams, a bamboo trough filling with the flow of the water and then plopping down to clack noisily against the stones in the stream bed...*

On a summer afternoon I had some reason to be back on the campus near the house on the quiet street and this time I ended up walking by the university's original Field House. It was built in the blocky "Progressive" style typical of government buildings — offices and schools and such — during the years before World War ii. It was a gymnasium that looked more like an armory, faced with squares of gray Ozark marble the color of a storm sky in February. One wing of the gym had contained an enormous wooden floor, the size of two basketball courts. It was, when the university was still just a local "normal" school for training teachers, the Women's Gymnasium. It was a place where coeds in demure bloomers had once batted volleyballs and twirled Indian clubs. In later years, when I was first there, the floor was the haunt of dancers, straining at the *barres* mounted along the walls, perfecting their *pointes* and *pliés*. In the evenings the place was empty and Sensei's lessons for me were conducted there when the weather was too inclement to practice outside or when the dojo in his home was too small for the techniques we were doing. Looking at the gym from the outside, it looked the same as it had when my teacher and I had exercised there; the same, for that matter, as it had back in the days of the coeds in bloomers. As I came closer, though, I knew that it was being changed.

Like the nineteenth-century mill at Riverdale, the gymnasium was under renovation. But instead of restoring it (not that it needed restoration at all: as with most buildings of that style it was virtually bombproof, as solid, as draughty, as fiendishly unventilated as the day it was completed in—so said the corner-stone—1940), the university had decided to remodel the Field House. The planked floor in the Women's Gym, carefully laid by WPA workers struggling to bring America out of the Depression was splintered and gaping with holes now. It was in the process of being ripped out to accommodate, I discovered, some state-of-the-art synthetic flooring which was in turn designed to accommodate a generation of student athletes unaccustomed to such dated and quaint concepts as natural materials and things old, well made, and long used. Or at least it was with such vinegar thoughts that I soaked my anger and sorrow at such thoughtless, sacking destruction. The stout planks of that floor were seasoned, more than a little, by my own perspiration, my tears, and on more than one occasion, by my blood. I was outraged and grieving at the razing of my memories. I retreated to the stone steps of the Field House, sat under the shade of the maples there and cried for all that was gone, all that had never been quite fulfilled in my life. Behind me, the demolition went on. Workers wrenched up another part of the floor and it gave way with a horrible, groaning crackle...

> *a sound hollow and wooden, like the bones of one's ancestors, rattling... and reminding...*

And I knew it had come time to go to see my teacher. To go to Japan.

For a few years I had been writing for *Winds,* the in-flight magazine given to passengers on Japan Air Lines. When I brought up the idea of going to Japan to the editor there, Tom Chapman, he made arrangements for me to take the fourteen-hour JAL flight from Chicago to Tokyo. Good editors have a talent for tolerating writers and their strange ways. Tom Chapman asked me no questions and if he doubted my interest in the magazine and my future contributions to it, he was too polite to say so. He merely suggested some places I might want to see to write about later for his magazine. His suggestions provided for me an acceptable reason I could give others for my going to Japan.

Having that reason was more important than it seemed at the time it was offered to me by my editor. I found this out on the connecting flight from St. Louis to Chicago.

"Are you going just to Chicago or to someplace further on?" my seatmate asked me after we'd buckled in. Paula Simmonds was an auditor for a company that sold investment advice and supplied management consultation to big corporations.

"Further," I said. "To Japan."

"Japan? Tokyo? Really?" She popped the seat in front of her with her hand. "Bradley," she said, "Where's our office in Tokyo?" Sitting in front of her, Bradley didn't hear the question. He'd stuffed headphones into his ears and he went on scribbling notes on a yellow legal pad.

Miss Simmonds wore a serge suit of the cut popular with professional women in the financial trades. She tugged at her paisley bow tie, then shot her cuffs. "What sort of business do you do that takes you to Japan?"

"No business," I replied. And suddenly I felt just a bit too casually attired in denim pants and an old blue broadcloth shirt. Miss Simmonds' Vuitton attaché case was tucked under her seat. Under mine was a hiker's daypack with a notebook, books, and a soon-to-be smuggled tape of the soft-porn movie *Emmanuelle* for a Japanese friend. "I'm going over to see some people I used to know," I said. "Travel around some. See the country."

Miss Simmonds pursed her lips and shook her head, looking at me sideways. "Must be... nice," she said and I detected a hint of disdain. We were close to the same age. She and her two associates sitting in front of us, Matt and Bradley, were on their way to Chicago to attend to the needs of a company that manufactured credit cards. I, on the other hand, was going from O'Hare off to wander around a foreign country that was hardly a popular tourist destination to renew old acquaintances. My plan, from her perspective, was neither business-related nor a proper vacation. It was, well, indolence.

"There must be a lot of work for your company to be sending three people up to Chicago," I said, to change the subject.

"Um-hm," she said. "And we've contracted to have it done in a week. This is a tough client."

Miss Simmonds and I talked over the greater length of the state of Illinois, largely about her occupation, and she constantly referred to the company she and her friends had been hired by as "the client." For all I know of the corporate world, this may be normal. But it reminded me of the bloodless way professional killers in novels will refer to their victims as "the targets."

"This client has, to put it politely," she told me, "a lot of waste in their middle management levels. They are expecting us to play a very tough ballgame in getting some of their internal problems straightened out."

I remarked that one of the auditors in her particular firm had recently acquired some notoriety in St. Louis for a dalliance in a different kind of sport. His wife had suffocated during a bout of sexual bondage and he'd fled in a panic after burning down the house and her body in it. His trial, just completed, was a sensational one in the city.

"Sore subject," said Miss Simmonds, and then we were righting our seats and gathering up our things in preparation for landing.

I learned from my conversation with Miss Simmonds. I was ready when I met Bill Foster and his wife June, from Russellville, Arkansas. The Fosters were on their way to join a month-long tour of China. We stood in line together at the JAL counter at O'Hare. Mr. Foster, who had a golf cart dealership in Russellville, asked me what I planned on doing in Japan.

"I'm a writer. Going over to gather some material for magazine articles."

"So Japan's a business trip for you?"

Right. It was a perfectly acceptable reason to him and I didn't have to squirm and feel like an idle playboy.

Mr. Hideo Tanaka, returning to Nagoya after a visit with his daughter and grandchildren in Oak Brook, asked me the same question soon after he settled down into the seat beside me on the plane.

"Why are you going to Japan?" he asked, in impeccable English.

"My sensei is there," I said. "I have *on*." Obligation.

Mr. Tanaka nodded. The explanation was as acceptable to him as my other had been to Mr. Foster from Russellville. Tanaka-san said nothing more about it and showed me pictures of his granddaughter in Oak Brook, only a month into the first grade and already through the first reader.

Tokyo began for me with a skyline studded by cranes and platform docks that looked like the nests of some giant prehistoric birds. I saw the skyline through the window of the shuttle bus that brought travelers from Narita Airport into the city. But Japan; Japan began for me miles before I saw anything of the city. The highway that was taking us into downtown Tokyo, to Shinjuku Station, curved back and forth in long arcs through the country outskirts of the city and we passed a farmhouse set off the road. Its roof tiles were burnt-red, its walls shuttered by door-sized plates of wood. The farmhouse stood by itself on the knob of a hill that was surrounded by fields of rice stalks that were brown and cut to a stubble. Beside it were a couple of pines, black-green in the fading light. Two crows, black as old oil, leaped off their perches in the pines and flapped silently over the wide plats of rice, like a haiku come to life.

Keiko Yoshikawa was waiting for me at Shinjuku Station. She was dressed in a heavy sweater, woolen skirt, and knee socks, even though the evening air in downtown Tokyo was still moist and warm with summer. Keiko-san had suffered a bout with rheumatic fever when she was in her early twenties, she explained after introducing herself to me. It left her susceptible to chills. Before the fever she had skied, rock-climbed. Her parents used to say she was not really their child, she told me, but a "daughter of the mountains." A mutual friend in the States had written her and her husband on my behalf, asking them to put me up since I knew no one in Tokyo.

It is one of the delights of travel that the strangers one comes across from time to time will launch without hesitation into explanations of their lives' particulars that friends who have been around them for years might not know. Once, on a bus in Spain, I listened while a woman told me about everyday life as she remembered it during the Spanish Civil War. "My," she had finally said, "I've never spoken to anyone about that!" I wondered if Keiko-san's closest confidants knew that she had been a "daughter of the mountains."

While Keiko told me about herself, we were being tumbled into the army ant throngs that funnel and churn through cavernous Shinjuku Station. Then, because she had some errands to run before we went back to her family's apartment, Keiko led me onto a dizzying series of local trains that took us into the heart of Tokyo. I plunged along beside her, trying to keep up, my thoughts spinning. Maybe it was the speed and sterility of air travel. The morning had begun in a city in the middle of America, talking with my wife about the most mundane matters. Now it was not yet sundown on the same day for me and I was aboard a train on the red Marunouchi Line, clicking past Yotsuya Station, chatting about trivial matters with a woman who had just plucked me from the anonymity of metropolitan Tokyo, a woman pressed so tightly against me by the crowds of passengers around us that our noses were no more than a foot apart and we both crossed eyes if we looked directly at one another too long. Bright strips of advertising on the train car's walls above our heads touted beers, cosmetics, and other products in kanji, displayed in a kaleidoscopic array that distracted me, as I tried to decipher some of the seemingly endless ways in which Japanese characters can be written. "That woman with the *gaijin*," I overheard a mutter. "Now what can they be up to?" I felt a ballooning sensation of the unreality of it all. Keiko-san noticed it in my expression. She stopped talking and smiled broadly at me, her black eyes dancing with amusement.

"It's different, isn't it?" she said.

The Yoshikawas, Keiko, her husband Taro, and their twelve-year-old son Esuke, lived in the Meguro neighborhood of south Tokyo, on the fourth floor of a complex of apartments that had an eel restaurant on the ground level. Their home was three rooms large: kitchen, living room, and a single bedroom, along with a tiny bathroom, postage stamp toilet room, and an alcove for storage. All of the Yoshikawas' Apartment #403 would have fit comfortably into the two-car garages of many American homes with room to spare. Keiko-san steamed brown rice and grilled chunks of chicken marinated in soy sauce. I sat in the kitchen and watched and talked to Esuke.

"Please speak English to Esuke," Keiko asked me. Like all schoolchildren in Japan, Esuke learned English in class. Like most of them, I was to discover, his instruction was confined primarily to written exercises and to the rote memorization of basic sentences.

"How are you?" inquired Esuke.

"I am fine."

"What do you like best about Japan?"

"The monster squid I saw climbing out of the harbor in Tokyo this evening."

Esuke's face screwed up as he tried to translate. His mother gave me a quick smile and translated the remark for him.

"What!" He gave a moment's consideration to the possibility of a mutant squid attack on the city, then recognized he was being teased by the guest for whom he was giving up some of his privacy. Normally, the single bedroom in the Yoshikawas' apartment was his. It was kodomo tame ni—for the sake of the child—that Keiko-san and her husband slept in the living room area. With a visitor staying there, they all crowded into Esuke's bedroom and I slept in the living room.

After dinner, Keiko-san unfolded a futon and quilts on the floor for me. She sprinkled herb powder, which was supposed to heal the aches of travel, into my bath. I soaked in the brew, eyes closed, then slipped on a cotton *yukata* and stood out on the Yoshikawas' narrow strip of balcony, watching the Meguro street that went past four stories below. Meguro — "black eyes" — takes its name from a dark-eyed statue of Fudo Myo-o, a divine protector of the Buddha's laws, erected within the precincts of a temple. Legend has it the shogun Tokugawa Ieyasu had four identical temples built in this neighborhood to help protect the southern boundary of what was then called Edo — modern Tokyo now. Time and misfortune had seen the destruction of every temple of the four but the one housing the black-eyed Fudo. And so the neighborhood had its name.

Late diners were arriving to duck into the eel restaurant below for appetizers of eel liver and bellies, and meals of lean, meaty eel fillets heaped atop bowls of sticky rice. Even though it was nearly midnight, the sidewalks were busy. Office workers were hurrying home, some after having just left their jobs at that late hour; others coming from the bars and snack shops where much of the social interaction of the Japanese business world takes place. Taro Yoshikawa, my host, was among them somewhere, his wife had told me. Over beer, he and his colleagues would have discussed the day's business and office gossip. It would be another hour or so before he got home, long after I had drifted off to sleep on the futon. The last sound I heard before sleep was the *clop-clop* of geta clogs strolling past on the street below.

"Where do you want to go in Tokyo?" Keiko-san asked me the next morning.

"Yasukuni Jinja," I replied.

Keiko coughed gently into her palm. Her eyebrows furrowed just slightly. "Are you sure you know what that place is?"

Visitors to foreign places who have some special interests in those places must become accustomed to this kind of polite reticence and skepticism on the part of the natives. You want to see the only pigsty left in Paris? You want to visit a nunnery in Rio during Carnival? Or, in my case, the first place you really want to go in Tokyo is the Shinto shrine Yasukuni, the home of the spirits of those who died in Japan's expansionist wars?

"This place where you want to go," ventured Keiko-san. "It is a *jinja*. A Shinto shrine."

I nodded. We'd taken seats on a Hibiya Gray Line subway that wasn't nearly so crowded in the late morning as it had been earlier and would be again, during the evening rush.

"Yasukuni is a very special place to Japanese," Keiko-san said.

I closed my eyes and mentally whacked the side of my head. Suddenly I thought I understood the cause for her hesitation in taking me to the shrine. Yasukuni is a site where the gods could be called down, where they lived and where with them were the spirits of the men who died for Japan's imperialist cause in places like Midway and Baugio and Saipan. It could be that she was trying to tell me that an American clomping through the grounds of such a place was poor form. As boorish as a travel tour of Japanese snapping photos of each other before the monument of u.s. soldiers hoisting the Stars and Stripes at Iwo Jima. Oh jeez. In Japan less than twenty-four hours and I was already traveling at Gray Line speed towards an insult and social gaffe of international proportions.

"Keiko-san, um, is there—will there—be a problem if I go to Yasukuni?"

Keiko wrinkled her nose and looked at me sideways. "Why do you think there would be a problem?"

"I'm gaijin."

"That has not escaped my notice, Dave-san."

"The war," I said. "Maybe if I go to Yasukuni it will be misunderstood. I'm thinking maybe that's why you want to know why I want to go there."

Keiko-san almost choked on the spurt of laughter that she just barely managed to hide behind her palm. "What are you *talking* about?" she asked. No offence was going to be taken to my being at the shrine, she assured me after she quit laughing. "I just can't imagine why *any* foreigner would want to go to Yasukuni."

I told her. "I have a responsibility to go there."

My sensei's eldest brother had died in some nameless battle in some nameless corner of humid jungle somewhere in the Philippines during the Second World War. His body was never recovered. But like so many others from that conflict, his spirit had been invested at Yasukuni, a government-sponsored shrine built during the early part of the twentieth century, during the Meiji era. Sensei had rarely mentioned his brother. Once, only once, when he was telling me about his school years in Tokyo he had asked that, should I ever go there I would pay a visit to Yasukuni and remember his brother. It was not Sensei's habit to ask me to do things. I was his student; he *told* me what he wanted me to do, or showed me. So even though he mentioned it only that single time, I did not forget. Fulfilling his request was my first concern in Japan. I was relieved I was going to be able to accomplish the task without creating an incident that would wind up being arbitrated by the United Nations.

Keiko-san and I strolled down the long gravel path at Yasukuni under a colossal bronze torii gate with the dimensions of a railroad trestle. On both sides of the path, the walk to the main shrine was bordered by ginkgo and cherry trees; partially obscured by their branches all along the way were monuments to the war dead. Here, near Tokyo's heart, the chatter and roar of the city was muted. Yasukuni was built on the summit of Kudan Hill, once the site of a lighthouse used to signal ships in Tokyo Bay. Now the jutting buildings of Tokyo dwarf the little summit, but the trees and monuments and park grounds around the shrine seem to hold the city at a distance.

It is possible to learn a great deal about a city by the civic attitude it expresses towards its dead. That's why I am always comfortable in a place like Boston, a city which has never tried to hide or ignore the citizens that have departed from it. In the Puritan's City on the Hill, modern businesses snuggle right up to seventeenth century graveyards as familiarly as train riders there on the MTA will squeeze and shimmy together to let one more passenger aboard. Boston accommodates the spirits of its dead, humors them, regards them as part of the urban scene. The dead, in turn, do not seem to mind those who are still upright. Boston's cemeteries tolerate the visitations of the tourist or office worker eating his lunch with a crypt for a table, the lovers who stroll through rows of headstones. Can you imagine *that* in Los Angeles, in one of the tacky monument parks like Forest Lawn? Californians have no respect for death, save for the occasional and contrived martyrdom of one of their celebrities. Visitors to New England's cemeteries come there to immerse themselves in the past. At the graves of Marilyn Monroe and Rock Hudson, visitors come to gawk. In Tokyo, as in Boston, cemeteries are a natural part of the landscape. Shrines like Yasukuni are never jostled for space. They have a dignity about them and their presence lends that dignity right back to the city itself.

Reproduced on a display near the main shrine at Yasukuni was the last tender letter from an infantryman, written to his wife not long before he was killed in combat. As Keiko-san and I paused to read the letter, three others who'd come to Yasukuni joined us. Concentrating on the characters of the letter, I heard soft wet sniffles and someone swallowed as if they were gulping stones. It was that quiet. But none of us said a word. We stood together and read silently. As I turned away from the display, one of the men beside me pulled out a handkerchief and swiped at his eyes. I could see, when he looked at me, that he was old enough to have fought alongside the author of the letter.

"It was such a waste, you know," was all he said to me.

Two young girls with placid faces watched over a booth opposite the center shrine of Yasukuni. They sold mementos of the shrine and brocade *omamori* amulets meant to bring good luck or to protect the wearer against bad. Yasukuni, like most major Shinto shrines, is attended by *miko*, maidens who seem to float about the shrine precincts in long ceremonial robes of white and pastel blue. Their hair is pulled back and tied in long shiny spills of black, adding to their ethereal presence. Young miko need not be vestal virgins to qualify for the job, according to Shinto doctrine. Many are daughters of priests or girls from nearby neighborhoods. Still, one does not encounter women who could accurately describe their occupation as "professional maiden" on a regular basis in this century. I watched the pair of them with as much curiosity as they seemed to be taking in the sight of a gaijin among the late-middle-aged crowd at the shrine. Two other miko who walked past on their duties paid me no mind at all. They were conducting a special service in the vestibule of the shrine, waving wands of folded paper called *haraegushi*, exorcising any evil that might be lurking near the altar. With their flowing robes and hair swept back, miko look like the *ko-omote*, the archetypal young girl who is a stock character on the Noh stage. The effect is enhanced by their movements during the ritual, stately and dance-like, and by the tranquility of their expressions as they perform. The job of the miko must be among the most anachronistic of callings. Yet I cannot imagine any woman not envying them in their grace and composure.

I dribbled a palmful of yen coins into the slotted box in front of the main temple at Yasukuni, a contribution that is meant to assist the financing of deities residing there, then I tugged the thick bell rope to gain their attention. The tin bells clanked. It's a cacophonous sound, like badly-tuned cowbells. I pressed my palms together and clapped and genuflected. And then we con-templated each other in silence, the spirits of Yasukuni and I, in the middle of the busiest city in the world.

Asakusa, on Tokyo's north side, is an old section of the city, a network of avenues clustered with shops and stalls where all kinds of wares have been sold since the days of the shogun. Asakusa then was to the city what Carnaby Street was to London in the sixties, festooned with bright banners and gay lanterns—a ground zero zone of entertainment that catered to every taste. Street-corner jugglers and acrobats competed with "teahouse girls" who proffered diversions of a different sort, many of them plying their trade in a brothel that had once been a training hall for archery. There were shops that specialized in tortoiseshell hair ornaments, in silk brocade obi, or in scissors, sandals, or soap. If you wanted it in seventeenth-century Japan, Asakusa shops were likely to have it—in a variety of sizes. There was food as well, stalls peddling bean paste buns, grilled loach, and tubs of sake.

The shops of Asakusa are still there. They still carry most of the produce they once did and a lot more besides. Cheap rayon kimono, plastic "jade" statues of the Buddha, and wildly decorated T-shirts are for sale there, along with rice crackers, syrup with shaved ice, and snacks of stringy dried cuttlefish. Some change, though, has come to Asakusa. The shops there no longer use unemployed swordsmen to advertise their products as they did in the old days. Back then, during the Meiji period, some of those warriors whose professional status had been outlawed with the end of feudalism turned to exhibiting their skills for pay. Fast-draw *iai* experts slashed with their swords at papier-mâché balls that were tossed into the air. *Jujutsu* exponents grappled before Asakusa's crowds and then hawked the mouth-watering delicacies that were available in local shops. The tawdry martial art carnival acts are gone now. Gone too, is the flourishing prostitution business. And the acrobatic troupes who formed themselves into human bridges as other tumblers did somersaults up and over them. But the merchants and their shops are as healthy as ever in Asakusa. Keiko-san wanted me to see the spectacle of it.

Asakusa is also the home of Sensoji, better known as the Asakusa Temple. Local residents rushed to its thick pillars for protection during the great earthquake that shuddered through Tokyo in 1923. Kannon, the temple's deity, showed the mercy for which she is venerated by Buddhists: she spared Sensoji and much of the whole area of Asakusa from the destruction wreaked upon the rest of Tokyo then. The local parishioners hurried there once again during the raging firestorms ignited by the Allies during the Second World War, and this time the goddess gave no sanctuary. The temple at Asakusa was roasted to embers.

An effigy of Kannon towers over modern worshippers today at the rebuilt temple. But perhaps better known at the Asakusa Temple is a much smaller Kannon that adorns an inner altar. This tiny statue is only one *sun* and eight *bu* high by the old method of measuring, scarcely taller than a little finger. Because of her diminutive size and distinctive shape, the *issun hachi-bu* Kannon-no-sama of Asakusa serves in idiomatic Japanese as an oblique euphemism for a woman's clitoris.

Keiko-san and I visited the temple, then browsed through the stalls. We stopped in a tea shop for bowls of *anmitsu,* a confection of starchy-sweet cubes of gelatin and gooey syrup. Then she tugged me in the direction of the Asakusa Tourist Information Center. I wasn't sure why. Keiko-san seemed to know the area well enough. She could have served as a good tour guide of Asakusa herself. She led me, however, straight to the information desk at the Center and spoke to the attendant behind it in a clear voice.

"My friend here is visiting from America," Keiko said. "He would like to know where he can purchase *fundoshi*."

The attendant's head cocked around so fast I thought for a second he'd hurt himself. His eyes went to Keiko-san, then to me. Then back to her. I was the only non-Japanese in the building and probably on the entire block of that part of Tokyo at that moment as well, so becoming inconspicuous would have been difficult. That didn't stop me from trying. Fundoshi are Japanese style loincloths. They are strips of cotton cloth worn wrapped around the waist. In old Japan men of every class wore fundoshi and having been introduced to them by my sensei, I could understand why. Fundoshi are remarkably functional. They are especially comfortable to wear in the summer, leaving the hips nearly bare under one's pants. The cloth pouch of a fundoshi cups the genitals more loosely than even a pair of boxer shorts, yet it can quickly be snugged up—girding the loins, so to speak—for the sort of heavy work or strenuous effort that might require a jockstrap. In spite of these advantages as an alternative to underwear, fundoshi have fallen out of favor in Japan except as wear during certain kinds of festivals. They have been replaced by Western kinds of underwear except among a few old-timers and eccentrics. Like me. Asking where to buy fundoshi in modern Tokyo is rather like going into a clothing store in mid-town Manhattan to ask if they have any spats in your size.

The night before, while I was drowsily soaking in their tub, Keiko-san's son Esuke had talked about me with his mother, she told me later. "That guy is really old-fashioned, isn't he, Mom," he'd told her. He was referring, she said to me, to my sometimes dated Japanese and to my interest in areas of Japanese culture that were to him, relevant only to samurai action-type programs on the TV. "Gee," he'd said to her, "you think he wears fundoshi like Grandpa?" Keiko had repeated all of this to me while we were out wandering around Tokyo. As a matter of fact, I told her, I *did* sometimes wear fundoshi, especially when I was training in swordsmanship or another martial art during the sweltering months of the summer. I told her my sensei's wife had made some fundoshi for me and then when she returned to Japan, I got an aunt who was handy with a sewing machine to make some more. Then I forgot about the conversation until we were standing at the information center desk.

The attendant motioned another worker over. "This foreign fellow here wants to buy fundoshi! What do you make of that?"

"No!"

"Yes, yes! Bizarre, isn't it?"

"Really, it is that," replied the other worker and they launched into an animated discussion of the matter while I suddenly found myself profoundly interested in a pictorial display about the district's old fire-fighting regiments, which was mounted on a wall of the Center. An elderly man in a suit and wearing *zori* sandals tottered over to join the conversation.

"Did I hear you right? That gaijin wants fundoshi? My, I've never heard of such a thing. Sure he hasn't made some error in pronunciation? You know how it is with them when they try to speak Japanese."

I felt the collective glance of the three of them on me. "You know," one of the attendants said to Keiko-san and the others in a hushed tone, "I've heard that foreigners are bigger, you know, 'down there.'"

"Yep, I've heard that too," said the other.

"Maybe he'll need a bigger size."

Keiko-san murmured a "perhaps" and the old man nodded sagely, I saw from the corner of my eye. I could see that all of them were relishing the opportunity to discuss matters of such a cosmopolitan nature.

Which is how I found myself in Tokyo's bustling Asakusa district, the center of an enlightened conversation on the probable volume of my "down there."

3
Mountains

$\mathcal{J}$apanese trains—they have become something of a metaphor for the postwar successes, efficiency, and reliability of the entire country—leave on time. They do so with a consistency that intrigues the visitor to Japan and makes him wonder what sort of punishment awaits those responsible for fouling things up. If ever they do. When a train is scheduled to depart from Shimbashi Station at, oh, say 9:35, then that is not to be construed by the would-be passenger to mean 9:34. Or 9:36. Or any other time thereabouts. It means 9—set your watch by it—35. And if you are that would-be passenger then you'd better plan your boarding accordingly. I did and found my seat just as the train was pulling out of the station.

I was thinking about this very Japanese penchant for promptness while I shared a snack of dried, shredded squid with a teenaged boy who was sitting beside me. My share of the snack was earned because it was my knife he'd borrowed to slit open the package. My seatmate was animated, excited he told me, at having a gaijin companion from the land of the Yankees and Pirates that he could talk to. His enthusiasm waned as, during our conversation, it quickly became clear that he knew a great deal more about American baseball than did I.

"Your town's team is really strong this year," he told me. Yes, they were, I agreed, much to my consternation. Whatever interest

I'd always had in baseball had been largely confined to an intense and nearly lifelong despising of the St. Louis Cardinals. It would have been something of an exaggeration to say that I planned my trip to Japan to escape all the hoopla of the Cardinals possibly making the playoffs back in St. Louis, true. But I was content to be as far as possible from the contest without having to leave the planet entirely.

My young baseball fan friend left me at Chofu, one of the satellite suburbs of Tokyo. His seat was taken and then some by a bald and genial beer barrel of a man. He introduced himself as Dr. Yaga, an optometrist, now retired, and current president of the Nagoya Rotary Club. He had been, he told me, a former first officer aboard a frigate and had seen action at the Battle of Midway. The entire bridge of his ship was sheared off at deck level, he recounted for me, when a disabled Mitsubishi shucked a wing and cartwheeled into the ship.

The urban sprawl of Tokyo dropped away behind the train as we talked. Chunky blocks of ferroconcrete apartments dominate the view for a while, their balconies decorated with bright futon draped out to air in the sun. Then, gradually, the land becomes green and brown and the stretches between houses and other buildings grow longer and longer. Dr. Yaga gave into the pull of his heavy eyelids. He blinked slowly for a while, like a fat frog happy on his lily pad. Then he was dozing, his exhalations a steady hum. I was interrupted from my reading by a tap on my shoulder from another passenger sitting behind us. When I looked up, he pointed out the window, past the knobby hills that snaked by. Behind him, so far in the distance it was gray and hazy and barely discernible, was the pyramid of Mount Fuji. I watched the mountain, much too far from it to make out distinctly the gullies of snow and ice fingers that streaked its flanks even in late summer.

In the distance, the eternal coned shape of Fuji-san. Beside me, the contentedly slumbering bulk of Dr. Yaga, his face a study in stillness as well.

4
Suwa, Home of the Past

Out of the primordial clouds of mist that drifted through the universe, the Earthly Deities created the islands of Japan. That's what the ancient texts there say. The kami, the deities, set about giving forth a whole population of others like themselves, who spent their time sporting and hunting and—being Japanese gods and the earthly sort at that—copulating, all over Japan. The growing band of earthly deities were led by a kami, the texts have it, named Okuninushi.

The earthly deities, however, had begun to bicker amongst themselves. They squabbled so much that when the heavenly deity Amaterasu Omikami sent down her august child on the Floating Bridge of Heaven, the child returned in short order to tell her that the country below was in turmoil. It was, her child reported back, filled with rambunctious kami who "glowed with the luster of fireflies; evil kami who buzzed like flies."

Amaterasu convened eight hundred other heavenly deities. All of them met in the bed of the Divine River of Heaven, and all present agreed that her other child should be sent on a mission to take charge of the rebellious earthly kami. It didn't work. The child she sent "curried favor" with the earthly kami leader Okuninushi and for more than three years after he was sent, nothing was heard back from him.

The heavenly gods met once again and this time they selected another of their own, Amewakahiko, to go on the mission of subjugation. Armed with a magical bow and arrows, he left for Japan but soon after he arrived, he was seduced by the daughter of Okuninushi. He married her and they disappeared. A third time the heavenly kami came together. This time, a pheasant was sent down to spy, to determine what it was that was making the earthly kami so troublesome to control. The bird was killed, though, and the heavenly deities were forced to meet yet again to try to solve the problem.

"Which of us shall be sent now?" Amaterasu asked. In response, the other kami offered two names. Takemikazuchi (whose full name is Takemikazuchi-no-wo-no-Kami, the Brave Awful Possessing Thunder Male Kami Whose Name May be Written Five Ways) was mentioned. And so was Toribune-no-Kami, the Heavenly Bird-Boat Kami.

These two heavenly spirits made their way to the dwelling lands of their earthly counterparts in Japan. A number of battles followed; they are recorded in detail in both the *Nihon Shoki* ("The Chronicle of Japan") and in the *Kojiki* ("The Record of Ancient Matters"). Finally the two met the leader Okuninushi.

"Amaterasu wishes to invest her august grandchild to rule over this country in your place," the pair announced to Okuninushi. "Will you step aside and allow him to take your place?"

Okuninushi was a crafty kami. "It is not up to me to decide such a matter," he told the heavenly deities. "You must ask my son, Kotoshironushi, who is now at the Cape of Miho, fishing." And so Toribune-no-Kami dispatched herself off to Cape Miho.

"I will obey the request of the heavenly deities," said Okuninushi's son when he was confronted, and he promptly left the marshes where he had been fishing and disappeared forever. The heavenly kami returned to Okuninushi. "Now will you abdicate your rule?" they asked him.

"Ah, but you see, I have another son," said Okuninushi. "He is Takeminakata-no-Kami." As Okuninushi spoke, this son happened onto the scene. He was balancing on his fingertips a rock, as the myths have it, that would have taken one thousand mortals to have budged.

"Who is it who wishes my father to abdicate?" he demanded. "Let us first have a test of strength here," he said. "Let it begin by taking my hand for a contest of our grips." Takeminakata-no-Kami extended his fist then and the heavenly deity Takemika-zuchi seized it. The grip of the heavenly kami was so powerful it turned Takeminakata's hand into an icicle. Seeing his strength was no match for the deities of heaven, Takeminakata fled, pursued by Takemikazuchi, who caught him at the shores of Lake Suwa. There, the earthly kami Takeminakata-no-Kami surrendered.

"I cannot go against the will of my father," he said. "I will yield up this central land of reeds and plains according to the mandate of the august representatives of the heavenly kami."

And so it was then, according to the *Kojiki* and *Nihon Shoki*, that the heavenly kami descended and took control of the lands of reeds and plains and later on, of Toyotas and pachinko.

Takeminakata-no-Kami's surrender occurred, if we can trust the reliability of the texts, a short distance from where the train station at Upper Suwa City sits, on the shore of Lake Suwa, deep in the highlands of Nagano Prefecture. All these divine events transpired some time ago, of course—quite a while, in fact, before the Japan National Railway on which I was riding laid its tracks up through the jagged trailings of the Japan Alps southwest of Tokyo to Lake Suwa. But if the JNR line had gone through back then, Takeminakata-no-Kami could have caught a ride when he made his escape from the icy grip of the heavenly kami Take-mikazuchi. The city of Upper Suwa, Kamisuwa-shi, is nestled right at the shore of the lake where the confrontation is supposed to have taken place. Suwa Taisha, the Shinto shrine erected to house the spirit of the defeated kami, is so close to the station that Takeminakata could doubtless have heaved that one-thousand-man boulder he was carrying on his fingertips the entire distance to it without breaking a divine sweat in the effort.

I made Suwa, in Nagano Prefecture, a destination in Japan after leaving Tokyo because of that shrine and because I was interested in seeing small-town Japan. An acquaintance had friends there; she arranged for me to stay with an old Suwa family, the Fujiwaras, and to be shown about by some of the locals. These plans were informal. I'd only called from Tokyo the day before to let my hosts in Suwa know that I was on my way. I had no idea what to expect. What I did not expect was to be greeted at the Suwa station by a man playing a Toshiba synthesizer in my honor. The machine started blaring a heartfelt rendition of "Stars and Stripes Forever" as soon as I walked through the doors of the station.

I blanched. Even if you are the sort of person who craves attention, Japan for a Westerner can often provide more of it than you will want. The "Fundoshi Incident" back in Asakusa had been a bit embarrassing by comparison. This was wretched, like one of those dreams where you show up at work stark naked.

"You don't get many visitors up in these parts, do you?" I very badly wanted to say, but did not. Instead, I stood there in the station, holding my backpack, feeling terribly embarrassed and self-conscious. Probably a dozen travelers who'd come up on the train with me had gone on to do the various things they needed to get done, some queued up at the ticket window, others were at the newsstand. A wrinkled *obaasan* in kimono was perched on a bench with her belongings knotted in a dark indigo *furoshiki* cloth by her side. Every one of them, I saw, was frozen in place like the elements of a tableau. Every one of them was looking at me. I wanted nothing more right at that moment than to have been able to sink away right down into the concrete at my feet. It was just when I had begun to think that I had to do something to get out of this that all three and one-half feet of Miss Yajima materialized beside me.

"Do you like the music?" she asked me. "It is for you."

"Very... thoughtful."

Yajima-san, a local English-language teacher, had volunteered to fill in for the Fujiwaras to come meet me at the station, she explained. They were older and neither spoke even the most basic English, and while they were happy to have me as a guest in their house, they were worried they might not be able to communicate with me.

"I see," I said. The Sousa march continued to hammer.

"Excuse me," Miss Yajima said. "Could we go now?"

You bet. Gladly. Quickly.

As we drove through the center of Suwa, Yajima-san confessed that the welcoming salute in my honor was not exactly that. The synthesizer was at the train station as part of a promotion by a local music store. The welcoming stanzas of John Philip Sousa were an impromptu request from Yajima-san to the store's representative. Even so, it was already clear that Suwa was off the beaten track for non-Japanese tourists and it was obvious too, that Yajima-san was enjoying the chance to play tour guide to a visitor.

"Those orchards are full of apples," she pointed out, "just ready now to be picked. Suwa apples are famous all over Japan." She went on, but I did not hear much of her spiel. My attention was taken by the scene that had just unfolded in front of us. We'd turned a corner down a street that looked as if it ran right into the moat of a spectacular castle tower, one that appeared to have been transported directly from the sixteenth century. The three-storied corner tower of Takashima-jo and part of its inner donjon walls were all that remained of the original fortress, Yajima-san told me. Later on in my travels in Japan, I would see larger and older castles. But the sight of Takashima-jo's stately white tower made a striking impression on me. It was that rare sort of architecture that has the power to communicate, and driving past it in the late afternoon, I wondered what it might have to say to me if I explored it. So I was delighted to see that the Fujiwara house where I was staying was down a narrow lane just a few blocks from the castle. The tower's long afternoon shadow almost touched the roof of the Fujiwara home I noticed, as Yajima-san and I drove up to their front gate.

"How! Are! You!"

The giggles and shouts of Tomoko and Akiko Nagata came bubbling in through the back doorway a full minute before they did. The two paused only as long as it takes a six and seven year old to bounce around wrenching off their shoes at the threshold step. Tomoko and Akiko were brought up short at the sight of a foreign stranger being shown through their grandparents' house. They were instantly reduced to whispers, hurriedly withdrawing to peer out at me from the safe distance of an open shoji screen until their father came in and urged them out of their hiding place to make a proper—and loudly enthusiastic—welcome that took full advantage of their English vocabulary.

Rather a lot of print in the West has been devoted to the extravagant premiums on space in Japan, mostly quoting land or apartment or house prices in Tokyo, and so there are horror tales of twenty million dollars or more being paid for a skinny strip of land barely big enough to build a single family house on. The stories are true; land available for building anything on has always been in scarce supply in Japan. But away from the major urban areas, out in places like Nagano Prefecture, land is not quite so precious. The Fujiwaras lived in a spacious, two-story house, not much noticeably smaller than the typical two-bedroom bunga-low in the United States. Unlike during my stay in Tokyo, where sleeping arrangements for the Yoshikawa family had to be altered to fit me in, I didn't dislodge anyone at the Fujiwara home in Suwa. I had a room to myself, the size of four tatami mats. Mr. Fujiwara showed me to it, and left me alone to nap until dinner. I did doze, eventually. But I sat for a few moments and took in the space around me.

There was nothing in the room save for a couple of closets built into the wall on one side and a tokonoma alcove on the other. The only decorations were a wall scroll hanging in the tokonoma, a poem brushed by Mrs. Fujiwara, she shyly admitted to me when I expressed an interest later that evening, and a quietly beautiful display of chrysanthemums she'd composed, on the shelf below the scroll.

Such emptiness, such an apparent void and blank space, is unsettling to many Westerners, accustomed to rooms busy with furniture, shelves and tabletops busy with knickknacks; living space devoid of such distractions can look forlorn and somehow incomplete. "A Japanese house always looks like someone has just moved out," one tourist in Japan told me. To become comfortable with all this emptiness, to resist the urge to fill it in, one must be comfortable with the concept of *ma*. Literally, ma refers to an "interval." The gap between weapons held by two swordsmen facing each other is one form of ma. The pause between beats on a taiko drum has its own specific ma; the hesitation between the first splatter of raindrops and the electric crackle of lightning, the resonance of thunder that follows: all have their own ma.

Ma plays a vital role in Japanese architecture. The severe simplicity of my guest quarters at the Fujiwara house was not a disregard for beauty. It was an example of ma, a deliberate aesthetic device to emphasize the accents that were in the room. In a space cluttered with paintings, sculpture, and other decorations, the spray of three chrysanthemum blossoms at the tokonoma and the scroll above it would have been just two more. But placed as they were, at one side against a spacious ma with nothing else to interfere, they drew to them anyone entering the room. Without competing distractions, the flowers could be appreciated in full. The vase they were in, a muddy brown pot in other circumstances, was highlighted and it was possible to notice how the color and texture of the vase were complemented by the soft, golden blossoms. The scroll was only a couple of lines of calligraphy, only a dozen or so characters. But because they were arranged on the hanging scroll—and the scroll itself arranged on the alcove wall—with a sensitivity to ma, they became objects worthy of study and appreciation, the inspiration for a meditative introspection. My room may have seemed empty. It was not. The deep expression of ma filled it wonderfully.

Mrs. Fujiwara answered the phone's ring as we finished dinner.

"Dave-san, this is Mrs. Mizuno on the line. She wants to know if you'd like to take a bath with her."

Mrs. Mizuno, I was told, was a widow who lived a few houses further down along the lane. She was as well, and had been for sixty years, a member in good standing at a local bath club. She'd heard I had arrived in Suwa and thought a perfect introduction to both herself and the town would be a trip to her bath club. Was I interested? You bet.

Mrs. Fujiwara gathered for me a heavy padded cotton yukata, a plastic rinsing bowl, soap, and a washcloth towel called a *tenugui*, and then Mizuno-san's wooden geta were clopping down the stone footpath to the front door to escort me. Minutes later, I found myself scrambling along a rice field dike path to keep up with her. The air was chill and hard as a marble slab and it had the smoky scent of burnt leaves and rice straw on it.

"You're from America," Mizuno-san said over her shoulder. Her gait was a remarkably fast, mincing shuffle.

"Yes, from St. Louis."

"Is that near Tu-peru-oh?"

Mentally, I did a fast translation. Tupero. Tupelo. Mississippi. I'm walking through a rice paddy in the dark, going to a Japanese bathhouse with an eighty-year-old daughter of Suwa, Nagano Prefecture, who's a God-help-me devotee of Elvis.

"No," I said. "Tupelo's a city farther south, in the state of Mississippi."

"Oh yes," Mrs. Mizuno nodded, still walking at the same furious pace. "I would certainly like to see it someday," she said. But it turned out that her interest in Tupelo was not fueled by a passion for the King. "My daughter had a pen pal from there," she told me. "Every year she sent us a jar of Tupelo honey." Mrs. Mizuno had developed a taste for the stuff.

Mizuno-san paused and looked back over her shoulder, her face as round and wrinkled as a dried apple. "I believe that city," she said — Tupero — "must taste good."

I laughed with her. This was before I had met Nakanishi-san, the innkeeper in Nara, and heard his equally creative use of that same word.

"By the way," Mizuno-san pointed. "There's the castle, Takashima-jo."

Takashima-jo's alabaster tower and dark tiled roof were illuminated against the night. Floodlight shined from the base of the moat. Viewed from the rice field we walked through, it had about it an even more stately and medieval atmosphere than when I'd seen it in daylight.

A broad, mossy brook ran beside the castle, part of its flow checked and diverted to fill the castle moat. On the opposite bank, hunkered down in a copse of pines, was Mizuno-san's bathhouse. Slatted windows with translucent panels suffused a pale glow, welcoming us with a promise of warmth in the cool night.

Our visit to the bath club was not a hygienic necessity, of course. Mizuno-san had a perfectly good *ofuro* tub in her house, as did the Fujiwaras. Simple cleanliness is important, but it's far from the sole motivation for bathing in Japan. There is a sociability attached to bathing, a convention going far back in Japanese history. In even the smallest neighborhood or hamlet in Japan there is at least one public bath, or *sento*, within walking distance of every resident. In places like Suwa, with its abundant hot springs, there are also sento maintained as clubs or social groups, with members paying an annual fee to keep up the bathhouse and grounds. A plaque in the men's dressing room informed me that I was peeling out of my pants in the Shokodachikai (the "Pine Grove Club"), built in 1810, during the sixth year of the era of Bunka. The names of the founders of the club were listed as well. I folded my clothes into a bamboo hamper and left them, trusting there were no thieves in the fraternal ranks of the Shokodachikai. Actually, it was not quite a fraternity in the strictest sense, as I was reminded when I stepped through the dressing room door. Shokodachikai was thoroughly co-ed.

"This is Mrs. Matayama," Mizuno-san said, nodding to a woman in her early thirties, I guessed, with a toddler playing at the edge of the tub beside her. "And this old geezer is Mr. Nishigaki," she told me, pushing her chin at a stoop-shouldered fellow on the other side of the bath who grinned and bobbed his head at me. Mizuno-san was squatting on a stool on the tiled apron outside the bath itself, in front of a hot water spigot. "This is Dave-san. He's staying with the Fujiwaras," she announced. Then she lifted her arm to scrub a soapy tenugui across her ribs.

Since I was standing and the tub was sunk in below the level of the floor, I bowed low and my bathing companions nodded to me from their seated positions.

"*Hajimemashite dozo yoroshiku,*" I said, the most formal greeting I knew, although under the circumstances it seemed a bit out of place. Mr. Nishigaki agreed. He cackled, "Ahh, too formal? We're just simple country folk here. And the bath is not a place for formalities, after all, eh Mizuno-san?"

"No indeed." Mizuno-san had filled her rinsing bowl full and she tipped it over herself, flushing away the suds and lather. She stood with surprising grace for her age. Almost casually, she gripped the hem of her tenugui in front of her pubic patch.

"Still, it's nice to hear good manners," said Mrs. Matayama. Her boy was crawling along the bath's rim behind her shoulder. She turned and grabbed his chubby leg and gave it a playful shake. He laughed and looked wide-eyed at her. His genitals were no more than pink buds of flesh.

"Yes, yes," agreed Mr. Nishigaki. "But he's a foreigner, you know. He must feel a touch awkward. No need to have him be so formal."

I pulled up a stool and drew my bucket full of steaming water from the spigot and wonder just how formal I could be like this.

If one knows anything about bathing Japanese style, he knows it is a gross breach of etiquette to soap up and rinse off in the bath water itself. That water is kept clean, to soak in. Water for washing and rinsing comes from another outlet entirely. A Japanese bath is a gloriously, hedonistically sloppy place. The floor, if it is wooden, is slatted, or, if it is tiled like the one in the Shokodachikai, is canted slightly to allow water outside the tub to runnel away. Once lathered up, soap starting to drip into your eyes, you may tilt your rinsing bowl up and over, luxuriating in the flow as the excess splashes all over and gargles merrily out the drains. Japanese who are washing off in preparation for soaking look like happy children at the beach, dumping bucket after bucket of water over themselves as they squat, sloshing away the dirt and perspiration—along with the stress and strains—of the day.

Clean and shivering, since the bathhouse had no heat aside from that used to keep the water at a fine simmer, I slid in and joined the stew. The bath itself would have accommodated a couple of Honda sedans side by side, it was that big, and it was deep enough that the waterline would have been level with the top of their trunks. Instead of automobiles, though, the bath at Shokodachikai was holding Mrs. Mizuno and Mr. Nishigaki, both neck deep and with folded tenugui on the crowns of their gray heads, me and Mrs. Matayama, and for short dunks that left him steaming like a lobster just hoisted from the pot, her little boy.

"Do you have anything like this in America?" Matayama-san asked me. She had pulled her hair up and clenched it with a clip into a chignon and I studied the effect carefully to avoid looking anywhere else in particular. Before I could answer her that no, we most definitely did not have anything remotely like this in America, not to my knowledge, we were joined by the Fujiwaras' son-in-law, Mitsuo Nagata.

"Listen," Nagata-san said to me as he squatted near where I was soaking and began soaping himself. "I have a friend coming over who's a member of the club here, too. He's an amateur photographer and he'd like to take some pictures of you here."

"Yes, yes; grand idea," applauded Mr. Nishigaki.

"You know," Mizuno-san said, "you're the first non-Japanese in the hundred and seven years of Shokodachikai to bathe here. It's quite an historic event for the neighborhood."

Perhaps, but I wasn't so sure I wanted the festivities recorded on film. In the time I'd come to Suwa, I had gotten the impression foreign visitors were a rarity. I had a quick mental picture of my bath being a front page item in tomorrow's local edition of the prefectural paper.

"*Konban wa! Konban wa!*" came from the women's dressing room.

"My, we have more visitors tonight," exclaimed Mrs. Matayama.

And so we did. With smiles and bows and nothing else save six strategically wielded hand towels, we were joined by a gaggle of women — high school teachers, I learned — who were in Suwa on a holiday trip, one of whom was a sister to another Shokodachikai member.

It was, all in all, a perfectly wonderful introduction to Suwa. And if I had not found the real Japan or at least a small part of it within the cypress-scented walls of the Pine Grove Bath Club, then I was that evening completely satisfied with the imitation.

The small fencing dojo in Suwa was on a spur of alley off one of the town's streets. It was near the center of Suwa, between a tiny grocery shop and an equally tiny hardware store. Despite the setting, the dojo had obviously been placed with some attention to aesthetics, situated off by itself, separated from the city and the world by a tall hedge of bamboo and a stockade-type fence. Like the bathhouse, the dojo was so old that moss had furred the tiles on the roof and the cypress walls outside were bleached and faded by the sun. Inside, they were dark with years of polishing. Hanging from a beam in one corner was a drum head that had been struck to signal the start of training sessions at the dojo. It had boomed for the last time in 1912, on the final day of kendo practice during the Meiji era.

"I trained at the dojo when I was a boy," Fujiwara-san told me while we were eating dinner the night before I went to fencing hall. His father had trained there too, and was there when the great drum was struck for the last time, to commemorate the death of the Emperor Meiji. "I used to go there at dawn four days a week," Fujiwara-san said, "with my brother. I'd tote him on the bumper of my bicycle." This was back in the twenties; Japan was emerging as a global military power. Kendo and other traditional martial ways were considered by the Imperial Government to be methods for teaching loyalty, for instilling patriotism and *Yamato damashi*—the "Japanese spirit."

"It was so cold, that's what I remember about the training at the dojo before the war," Fujiwara-san went on, reminiscing. "I used to cry when we'd get out onto that frozen wooden floor in the wintertime."

Fujiwara-san hadn't continued on with his practice of kendo once he left school. But one of his classmates at the dojo had gone on to become the chief instructor at the Suwa Dojo, with eighth dan rankings in kendo and in iaido, the way of drawing and cutting with the live sword. Armed with a letter of introduction from Fujiwara-san, I went to the dojo to meet Tsuchihashi Sensei.

Do you remember television's *The Muppet Show?* Remember the myopic Dr. Bunsen Honeydew? Dr. Honeydew was a melon-headed researcher who, with his dithering assistant Beaker, was forever elucidating some obscure point of science, usually culminating in a lab experiment that exploded the hapless Beaker. If you do remember Dr. Honeydew, then you would have had the same thought I did upon meeting Tsuchihashi Sensei: he was a dead ringer, surely the inspiration in fact, for the Muppet Dr. Honeydew. Bald, his perpetually smiling eyes mere slits behind thick, round-rimmed glasses, the senior teacher at the Suwa Dojo beamed amiably and chuckled when I bowed and handed him the letter of introduction.

"Sure, we've been expecting you," he said to me. "Go get dressed and introduce yourself to Toguchi-san. He's the fellow with the long hair over there. He's volunteered to loan you a *katana* while you're staying here in Suwa."

I dressed quickly, knotting up the wide cotton obi, the ties of my training jacket lapels, and the long cloth wrappings of my *hakama* overskirt. As I did, Toguchi-san came into the dressing room, a long canvas bag slung over his shoulder. We introduced ourselves and he untied the bag, drawing out a katana in its lacquered sheath.

Up until about the fourteenth century, the Japanese warrior wore his sword, or *tachi,* with the convex cutting edge turned downward, attached to his belt by silk or leather cords. It was a weapon well suited to be drawn and used from horseback. During the Muromachi era of the fifteenth century, though, military strategy changed dramatically. Instead of charges by massed cavalry, battles were increasingly waged by armies on foot. Warfare was conducted as a series of individual duels between samurai (as well as larger encounters by foot soldiers wielding spears or other weapons). Responding to these evolutions in fighting, the warrior altered his methods of carrying and using his sword. He reversed the way in which he slung the weapon, turning the blade over and wearing it in its scabbard thrust through his belt. This modification, from the tachi to the katana (actually the weapon itself changed almost not at all: the katana is generally shorter than the tachi, but the difference in terminology refers to the different way in which the sword was worn), brought about too, further developments in the warrior class itself. As the samurai became solidified as a distinct feudal caste, specific behaviors began to be expected of the warrior. An elaborate etiquette governing virtually all areas of interaction with others was cultivated. The warrior found himself accountable for all kinds of potential breaches in his expected conduct in daily life. If, for example, he allowed his blade in its scabbard to scrape or knock against that of another samurai's weapon while walking down the street, if he failed to bow properly to a superior, if by accident or deliberately he committed any number of gaffes, he risked immediate retaliation. This often took the form of a duel or a challenge.

It is important to understand, incidentally, that such challenges for the samurai during much of the feudal era were not typically those of the sort issued in the West in earlier times, the "demand for satisfaction" that preceded a duel in Hamburg or Verona, for instance. In the strict code of conduct of the Japanese warrior, the offence itself could be taken as an invitation to fight. Cross in front of my path without taking your right hand off your sword handle and extending it so I can see you mean no harm, and I will assume by your action that you indeed do have some hostile action planned for me. My response would not be to issue a challenge, since I would assume by your behavior that you have already challenged me. Instead, I might simply move to cut you down, instantly. True, too much can and has been made of the potential for this sort of violence. Fictionalized and some highly colorized historical accounts of the samurai often accent these "look at me the wrong way and you die" tendencies in the professional warrior class of old Japan. The potential was there. Yet in a highly stratified society, members know what to expect and how to behave within the rigid forms of conduct; while such forms made demands on behavior we might consider harsh, they nonetheless allowed everyone in the society a clear guide to what was and was not permissible. Even so, the demands of the samurai's sense of etiquette were, especially by today's standards, extreme. Even the manner in which a samurai sat on the floor, his sheathed blade resting by his side, became a matter of carefully-observed convention. Placing the katana down so the cutting edge faced out would have provided the swordsman a fractional advantage in quickly drawing it. To so do, and to keep it on one's left side which would mean an even faster access to the weapon, could be a serious insult under some conditions. The perpetrator, even if his action was entirely innocent (and seldom was it; those of the military class had an education in this sort of thing beginning almost from birth), was very soon likely to find himself answering for the breach. Such volatility may seem excessive. But it was the way of the warrior in feudal Japan and men died for not paying it adequate attention or ignoring its dangers.

To cope with these dangers, the samurai began to formulate techniques to allow him to use his sword, drawing and cutting with it immediately, with deadly precision under almost any circumstances. These techniques became known collectively by a number of names. Two of the most common were *battojutsu* and *iaijutsu*. Both terms describe the art or skills of taking the initiative with the sword, striking speedily and decisively with the katana before an enemy could draw his own weapon or make an attack. Whether standing, sitting, kneeling, or walking, the competent iaijutsu exponent could unsheathe and cut with his katana, no matter from what direction his opponent approached—or from what direction he approached his opponent. It was an important element in the art. Nearly all methods of iaijutsu involved techniques that called for an aggressive instigation. A warrior did not always have the luxury of resorting to violence only in "defending" himself. Notions of "self-defense" and other such ideas as applied to the Japanese combative arts are strictly a modern interpretation. The duty of the samurai, to protect and promote the interests of his lord, often required him to initiate combat. His iaijutsu was a means to that end.

The majority of the classical schools of *bujutsu*, the koryu, included a thorough study of iai in their combative curriculum. Each of these koryu engendered its own distinctive techniques for drawing the sword. With the eclipse of the feudal caste system in 1867, though, an historical evening set too, on the practical uses of iaijutsu and all other classical arts of the samurai. Iaijutsu and *kenjutsu* (swordsmanship, the art of wielding the katana once it was unsheathed) were relegated in early modern Japan to the status of antiques. Several *ryu* maintained their classical traditions—the Shinkage-ryu of my teacher's lineage was one. Other schools, however, produced swordsmen who were extraordinary in their ability to read the currents of the future. Drawn from the elitist warrior's iaijutsu, they believed, could be an egalitarian form of the sword-drawing art, one no longer devoted to lethal conclusions but to be used as an avenue towards spiritual enlightenment and self-discovery. This was the impetus for iaido, the "Do" or "Way" of the sword draw.

Today, modern iaido consists of ten basic draws and strikes. These are the *seiteigata*, the "established forms." Once these ten forms are learned and polished sufficiently, instruction is given to the practitioner in some of the older iaido styles of swordsmanship that flourished in the post-feudal era. These *kata* are from the Omori-ryu, the Hasegawa-ryu, and the Eishin-ryu which, while not technically ancient enough to be called truly classical, were methods of an age when *bugeisha* were still alive who had fought and killed with the katana. Finally, if he persists through the lessons of these movements, the iaido adept may be encouraged to train in one of the still-surviving koryu with their purely combative, essentially deadly techniques of iaijutsu.

Unlike most iaido exponents, I entered the art through its back door: I trained first in the drawing techniques that were related to the swordsmanship of the Shinkage-ryu. Only later did friends of my sensei introduce me to modern iaido. My early koryu experience has influenced my practice of iaido. My movements during the kata of iaido often snap when they should flow, crackle when they ought to glow. In the dojo at Suwa, Tsuchihashi Sensei noticed this right away. He asked me to perform the first draw of the seiteigata. Kneeling, I rose on one knee and loosened the unfamiliar katana from its scabbard. It arced out, cut with a raking, horizontal slash, and then I struck again, raising the sword above my head as I shuffled forward still on my knees, cutting vertically. I whipped the blade in a wide circle, a stylistic motion meant to clean the weapon of accumulated blood and gore, and then I returned it to the scabbard. It was a far from perfect rendition of the kata; probably two decades of training under the continuous guidance of a master would be the only way to attain anything resembling perfection in even this, the most basic movement of the art. But, I thought, considering it was a borrowed katana and I was stiff from a lot of travel, my performance was passable. Tsuchihashi Sensei did not.

"This isn't a battlefield," the master of the Suwa Dojo admonished me. "Instead of being so aggressive in your kata, try to make your fighting spirit come out in your presence."

What Tsuchihashi Sensei meant was for me to try to dominate my imaginary opponent, to control the space around me, with my feeling. Like the Noh actor, the iaido exponent must work to master not only himself, but to establish a sense of authority over the moment. The true expert can cut with his spirit, sending it out like a wave, to devastate and overwhelm. His power with the sword is far more than physical.

Tsuchihashi Sensei made some technical corrections, then, "Try again." I did. I made an effort to incorporate his instructions into my kata, concentrating completely on it. When I finished, clicking the katana into its sheath and coming up out of the kneeling position with a slow, focused deliberation, I looked up to see if I'd merited any approval with the execution. But Tsuchihashi Sensei had disappeared to the other side of the dojo where he was helping a woman member of the dojo with her *noto*. Noto—returning the blade to the *saya*, or scabbard—is perhaps the most dangerous aspect of iaido. It must be accomplished purely by feel, gripping the saya mouth with the left hand and sliding the back of the sword along the web of flesh between the left thumb and forefinger, then suddenly reversing the movement just as the razor tip of the weapon reaches the scabbard opening. Correctly done, the blade slithers swiftly home into the saya—or into the left hand or the side of the practitioner if the timing or coordination between left and right hands or the movement of the katana and the saya are off in the least bit. Even very good iaido practitioners are apt to have nicks and little cuts in the soft wood at the mouth of their saya, where the sword has cut upon being replaced incorrectly from time to time. Bad iaido practitioners are likely to have scars of a more anatomical nature as testimony

to their poor training. Tsuchihashi Sensei was demonstrating a
fine point of noto of some kind to the woman. He seemed to have
forgotten all about me. I knew better, though.

Unlike Western forms of education, the classical martial ways
like iaido are not learned in a concise and logically understandable order. There are no pre-set "black belt courses" or guaranteed
results. Quite the opposite. The budo, like all the other "do" forms
of Japan, are based upon a Confucian approach to teaching and
learning.

"I do not enlighten those who are not eager to learn, nor
arouse those who are not quick to give an explanation themselves.
If I have presented one corner to the square and they cannot come
back to me with the other three, I should not go over the points
again." That is the way Confucius himself expressed the idea
almost twenty-five hundred years ago, in his *Analects*, providing with his philosophy the framework of education throughout
much of Asia even today. The student of iaido, or any other "do,"
is expected to follow his teacher's instructions without question,
always exhibiting a flexibility of spirit, a willingness to give up
his own notions to incorporate those of the teacher. At times in
his training he will learn something new whenever he is with his
teacher — another technique, a deeper insight into the art. Other
periods of training may find him going on and on, coming to
practice and working under the eye of a teacher who gives him
little if any direct instruction or advice. The student may even
come to feel during these times that his teacher has forgotten all
about him. But there is no neglect; the sensei is merely waiting.
He has presented his student with a corner of the square. Now
he stands back, watching to see of the student can discover for
himself the other three.

I drew and cut, again and again, the constant mechanics of
repetition, working on the points Tsuchihashi Sensei had made to
me, oblivious to the ten other practitioners who shared the dojo
with me, until one of them stepped in front of my little space in
the corner. I only needed to glimpse his posture, relaxed, solid

through the legs and hips like the trunk of an oak, to know he was my senior in iaido.

"Okay," he said pleasantly, "take a rest."

It wasn't until then that I realized my jacket was weighted with perspiration. It runneled down my forearms and had stained the silk cord wrappings of the katana where I'd gripped the handle. The windows of the dojo were open to the cold air of the autumn evening but my face was flushed and throbbed with the heat of my exertion.

"And while you're resting," the senior went on, "show me the next kata please."

I glanced at Tsuchihashi Sensei. He stood across the room, arms folded, and he nodded his Muppet head slightly. I had not yet merited more of his masterful instruction. But one of his most advanced students, and then another after that, came over to watch my technique, to offer criticism and guidance. *Ukenagashi* ("flowing parry"), *ganmenate* ("striking the face"), *shihogiri* ("cutting in four directions"): I was worked at the Suwa Dojo through the whole of the basic ten techniques of iaido, each of them scrutinized by the senior members. Just when I thought one more kata would send me crashing to the floor on my face, Tsuchihashi Sensei clapped his hands to bring the group to order. We bowed to him, to the shrine at the front of the dojo, and to each other. In the dressing room I shrugged out of my wet uniform, already feeling the stiffness of sore muscles. Tsuchihashi Sensei, already dressed and looking even more Muppet-like in his sport jacket and tie, touched me on the shoulder.

"We will see you again?"

"Yes, sensei," I said, and thanked him for allowing me to train with his group. He nodded, but I could see the doubt in his eyes. It had been a long night for me, and many Japanese simply do not believe that gaijin have a serious interest in the budo.

I stopped at the bathhouse and soaked away the aches of the evening's training. My cranky muscles softened in the steaming water of the tub, but my head buzzed with all the instruction I had been given. Later that night, sandwiched between the futon and a fat, quilted coverlet, I dreamed of the angles and arcs of iaido and I traced them, my mind still at work long after my body had called it a day.

I woke to the rustle of the shoji screen panel gliding back along its polished track. I rolled over, blinking against the sunlight that cut through the open doorway and stared into the big, luminous eyes of six-year-old Tomoko. She sat in a flat-footed crouch to observe the alien who was sleeping in her grandparents' house. Akiko, her sister, would talk with me and even climb into my lap when I sat with the Fujiwara family watching television at night and drinking bitter brown barley tea. But Tomoko was silent and distant. She only watched me, and every day I stayed in Suwa, she came and let in the light to awaken me and crouched there in the doorway, fixing me with an obdurate stare, never saying to me a word.

5
Glimpses of the Warrior

*A*ccording to the JNTO, the Japan National Tourist Organization, the average tourist in Japan comes as a part of a guided tour, a group following either a guide or an itinerary supplied by a travel agency. That tourist tends to center time, attention, and spending in major urban areas like Tokyo, Osaka, or Kyoto. He confines his sightseeing to temples, museums, and the like. This sort of travel is relatively painless and without a lot of unhappy surprises, and it can be almost a necessity in dealing with a country like Japan where reading even a simple menu is beyond the capacity of most foreigners. But it insulates the visitor from exposure to small-town Japanese life as it unfolds in out-of-the-way places like Suwa. For instance, the visitor who never strays from the beaten track in Japan misses the quite extraordinary sensation that he is a transient from another galaxy just dropped in for a sojourn in this neck of the universe.

One afternoon, I was sitting at a table directly off the entrance to an inn in Suwa, waiting for the owner, Tsuchida-san, who was taking me out to dinner. A friend of Tsuchida-san, an old drinking buddy, came bounding in the front door of the inn, waving jauntily to the receptionist behind her desk and spinning around the corner to where I was sitting. He took one look—and I am not remarkably unattractive or malformed—and he hurled himself—actually launched—backward, staggering in shock as if he'd been shot. It was dramatic, like an entrance in a situation comedy on TV. At first I thought it was some kind of theatrical gesture, in fact; perhaps this was the Jerry Lewis of Suwa. But the man's face was a study in amazement. He looked stunned, and he circled around me warily, keeping a safe distance.

"He was surprised because you are probably only the third or fourth gaijin he's ever seen that close up," Tsuchida-san told me later. I was a bit startled myself at this. I associated such encounters more with explorers in New Guinea or the Amazon Basin. The inhabitants of cities even smaller than Suwa in the U.S. are exposed to different races, different nationalities. In Tokyo and other metropolitan spaces in Japan the same is true. But in rural areas, foreigners—anyone non-Japanese—are still not a common sight by any means. Every visitor to Japan is soon familiar with the word gaijin, "outside person." In places like Suwa, one learns what it really means.

Only one other gaijin had trained at the Suwa Dojo, a Japanese-Canadian kendo enthusiast who had been staying in Suwa while doing some sort of botanical research in the surrounding mountain ranges. I was the second. When I returned for the next iaido practice at the dojo I heard a few murmurs among the regular members. My return wasn't expected. As we changed into training uniforms, Tsuchihashi explained why.

"I was training myself in Kyoto last year with some of my seniors," he said. (Since he was ranked at the eighth dan—only nine are awarded in iaido—with over forty years of experience, I didn't even want to think about the standards and skill of those he considered *his* seniors.) "We had a couple of gaijin come to the dojo while I was there," he told me. "The way my seniors treated them was to correct points in the few first few kata and then to have them practice those for the entire training session." Tsuchihashi Sensei and his colleagues had found this method of instruction to be a satisfactory way of thinning out those less than completely sincere about training in iaido since, as he put it, "They quickly got bored and left us alone."

Many Westerners, too many who have come to Japan to follow the budo, have been dabblers when they entered training in their own country. They are what the Japanese describe as *chishiki wo kajiru,* "knowledge nibblers." They have taken up the budo because "things Japanese" are fashionable, or because of popular novels with heroes who are martial arts experts, or for dozens of other insubstantial reasons. They come to Japan with romantic notions of learning with budo masters who spend their days spouting aphorisms and pruning their bonsai, and they are swiftly disillusioned. The martial ways are, at their most basic level, an awfully lot of hard and repetitious work. One cannot nibble at the edges if he expects to get anywhere. The *budoka* must plunge right in and gobble up as much as he can. Further, Western budoka cannot afford to indulge themselves in romanticism. The budo master in Japan is not likely to be the master portrayed in novels or on the screen. More typically, he is an accountant or a carpenter or, as in Tsuchihashi Sensei's case, a manager in a nearby Seiko watch factory. He is not an all-knowing guru with the answers to life's problems. He has struggled along the way himself and in return for the kindness shown him by his teachers, he shows you the methods by which you can make the same journey for yourself.

Just as the budo sensei is no wizard with the power to provide easy solutions or shortcuts to the process of treading the way, the dojo does not offer a sentimental escape from reality, as it is sometimes depicted. The experience there is just the opposite, as real as the two dozen stitches laced up the forearm of one of the younger practitioners at the Suwa Dojo, the result of a hasty and ill-timed draw a week before my arrival. The budoka must be willing to endure danger in the training hall—and boredom as well. He must be able to accept too, that his seniors and teachers are travelers on the same path he's walking, a little or a lot further along the trip than he is. All are following the way as best they can. They know that the dojo is not the place to escape life's rigors. It is the arena in which they are confronted. To come to the dojo with any other attitude is to take the path of the nibbler, who wants to taste briefly and then leave, wanting to believe he has benefited from a full and nutritious meal.

Perhaps it takes Westerners coming to Japan a bit longer to prove to the Japanese that they are serious about following the martial ways. Tsuchihashi Sensei was surprised, pleasantly so, at my return. But still, he offered no further instruction to me. I hadn't yet merited it and would not, not for the short time I was spending in Suwa. The senior adepts at the dojo, however, generously took turns working me up through the more advanced kata of iaido, movements with esoteric names like "A Floating Cloud," and "A Rock Against the Waves," with subtleties and technical points of performance that are elusive as well. For every detail the seniors explained to me that I remembered, I felt as if I was forgetting at least three others. I had the urge to scamper off to the side of the floor and scribble notes. But that is not the way learning goes on in the dojo, either. The student must absorb with his body, not with his intellect. "What your body remembers is what is important for you at your particular stage of development," Tsuchihashi Sensei told me when I bemoaned how much information was slipping out of memory right away. "What your mind forgets, your body is telling you it couldn't use at this time." The loss seemed a waste, yet it was only a reminder of how much I still had to learn along the "Do," the way of iai.

One night at the dojo, Tsuchihashi Sensei asked me to demonstrate for the rest of the members some of the unsheathing and striking techniques of the Shinkage-ryu. It was a change to be demonstrating in Japan instead of watching. Ever since I had arrived, it seemed I had been learning, soaking up information. Now the iai I'd been taught long ago by my sensei came back to me. (To be entirely accurate, the Shinkage-ryu does not have its own sword-drawing methods in its curriculum. It incorporates those of another ryu, the Seigo school of swordsmanship, into its training and refers to the art by another of its names, battojutsu.) The movements were as comfortable and familiar to me as old friends. When I had been a student of my sensei's, and I was traveling, I would try to take the time to go out someplace private, into a field or a clearing in the woods, and perform the battojutsu he had taught me. Part of the enjoyment I had in these solo sessions was in reflecting upon the fact that nothing even remotely like what I was doing with the sword had ever been done in that space before; it was a moment unique. "I am fairly safe in betting," I would say to myself while practicing in an open meadow between soybean fields in Kansas, for instance, "that I am the only person in this whole state who is doing these techniques, indeed, I am the first and only person ever to be doing them here." Kneeling in the Suwa Dojo, I had the same sensation. I had never done the movements of unsheathing and cutting with the sword in this way in Japan before. And yet it was not, I had to remind myself, a novel occurrence there. I was in the country where these methods were created. And then I scolded myself for not paying attention to what it was I actually was doing. It would not do at all, I reminded myself, to cut off my thumb or to stick myself in the side right here in the dojo in front of all these people, when I am supposed to be demonstrating an art from their culture, one I am supposed to know.

After iaido practice that evening, I stopped by the bathhouse for my regular evening ablutions, now greeted with friendliness but none of the attention I'd first gotten, and then I hiked back to the Fujiwara home.

"Dave-san, come in here." Fujiwara-san called me in as I was hanging out my training uniform, heavy with perspiration once again, on a bamboo pole under the eaves where the laundry was hung in good weather. He and his wife and the grandchildren, Tomoko and Akiko, were sitting at the low table with tea, immersed in the NHK television series that was playing in Japan at that time, recounting the life and exploits of the first of the Tokugawa line of shoguns, Tokugawa Ieyasu.

These elaborately and expensively produced series appear about every other year on Japanese TV, devoted to the lives and adventures of one or another of the great military leaders of the feudal era. Date Masamune, Toyotomi Hideyoshi, Takeda Shingen: all of these and more Japanese warrior heroes have had their lives documented, soap-opera fashion, in television series. Now it was the turn of the brilliant and enigmatic unifier of Japan, Ieyasu. Typically, these thirty-minute programs last nearly a year in telling their tales, with new episodes appearing weekly. They go into convoluted and intricate details of personal relationships as well as the public aspects of the leader's life. The series too, must go to considerable lengths to maintain historical accuracy. If the style of armor depicted is not correct for the specific period of time covered in the series, there will be letters of complaint to the network. If a lord mentions his three concubines when, according to historical fact he had four, it will be noticed. (Japanese viewers were both amused and critical when the American-produced TV drama "Shogun" appeared some years ago in Japan. While the figure of the high-ranking lord played by actor Toshiro Mifune had a lush growth of hair to make him more appealing to Western audiences, the Japanese conversant in their country's sartorial history knew that lords of that rank would almost have invariably been shaven-headed.) The series on Ieyasu was no exception. It had progressed to the point in the life of the ambitious *daimyo* Ieyasu when he had made a minor military foray to take over the province of Shinano. A small castle there had been erected by the lord of the Hineno clan. While they were allies, ostensibly, of the Tokugawa family of Ieyasu's, just to be sure they stayed in line, Ieyasu sent one of his sons to the castle to serve as its administrator.

The episode we watched at the Fujiwara house that night depicted fact. Ieyasu had indeed made a number of appointments that were designed to consolidate and maintain his power over virtually the whole of Japan. The difference to us watching at the house that night was that the castle in this particular episode still stood; still stood so close to us, in fact, that the moonlit shadow of one of its towers nearly touched the roof of the house.

I sat and watched the drama on Ieyasu with Akiko-chan curled up in my lap and stealing sips of tea from my cup. The next morning, I walked down the lane in front of the house to the castle, Takashima-jo. I stopped, though, before going around to the main gate. Instead, I stepped into a field of brown rice stubble. I crouched, the dank aroma of farm dirt filling my nostrils. My squatting posture was that of the bugeisha, a sort of sprinter's crouch that kept me close to the ground, not much of a target, but still able to use a sword quickly if the need arose. And if I was carrying one, which I was not. But even unarmed, I was approaching the castle Takashima as one of its enemies might have, four centuries ago, no longer viewing it as would a tourist, with an aesthete's eye for design and beauty, but as would a foe who sought to penetrate and conquer.

Chikujojutsu is the science, the *jutsu*, of fortifying a castle or a battlefield position. It is one of the myriad corollary *martial* arts that is not precisely a *combative* art. *Noroshijutsu* (the employment of signal fires), *suijohokujutsu* (methods of ferrying troops across bodies of water), *senjojutsu* (deployment tactics): all are true Japanese martial arts, as valuable to the bugeisha as his fencing or spearmanship. My sensei had introduced me to the basics of fortification and penetration of the Shinkage-ryu — the teachings of the ryu were specifically intended for use in large-scale tactics as well as in individual combat. Many of these techniques enforced the concept that the strategy for defeating an opponent with the sword in single battle could be implemented on a larger scale to break through and defeat the defenses of a castle. Facing a swordsman or contemplating an attack on a fortress, the key to victory according to the ryu, was to know the weak spots.

The principles of chikujojutsu, contained in the secret scrolls of many classical ryu, classify castles according to their location. There are *hirajiro,* castles built on a flat plain, and *yamajiro,* or those situated on mountaintops. Takashima-jo, the fortress that had once protected Suwa, was a rarer sort of castle. Constructed on an island just off the shore of Lake Suwa, Takashima-jo was an *ukijiro*, a "floating citadel." It was originally connected to the shore only by a narrow, quick-angled road, a lane that allowed not much more than a thread of foot traffic to move along it.

A castle's location figured prominently, both in its defense and in its possible defeat. If, for instance, an attacking force encountered a hirajiro on a broad plain, there was a chance they could erect siege towers beside the outer fortifications and above the height of its walls. The towers permitted assault forces to climb up and fire muskets and arrows down on those defending inside. A mountaintop fortress, on the other hand, was invulnerable to siege towers since its walls were invariably on the sides of steep slopes. However, a mountain castle could succumb to a siege that would starve out its defenders or deprive them of the water that would be easier for a castle on flat ground to keep and store.

Castles built on the borders of lakes like Takashima-jo were designed to foil both these common weaknesses. Since Takashima-jo was actually constructed on an island (or had been, originally), a siege tower could not have been successfully raised close enough to the walls to do the castle harm. And with the lake immediately at hand, an endless supply of water was readily available. Further, according to a history of Suwa that Fujiwara-san had taken down from a shelf the night before and given me to read, the defenders of Takashima-jo took advantage of its lakeside location in an ingenious way. The fortress at Suwa was built as a series of walled courtyards called *maru*. There were five maru at Takashima-jo, each one connected to the others by bridges even narrower than the road leading out to the main gate. Every maru was secured by the lake's water on all sides of it; each by itself could protect and house enough warriors to defend it for a very long time against a serious attack. It would have been, I decided as I stood and brushed crumbs of dirt off my knees, a challenge to have come up with a plan to defeat a castle like this. Fortunately, I did not have to. The main gate of Takashima-jo was swung wide open each morning to let in visitors. I crossed the moat bridge and went into the center of the remaining structure of the castle without having met the slightest resistance.

The majority of castles still standing in Japan (most of them have received at least a little and sometimes a whole lot of renovation) were built within a rather short period of time in that country's history, a few brief decades (ca. 1580-1610) during the Muromachi period. This Golden Era of castle architecture is known as the Azuchi Age, named after a formidable and spectacular fortress erected under the command of the warrior-general Oda Nobunaga.

When its devotees go on poetically about the virtues of the Japanese samurai's code of bushido, likening it to a Far Eastern rendition of European chivalry and such, it is almost certain they are not talking about men like Oda Nobunaga. Born in the latter part of the sixteenth-century Muromachi era, Nobunaga was the offspring of an undistinguished family of the ordinary foot soldiers who were known during that period as *nobushi*. Nobunaga was among the most successful of several men-at-arms of the common class who managed to exploit the turbulence of the times—and not incidentally the plentiful positions opened by the excessive mortality rate among the warrior caste—to his personal advantage. Through a succession of cutthroat, Byzantine maneuvers that would give the most hardened corporate raider of our century cause to blanch and hesitate, Nobunaga managed to double- and triple-cross his way into power. He began in Owari Province, with a band of nobushi like himself. In Owari, he soon made short work of any serious rivals in the immediate vicinity. He gained the admiration of the ruling military leader of central Japan in Kyoto, the reigning shogun of the Ashikaga clan. The shogun at first encouraged Nobunaga in the latter's military career. Very quickly, Nobunaga responded by deposing him. In doing so, Nobunaga put an end to nearly three centuries of rule by the Ashikaga family and set the stage for the eventual unification of Japan under the rule of the Tokugawa.

The hallmark of Nobunaga's reign (aside from ruthlessness and treachery, that is) was his creative use of plebeian nobushi in combat against classically trained, aristocratic samurai. It was an idea for waging war that at first blush seemed suicidal. Professional warriors who were descended from generations of warriors would have appeared to have had an enormous advantage in meeting foot soldiers of peasant origins whose training and discipline were mediocre at best. But typical of Nobunaga, he threw in a viciously brilliant twist in his strategy. He armed his troops with high-tech weaponry, which, in Muromachi era terms, meant smoothbore muskets, cumbersome and ugly, with a firing mechanism dependent upon smoky, sulfurous wicks that malfunctioned only slightly less often than they worked. The range of these early firearms was limited. A good archer could consistently place a killing shot from a greater distance. Then too, the firearms were a nuisance to load and prime. But aimed and fired in successive volleys by close-ordered ranks, the results were deadly. The musket did not require the courage and verve of the katana, nor the skill of a bow. Yet against withering blasts of firepower, the noble samurai went down like springtime rows of grain before a Sagami hailstorm.

Despite its undeniable military effectiveness (or perhaps, some historians argue, because of it), the samurai as a class continued to show a disdain for the bourgeois firearm as part of their armament for the remainder of the long feudal period in Japan. But after witnessing the carnage produced at the end of its barrel, they could not ignore its potential. Their response to this potential was in the development of chikujojutsu. The fabulous castles of the Muromachi period are structures conceived and built with the dangers of musketry in mind. Not surprisingly, Oda Nobunaga was among the first to implement features in castle architecture that offered protection against musket fire. His own castle, which he named Azuchi, was a prototype for virtually all of the fortresses built from that time on. Castle-makers began digging moats that were much wider than before, to take into account the range of the firearms. Stone walls that had served in earlier times only as a foundation for castle buildings were heightened dramatically to lift the structures above the threat of horizontally-directed volleys, and tall corner turrets were added to allow defenders to shoot down onto opponents massed outside the outer walls.

Takashima-jo, the castle at Suwa, incorporated many of these Azuchi-type features. Its chiseled stone foundation walls form a curving parabola that deflected bullets or cannon shot. There was no mortar or concrete holding these blocks, the size of mail trucks, together. They were fitted tightly and ingeniously, yet with just enough space left between the square stones so rainwater would drain through and not collect and stagnate. At each corner, the walls were corniced by much larger stones that were stacked in a graceful rising curve known as a "folding fan corner," which distributed the weight of the citadel towers they supported. The sides of the tower walls too, were specifically constructed to defeat bullets. Below a coat of gleaming whitewash, I could see a rough daubed plaster, a mixture of rock salt and clay, I knew, smeared over wattle. It was resilient as brick, fireproof against any incendiary devices that might have been hurled at it.

As I entered through the main gate at Takashima-jo, I could see remains of a low rock border, all that was left of a foundation where once a wall had stood. When the castle was occupied, visitors coming through the gate would have found themselves directly in front of the wall there. They would have been forced to make an immediate, ninety-degree turn to get any further into the interior of the castle. It must have been something of a nuisance for daily traffic, to have made that turn every time it was necessary to enter the castle compound. But the "right-turn gate," was a basic strategy of fortification. Attackers who might manage to smash through the sturdy main gate would scramble forward to find themselves not in the heart of the castle as they had planned and hoped, but face-to-face with another barrier to their invasion. They would have been stopped by the wall even before their charge into the compound began, forced to veer hard right. As they did, they would have been met with gusts of arrows blowing down from redoubts all along the top of the gate's walls.

The implementation of maze-like turns to protect castle entrances was not limited to the immediate precincts of the castle itself. I turned back from the remains of the right-turn gate and looked out across the moat bridge and into the city. Logically, a street should have been there, beyond the moat on the far side of the bridge, leading away from the castle. There was none, though. There had never been a street. There was only a row of stores and businesses. Once again, castle fortification strategy called for a sharp right angle, one more turn in the design of the area around the fortress that would have to have been navigated by approaching attackers. Without a long street leading up to the bridge, Takashima-jo was practically impervious to the momentum of a full-speed frontal charge. There wasn't enough room to have mounted such a maneuver.

The center courtyard of Takashima-jo is now a city park. A balsa-wood glider soared, a knot of children running underneath it. Parents dozed in the sunshine or read, stretched out on blankets. Trees and azalea beds had been fastidiously pruned. Walkways were kept neatly swept. The courtyard was something like Suwa's town common. Over near one of the castle's interior walls, beside an arch of wisteria, a pedestal supported a bronze bust of a World War II general. He was, the sign below said, a descendant of the Takashima family who, according to the inscription, had served the Imperial Empire of Japan in Manchuria. I thought it an odd memorial. Usually it is the victors who erect statues to celebrate their heroes. Was this a uniquely Japanese trait? Commemorating a loser and one who, for all I knew, had been one of the butchers who hacked China into a bloody slaughterhouse during the Japanese occupation? Or did other vanquished nations celebrate their defeated? Decorating parks in rural burgs in Germany are there graven images, greenish with age and streaked by bird droppings, of Wermacht commanders and Luftwaffe generals?

A corner tower of Takashima-jo that had long ago been a watchpost was now converted into a museum. Rooms connected by spiraling staircases held the heirlooms of the Takashima clan: softly faded kimono and formal silk hakama with the family crest embroidered on them (a crane stretching its wings, it is the official crest of the city of Suwa now); weapons and armor, and all sorts of diaries, documents, and personal letters that gave insight into the Takashima family and their castle. I was reading an account, drawn up in 1630, of the taxes paid in rice to the clan by farmers of the surrounding fief, when the museum's curator approached. He had the look and the heavy bounce in his gait of a genial sort of fellow. Thick glasses magnified his smiling eyes. Like many Japanese who came of age during the war, when dental care was not always an option, his smile was uncooperative with the rest of his features. His teeth leaned at unruly angles. It was a slow day, in terms of attendance, he said. Would I like for him to show me around?

The curator was obviously not much interested in the arts of medieval warfare that had brought me to the castle. With an "Oh, that's some kind of old spear," he brushed aside my question about the origins of a *naginata* on display. It was a long-bladed polearm that looked to have been from the early Ashikaga period of the fifteenth century. But he knew the history of the fortress and as we ambled through it, me pausing to peer at whatever caught my eye, he rattled off conversationally whole strings of anecdotes about the castle's past. Over there, where another corner spire once stood, one called the Moon Viewing Tower, the drama of a *shinju* had been played out. Literally, a "death to pierce the spirit," shinju is a form of lover's suicide. In this case, two centuries old, a married woman and her lover had leaped from the tower into the lake when her husband discovered the affair. The family of the woman was prominent, the curator told me in a confidential tone. Still is. They are distillers of a locally-brewed sake.

On another section of the castle fortifications, my guide pointed out a flat stone platform. An old man, he said, born of the samurai rank, had come here the morning after the Emperor Meiji died in 1912, and performed another form of self-immolation. *Junshi* is a particular kind of *harakiri,* a disembowelment carried out to follow one's leader into death. The old man had killed himself as an act of loyalty to the emperor who was the father of Hirohito. At the time I was visiting in Suwa, Hirohito himself was suffering from an advanced form of cancer and was not expected to live much longer. What grizzled warriors would follow him when he died?—the unspoken thought crossed my mind. Instead, considering the bloody events he'd described for me regarding the castle's past, I asked the curator another question.

"Were Takashima-jo's defenses ever put into use?"

The curator flashed his bad teeth in a smile. Well, he said, no. The castle had only been taken once. That was when the exiled daimyo of Suwa, Lord Takashima, mounted an expedition to retake his ancestral land around Suwa and to capture too, the fortress that had been built during his absence by an interloping daimyo of the Hineno clan.

"Was there a battle when the Takashima daimyo returned?"

No again. The curator explained that the daimyo of Suwa had entered the castle in much the same way I had, strolling through the front gate. The parapets of Takashima-jo had never, in their nearly four centuries, been blackened by fire or battered by missiles. Sieges never tested the fortifications. No defenders defended; no invaders invaded. In 1867, an Imperial decree ordered that Takashima-jo, along with hundreds of other castles throughout Japan, be largely dismantled, rendered ineffective militarily so they could never pose a threat to the newly-consolidated Imperial rule. Takashima-jo was gutted and abandoned and over the years it fell into a crumbled ruin as the city grew around it. Not until the modern era had Suwa rebuilt and restored this one section of the fortress.

That Takashima-jo had no test in battle might have tarnished the luster of its image for some. But not for me. For more than half of my own life I had been learning and practicing arts meant for battles, never once bringing them to the lethal conclusions for which they were intended. I could have taken out many of the sets of lacquered armor behind the glass cases at the museum at Takashima-jo and put them on. I recognized the knots and lacing that were used on them. My sensei had taught me, had given me scrolls detailing the mechanics of binding and fastening on the components of a samurai's complicated suit of body protection, even though such obvious antiquities are never to be worn again, nor even seen much, outside of museums like the one in Suwa. The only blood my sword had ever spilled—or was likely to—was my own, from my mistakes in training. Like all exponents of the koryu, the practical applications of my training were—what? As practical as maintaining—and on prime lake-front property, no less, right in downtown Suwa—an Azuchi-era citadel?

My history was not so different in ways from that of the castle Takashima-jo. Neither of us had been tested in life-and-death combat. To me, the castle (or what remained of it) was an anachronism, a relic floating serenely in the midst of all that was new and modern around it. The study and appreciation of ancient things, my sensei had taught me, was vital to understanding our own times. One cannot know where he's bound without a grasp of where it was he came from—this concept Sensei had expressed to me many different times, in many different ways. It was that sense of identification with the venerable and the patinaed and the anachronistic that had led me to his teaching in the first place, I suppose. Takashima-jo had never withstood the depredations and dangers of warfare but it had, in its own way, endured. Touching the stones of its ramparts and standing at the tallest of its tower redoubts overlooking Suwa, the flat silvery pan of the lake below and the mountains above, I felt the resiliency of its endurance. It was a quality that could not be explained purely in terms of architectural integrity or meticulous preservation. Takashima-jo, like the way of the sword I had chosen to follow, is a reliquary of the past, it is true. But that is only part of its value. The other half of its worth is as a landmark, a touchstone, a gatepost to the future.

Ragged clouds of autumn dragged their tails along the mountain ridges above the city when I awoke. They had crept down during the night and Suwa, as I explored it that morning, was muted, colors and sounds were stilled. In fog, I followed streets at my whim, turning left, then right at random. I worked my way along narrow lanes where houses and shops were side by side. There are no lawns in neighborhoods like this in Japan; a gutter and a few feet of concrete or brick of dark cobblestone separate the street from the buildings. Inevitably, I noticed, these little patches of real estate were used to aesthetic advantage, though. Some were occupied with shelves of carefully tended bonsai in their pots; others had received a wheelbarrow load of gravel and a trio or a quintet of stones were arranged in a miniature "dry landscape of water and mountains." Some had bamboo hedges or other plantings in boxes, others were decorated with nothing more than a flat rock used as a step-stone up into the house. Almost none of these otherwise unnoticed spaces were left unattended and bare, however. They reminded me of a gas station I'd seen once in Iowa City. It's a locally renowned site, as renowned as a gas station can be, I suppose, because every summer in a space between the premium and super-unleaded pumps is planted a couple of rows of corn. It is a cultivated plot the dimensions of an ironing board, but the stalks are green and tall in the growing season, golden heads tossing in the sun. The acres, the hundred thousand rows of corn on the way into Iowa City barely catch the attention of drivers going by them. But arrange a dozen stalks in an unusual and imaginative way or place and they take on, as they do at that gas station, a special beauty. The bonsai and scaled-down dry gardens of Suwa's doorways distilled the forms and energies of the enormous Nagano highlands that surround the city. A mountain range, a forest, all contained on a house porch. Between gas pumps, the vast acreage of Iowa's cornfields are reflected. Beauty reduced and thus personified and thus, to the limited grasp of our species, comprehensible.

A wooden signpost brushed with ink characters and fixed to a plank wall identified the building hidden behind the wall as the site of the oldest *ryokan* inn in the prefecture. Ryokan were a major industry in Suwa; all the way back to the mid-fifteenth century this part of Nagano was a popular resort that drew visitors from all over the country to the lake and mountain scenery. According to the sign that gave the date of the ryokan's opening, Columbus had been poking around the islands he christened the West Indies when the inn I'd found had begun receiving guests. Confident it could stand having one more for an hour or two, I pushed open the gate.

"Moshi moshi," I ventured, standing at the open door. "Coming, coming," I heard from the darkness within. Minami-san's slippers shuffled as he came out of the shadows, down a long cool hallway right beside the main door. At another, more contemporary ryokan, the owner's friend had been staggered by the appearance of my foreign face. Minami-san, who introduced himself as the proprietor, the direct descendant of the ryokan's original innkeep, and the guide who would for three hundred yen show me around the place, barely blinked at my showing up in his inn. His Japanese was quick and peppered with so many colloquialisms that I caught only about every third word. But I did my best to follow both his feet and his shuffling slippers as he led me down the dark hallway from where he'd come.

While the ryokan was now a museum that no longer took in overnight guests, none of the charm of a working inn was lost. It was a magnificent place, in terms of Japanese architecture. By which I mean it was more filled with shadows than with illumination. Transoms shunted the light, shoji screens suffused it; the sandy amber interior walls and black floorboards of the ryokan gathered in the light and aged it and returned it in a more mellow, subdued vintage. Minami-san shuffled ahead of me, keeping up his chatty and often incomprehensible monologue. Did I know about the utensils for the ritual of tea? was the question he asked me. I thought. Or was he inquiring about my familiarity with snake venom? The first is *chadogu* in Japanese; the second, *jadoku*. I took a chance and said yes, I was acquainted with it. At the same time, I looked around to see if there was any sign of snakes in the ryokan. But no, he was talking about *chado*, and he pointed out that here at this inn, the tea master Kitamuki Dochin himself had been a guest and had performed the tea ceremony in this very room. Here in this box were pieces of sandalwood incense that were used that evening four hundred and thirty-some years ago. Minami-san pulled the tight-fitting lid off the box and held it up for me to sniff. Faint, but pungent still. The sandalwood had retained its fragrance. Its odor lingered in the air as he led me through a pair of shoji screens into a larger room, one furnished with a spacious tokonoma alcove. Hanging in the recess of the alcove was a scroll painting that looked somehow familiar. It was a portrait of the Daruma, the fierce, bug-eyed patriarch of the Buddhist faith who had crossed over from India to bring the discipline of Zen to China. His likeness was less than simple, carved with just a few strokes of the brush out of the yellowing ivory of the scroll paper. A masterpiece of *zenga*, the bold black and white artistry of Zen ink painting. The master painter, I recognized after reading only the first character of his distinctive signature. I knew then why the painting, or at least its style, was so familiar.

Tsukahara Bokuden was a legend among legendary swordsmen in old Japan. He was a prodigy of the early years of Japan's long period of civil strife, one who defeated his first opponent (a swordslinger twice the young Bokuden's age) in a duel when Bokuden was still in his teens. Bokuden had apprenticed in the martial arts of the Kashima-ryu, one of the oldest schools of swordsmanship, under his father. Throughout the sixteenth century, he put his martial abilities to use in a variety of exploits. Many of his adventures are the stuff of novels and folk tales. A goodly number are historically quite improbable. Bokuden's life was saved *à la* Androcles and the Lion, for instance, by a band of monkeys, one of which Bokuden had earlier set free from a hunter's snare. Afterwards, Bokuden was captured himself, by disciples of a fencing school who were angry that Bokuden had slain their master in a duel. Vengeful students left Bokuden suspended, bound and upside down, over a gorge. A troop of monkeys happened by, fortuitously including the one he'd rescued. In return for his kindness, the monkeys gnawed through the ropes, saving Bokuden from the slow starvation his enemies had intended.

Other tales of Bokuden's life and times are less distantly-fetched. He was challenged once by a fearsome expert with the naginata, Nagato Kajiwara. Casually misidentified as it had been for me by the curator at the Takashima castle, the naginata is not a spear. It is a long polearm of a weapon, with a balanced curved cutting edge fixed to one end. Its length intensifies the power of its cut. One sweep with the naginata could take off both a man's legs as well as the legs of a charging cavalry mount. Nagato was alleged to have been able to swipe a darting swallow out of the air with the blows of his naginata, and to whirl his weapon in arcs and circles defensively about himself so quickly it looked to observers as if he were in the center of a protective blur. In spite of the fame Bokuden had acquired by the time he met Nagato in the duel, the smart money was on Nagato. The naginata, over seven feet long, could reach Bokuden before the swordsman's three-foot katana came into effective range. Even Bokuden's own students were in doubt. But Bokuden placidly noted that while the naginata was longer than his sword, the business end of the naginata, its blade, was only a couple of feet in length, shorter, actually, than Bokuden's weapon. His students had the chance straightaway to see the wisdom in Bokuden's tactics. No sooner had the fight between Nagato and Bokuden begun than Bokuden directed a zipping strike, not against Nagato, but aimed at the naginata itself. Slash! The last two feet of Nagato's naginata were cut off. Another slash, and another section of the shaft was gone. Nagato was deprived of the tornado-like centrifugal force of his long polearm. He fell dead when Bokuden's final slash opened his skull. (Naginata exponents, it should be noted, immediately repaired, after the results of this duel became widely known, to devise new methods of wielding their halberds to guard against techniques like those used so unexpectedly by Bokuden. Some of their modifications in the art of *naginatajutsu* can be seen today in the kata of the various koryu that teach naginata in their curriculum.)

Tsukahara Bokuden is credited by more than a dozen fencing ryu as having founded their combative traditions. All of these have descended from students of Bokuden to be more exact, and all of them have incorporated, in one way or another, the legacy of his principle of *hitotsu-tachi*. This "one stroke sword" method calls for enticing an opponent to attack and to then counter at the very last instant, just as the opponent's blade is a hairsbreadth from finding its target.

"Is this painting actually an original by Bokuden?" I asked.

"How do you know about Tsukahara Bokuden?" The innkeeper guide appeared to have taken notice for the first time that afternoon that I was not exactly from these parts

"Hitotsu-tachi," I replied, both to show off my knowledge of arcane Japanese history and to sound out his own. How much did he know about the painter of this portrait that had been hanging in his family's inn? He knew. He knew enough to smile and nod when he heard me use the term and he raised his fists as if bringing down a katana, slowly, slowly, then with a quick snap as it reached a target. "Hitotsu-tachi," he said. Then he pointed to the portrait hanging in the tokonoma and added, *"Hitotsu-fude."*

It was a pithily accurate observation. Bokuden's timing and celerity with his katana had been translated into the *fude* or ink brush. Hitotsu-fude: "one strike of the brush." Bokuden's interpretation of the Zen patriarch had captured the essence of Daruma's fierce piety, gone straight to the artistic bull's-eye with an almost abstract economy of brushwork. The stare, furious and wide-eyed (Daruma, the hagiography of Zen has it, sliced off his own eyelids after having become enraged at falling asleep during a period of meditation), was the glare of a swordsman entering combat.

Bokuden had melded his art of the sword into the art of the brush. His likeness of Daruma was painted with such passion that the artist and his subject merged as well, and one could imagine the figure in the portrait about to roar forth with the Zen shout of enlightenment, *"Katsu!"* or the warrior combative *kiai* cry, either one with an equal and ferocious energy.

Later, after Minami-san had finished his tour, he led me to a storage room and, squatting down on his haunches, he dug through some low shelves, pulling out paulownia wood boxes that held, he told me, stoneware jugs, hanging scrolls, ikebana containers and vases—Minami family heirlooms. Among the collection was a brocade bag protecting a wooden practice sword.

"My great-grandfather's bokuto," Minami-san said. He slid it out of the bag and handed it to me to feel its heft and balance and we took it out into the garden so I could swing it and cut the heavy gray air of the still damp and cloudy afternoon. The bokuto was nicked and dented and shiny-slick at the handle from the years of polishing with sweat it had, and as soon as I took it up in the swordsman's loose-fisted grip, I could feel a quiver snake through the curve of its spine. The incense sticks in the tea room of the old ryokan had for so long retained their pungency. Great-grandfather Minami's bokuto retained something of its essence, too. It was animated, alive, and when I finally put it down to accept a cup of tea that Minami-san had brewed and brought out on the veranda for me, I felt my arms still twitching, as if I had just unplugged them from some electrical source.

Takemikazuchi was the heavenly deity who defeated the earthly kami Takeminakata on the shores of Lake Suwa. His icy grip had forced Takeminakata's hand (literally, in their hand-clasping duel of strength), and the second son of the leader of the earthly kami had surrendered Japan in that mythic age, to the heavenly forces. The victor, Takemikazuchi, is enshrined as the principal deity at Shinto shrines located throughout Japan. His spirit is said to dwell at the Kashima Shrine in Ibaraki Prefecture where Tsukahara Bokuden secluded himself for months of intense physical and spiritual austerities. Bokuden credited the divine assistance of Takemikazuchi for his "single stroke" sword strategy. One of the ryu of that era is called the Kashima-ryu; its dojo is still in use by members of the school, on the precincts of the Kashima Shrine. Takemikazuchi is considered by those who travel the path of the warrior to be a patron kami of sorts, prayed to and venerated.

But what of Takeminakata, the kami who surrendered the Land of the Luxuriant Reed Plains? Save as martyrs or tragic heroes, myths do not afford much room for the losers. Take-minakata, the earthly deity whose name means Brave August Name-Firm Kami, is an exception. A temple at Suwa, Suwa Taisha, is set aside to honor this vanquished kami. Suwa Taisha is on the north shore of Lake Suwa, set right at the foot of a mountain. It is typical of Shinto jinja, surrounded by a forest so thick the ground beneath the trees is bare, packed like umber concrete along the paths worshippers tread, elsewhere, soft and fluffy with layers of feathery russet cryptomeria needles. The cryptomeria forest around the shrine must have been there at least since the two kami had fought it out on that very spot. They are primordial, a species related to cedars, with a thick, straight trunk and flat olive-green needles like a cypress. Their size makes them look like the redwoods of California. Branches of cryptomeria do not emerge from the trunk of the tree until far up along the height; they interlace to form a dense canopy overhead. Walking through the glade of them enclosing Suwa Taisha is like strolling through an expansive and shadowy cathedral, a sun-dappled, green-brushed ceiling supported by massive pillars with shaggy bark.

There is a wealth of lore about the shrine at Suwa. The wife of Takeminakata has her own jinja on the opposite, south shore of the lake. When each spring comes to this part of Nagano Prefecture, there is a fissure that appears in the frozen tabletop of ice covering the lake all winter, a crack that channels its way from one shrine to the other, heaving up the ice in big chunks. It is the passage made, local folk belief insists, when the wife of Takeminakata makes her way across the lake to visit at the shrine of her husband. Another legend has it that the original Suwa Taisha was nothing more than a clearing in the woods, set aside by four great cryptomeria trunks that were felled and then erected in a square. Once every seven years even today, a similar primitive worship rectangle is erected on the grounds of the shrine. From far up on the mountainside, four trees are selected under the direction of a priest, then cut down with ceremonially purified axes. Straw rope cables girdle the trunks and the ritual turns from religion to festival as intrepid townsmen (no women have volunteered so far) straddle the huge logs and ride them, hanging to the cables for their very lives, as they go careening and sliding down the mountain. It is an event very much like a Japanese version of Pamplona, and as with the running of the bulls, severe injuries and deaths are not uncommon. The logs reach the shrine eventually. Along the way, they plough up rocks and flatten smaller trees all along their path, carrying a complement of increasingly bedraggled and exhilarated riders with them. The logs are erected in a sacred square where they stand for the next seven years, festooned with woven rope bands and lightning-shaped paper streamers.

According to the esoteric traditions of the Shinkage-ryu, the victorious Takemikazuchi is honored as a martial deity as he is in many other koryu. But the Shinkage-ryu affords too, veneration for the loser. Sensei had explained to me years before that Takeminakata was a kami worthy of the warrior's respect and that a commemoration of his spirit should never be neglected by a swordsman. Why? Because Takeminakata was a kami who understood the vital connection between *heiho* and *heiho*.

In English, the distinctions between the two words are impossible to make. One heiho, the one known to all bugeisha, refers to "military methods" or "martial strategy." The other, pronounced the same way yet written with different kanji, means "a strategy that benefits the populace." *"Heiho ha; heiho na,"* goes a proverb handed down in the ryu: heiho is heiho; the strategy of the warrior is the strategy that will also encourage harmony in mankind. Takeminakata could have continued fighting against the heavenly deity who demanded his surrender, of course. Struggling against overwhelming odds in the face of certain failure strikes a chord deep and responsive within the Japanese character. But heiho, as Takeminakata demonstrated, can also mean knowing when to submit in order to promote the greater good. To die uselessly, my sensei had taught, was romantic perhaps, but it was not necessarily always the proper application of true heiho. Not according to the teachings of the Shinkage-ryu.

Heiho ha; heiho na. That is why Takeminakata has always been admired and respected by generations of Shinkage-ryu exponents. Which was why I was at the Suwa Taisha, there in the midst of a dark cryptomeria grove that smelled like a cedar chest. I had visited at the Yasukuni Jinja in Tokyo to fulfill an obligation to my teacher. I came to Suwa Taisha to fulfill the obligations I had to *his* teachers, and their teachers before them. It was not a legal debt I owed them, of course. Or a rationally explicable burden I had taken on, for that matter. It was an obligation of shamanistic origins, one that went back to before a time when the principal weapon in Japan was a Neolithic stone club, back to when time itself was not measured in astrological cycles or years, but in the most elemental of terms: the clatter of frost-cracked rocks rolling down a slope in spring, the trickle of water exactly like that splashing between my fingers. I rinsed them under a scoop, a part of the purification process at the "hand-washing place" that is a customary stop before approaching a Shinto shrine. The obligation to pay respects at Suwa Taisha went back to a time when gods walked across the land, kami who slung about boulders it would have taken a thousand men to budge. It was an age of deities too, who conceived of ways of combat that were also a way of resolving conflict, providing in those ways an inheritance for me to struggle with eons later, in the dojo and elsewhere in my life. In the mystical stronghold of these spirits, a shrine guarded by a hoary, totem pole forest, it was an obligation I felt drawing me nearer to the past. It was a past esoteric, stretching back — so far back that when I clapped my hands together and bowed before the central altar, the sound echoed and seemed to reverberate down a silent passage, the length of which I could not begin to fathom.

One of the last nights I spent in Suwa, I was the guest of honor at a banquet held in a sixteenth-century restaurant on the outskirts of town. The restaurant specialized in *robata ryori,* a method of grilling over oak fire coals that glowed in a brick pit around which all the guests sat. It was a convivial gathering, hosted by a city official who had befriended me, and attended by a dozen or so of the people I had met during my stay. A couple of training partners from the iaido dojo, some fellow bathers at the bathhouse club, and others I had come to know there were all around the grill. Trout from a nearby stream were gutted and spitted over the coals. While they cooked, the table was loaded with platters of sushi, sweet potatoes boiled in soy sauce, vinegared lotus root, and other appetizers, and sashimi of the very freshest kind. Whole sea bream were scored back in the kitchen with razor knives so sharp the fish were still twitching, their gills flapping as we picked up slivers of their meat with chopsticks. Later courses included another entree still kicking, or at least crawling: freshwater prawns the length of my hand, their fleshy tail sections sliced off and, before their nervous systems reflexively led them scuttling away, shelled and eaten along with fiery wasabi paste. (This is, admittedly, unusual culinary fare by the standards of daily Japanese eating habits, it should be noted by those not familiar with it. But there is among most Japanese what many Westerners would consider to be a preoccupation with freshness. The true sushi or sashimi aficionado will not eat either of these dishes after noon, for instance, since by that time the fish that was caught early that same morning, even if cooled on ice, will have passed its peak.)

There were other delicacies that were specialties of robata-style cooking. *Suzume,* or field sparrows, were split open and skewered and fricasseed like tiny chickens. (The taste—they are eaten little bones, beaks, and all—is nutty and faintly sweet.) Accompanied by what I thought of as a stunningly prodigious amount of sake, the feast was demolished, nibbled, chomped, and munched right down to the cleaned carcasses of the bream that were laid out on the grill until the bones were crispy-crunchy. Only one entree brought about any comments such as might be expected at a Sunday supper table in Kansas if, oh, say a heaping plate of roasted sparrow were plunked down among the mashed potatoes and three-bean salad. The finicky reaction came when a waitress brought out and stuck into the ashes beside the fire, skewers of several pairs of frog legs.

"You like *those?*" asked an astonished Tsuchida-san. He took only a mincing bite of the frog thigh I offered to him. Frogs are popularly regarded in much of Japan with the same squeamishness and loathing as are snakes in the West.

"That? That?" A menu that included fricasseed finch, crustaceans that went down still wriggling, fish that hadn't finished twitching, and he was queasy at the thought I'd eat frog legs? Food prejudices have always been difficult for me to understand. But at that moment they seemed positively ludicrous.

The sake flowed on, the evening progressed happily, lubricated too, with good-natured, animated accounts by the guests of my encounters with the local citizenry. These stories were punctuated by numerous imitations of my Nihongo, which I had learned from a very old-fashioned sensei, often a medieval version of the language. And there were uproariously received pantomimes of the reactions of those in Suwa who had heard a gaijin speaking, and often—I was generously reminded—*mis*-speaking Japanese. I got in equal time. Tsuchida-san laughed so hard he rolled back onto the tatami and hugged his sides at his own fumble-tongued efforts to distinguish, with my coaching, the varied pronunciations of "bus," "base," and "bass." All three sound alike to Japanese ears.

Someone took up a folksong of old Nagano, about a barley crop that ripened so luxuriously one season it had to be harvested with axes instead of sickles. I flirted with a waitress, the daughter of the owner of the restaurant, it turned out. By the time the banquet broke up and I got back to the Fujiwara house, the floodlights illuminating Takashima-jo were turned off. The tower of the fortress was a dark silhouette against a cold black sky of glittering stars.

The owner's daughter at the restaurant had been attentive and the kind of beautiful that made me wonder if I wasn't leaving Suwa too soon, before I had seen all there was to see in this part of Japan that is so little visited by foreigners. Standing alone and looking up at the silent, empty citadel of Takashima-jo, I was reminded that it was time for me to go.

6
Snowy Heron at Dusk

*T*he train south to Kyoto passed across a bridge in the highlands of Shiga Prefecture. The mountains, weathered through time and erosion to smooth round mounds, were shimmering near their summits under blankets of golden birch. At their bases, where the tracks ran, it was cool and shady. The smell of pine in the air was almost a musk.

A broad river with a current so patient, the placid surface was a perfect mirror. Reflected in the still water was a sheer boulder jutting like a cliff from the bank beside the bridge, a pair of tenacious pines leaning out from the angle of the rock. Around the river's bend flapped a snowy heron. His long-fingered wings heaved with an imperturbable see-saw rhythm. He rolled in mid-air, braked, and poked down a black pencil leg to snag his perch in one of the pines. The heron settled, stretched, then curved his neck into a tight, hunchbacked S, an upright exclamation mark of white against the sombre, still riverbank.

In another moment, the bridge was crossed.

7
The Sound of the Rocks

*I*n the sharp morning air Sensei's bokuto whirred. The weapon, a dull-bladed oak substitute for a real sword, whipped down. Its path was impossible to gauge by trying to follow it with my eyes. Instead, I judged its approach by "feel," a combination of senses—whetted through long practice—that judged the length of the bokuto, the effective reach of the opponent, the range of his step toward me as he cut.

It is possible, of course, to jump away from the strike entirely. But these kata were all representative of what in the curriculum of the ryu are called *tai*, or "waiting." Against the advance of my teacher, who took the role of the attacker, I waited, sometimes motionless, deliberately offering a tempting target, a shoulder, perhaps, or my wrists, or the bokuto itself extended in my hands, inviting the attempt to knock it aside. Only after Sensei committed himself, initiating the attack that was inches from completion, did my counter begin. I shifted marginally to cheat the blow and then replied in the same motion with a responding strike. If I leaped back away from the attack I would be out of range to make my counter; if I shifted too little or too late, my responding strike would be useless. I'd already have been struck.

It was my first morning in the little cluster of houses in Sensei's countryside neighborhood outside Nara. Before the light had edged up over the hilltops surrounding us, we had begun, working our way through the two-man sword kata that are distinctive to the Shinkage-ryu, reviewing them slowly and carefully for my sake. In between them, I shivered and bounced my legs inside my hakama to keep the circulation flowing. Dawn isn't warm in October in this part of Japan, not this high in the mountains. But the sun inched upward and we went on to the second level of the kata. My breathing lengthened. My face flushed and began to glow. Sensei drilled me with constant repetition. While he paused to correct a detail of technique here and there, he ignored most of the minor flaws in my execution of the movements, concentrating instead to see what I remembered of his teaching.

The rhythm of a set of kata of the older fighting arts is not unlike that of war. The enemy draws within range, the battle is joined, decided; the combatants part, each wary of the other, readying for the next engagement. Unlike a boxing match, when the gloves drop at the signal of the bell and contenders slump into their corners, the kata of the bugeisha does not finish at the close of the observable action. He must continue to keep *zanshin*, a spirit of alertness expressed in his posture and his gaze. Zanshin is sometimes translated as "concentration," a potentially misleading choice of words. Concentration implies a narrow focus of attention. Zanshin is diffused attention, an awareness of diverse elements. The footing of the battlefield ground, the position of the sun, the possibility of another opponent coming up from behind; zanshin takes in all of these and more and evaluates their relevancy without "concentrating" on any one. To sustain zanshin is at least as exhausting psychologically as the exertions of the kata are physically. After two hours at it, I was feeling the strain. The sunlight had hardened and pressed in and I squinted against it. My legs and arms trembled, not from the cold now, but from weariness. My attention slackened. My mind was drifting from the stern and tight hawsers of zanshin.

I'm not really here, I started to tell myself. I am only remembering, daydreaming about the past so well I can see it, training as I had been when I was a boy with Sensei in the Ozarks countryside. There, peppered across the horizon was a flock of the same crows I remembered, cawing their raucous kiai in the sky above our practice. A couple of Taney County farmers had paused, as they always did when we practiced outside, to stand and watch us from the road at the border of the field...

We were well into the advanced levels of the kata now, the ones known collectively as *tengusho*. They were a series named after the *tengu*, the mountain goblins who had imparted their secrets of strategy, Japanese martial tradition had it, to the founder of the Yagyu Shinkage-ryu, Yagyu Munetoshi. Arms stretched out beside my head, I raised my bokuto so its blunt tip angled to point at my sensei's throat. In slow and measured steps, I paced towards him. In the earlier kata I had been waiting for the attack. Now, I elicited it, forcing my opponent into an attack. He poised, then burst forward with an overhead stroke. I slid to the side and countered. I sliced my weapon across his forearms with a diagonal blow that, had my blade and intentions been real, my distancing complete, would have laid both his arms open with a lethal cut. Sensei dodged to his rear. Then he jumped in again with another vertical cut. This time I responded with a simultaneous pushing strike that slid past his weapon and penetrated, a thrust to his belly. We paused, then moved apart. I lifted my bokuto high above my head, ready for another opening to present itself, my sensei giving me none, his own sword pointed low to flick out against the arteries in my legs should I make an offensive motion in his direction. We retreated from each other without hurry, still locked together in an intense combative spirit...

It was not a mere reverie, I realized then. That was not the papery rustle of mown cornstalks in a harvested Missouri field I felt underfoot as I backed away from the completion of the kata. It was the stubbly cut stumps of a rice field. Those weren't crows here; they were *karasu*. Unlike the farmers who'd watched us back home, the billed caps of these farmers sported logos of a firm of automated rice-planting machinery. In place of work boots, they wore split-toed *jikatabi*, calf-high cloth moccasins with rubber tread soles that were the perfect footwear for mucking about in the soggy ground. Traipsing back to Sensei's house after our morning practice session, I saw that his hair, gray when I had begun my training with him back in the sixties, was now all white. The lines that creased his face when he laughed now, those too told me that the years were different. The crows were not any the less black or less boisterous for their being karasu here. The farmers still watched silently from a distance and shook their heads in puzzlement at the strange scene we presented with our wooden swords and fierce exchanges. But time had passed; I was now in Japan. It was not the same.

Kokoro kagami, the innkeeper in Nara had called the classical military arts of feudal Japan, the "mirror of the soul." An apt description. The late Donn Draeger, one of the first Westerners to delve into the combat methods of old Japan, was also their foremost non-Japanese historian. His books on the subject introduced the bujutsu to the West. Draeger once observed that while archaeologists may spend hundreds of hours scrutinizing shards of pottery and anthropologists might devote years to an exploration of the fertility rituals of primitive tribes, the serious study of man's weapons and his approaches to fighting with them are rarely given more than the most cursory attention in academia. This is a significant oversight, Draeger maintained, for conflict and the use of weaponry are universal, common to all civilizations in all times. The arms devised by a particular culture or society and the ways in which their inventors took them up can tell us much. An informed researcher—their proper title is "hoplologist" and the science they pursue is called "hoplology"—can make several very accurate deductions about Japanese life and technology, about the social structure of Japan and its aesthetic values during any particular period, just by examining a sword of that period. He can deduce even more by watching the traditional training of the koryu, its etiquette, teaching methodology, and so on. This is hoplology on the etic level, the perspective of the dispassionate scientific observer. One important step further in understanding is to actually take that sword from its scabbard or display case, to take up the training itself. This involves seeking an apprenticeship in a koryu, learning its approach to combat from the inside out; to "go native" in a sense or, as the hoplologist would put it, to study on an emic, or participatory level.

Understandably, it is often impossible to pursue the use of some weapons and fighting systems from the truly emic angle. Hoplologists have only the vaguest of ideas as to how the Scandinavian berserker wielded his battle axe, for instance, how its methods might have been learned or how they were passed on from one practitioner to another. There are gaps in the resources of hoplology. Important aspects have been lost. Anyone who has ever read tales of Robin Hood knows of the famous English longbow. But scholars had no exact description of this weapon until a centuries-old shipwreck off England's coast was discovered, with some waterlogged but otherwise preserved longbows in the hold. In these cases, the hoplologist can do little more than research weapons or a fighting system from a limited etic perspective. The remaining weapons available to him may be only museum specimens, the systems behind their development completely extinct. In this regard, the fate of many traditional fighting arts of Japan is more fortunate. They have been preserved in more than three hundred schools of classical martial arts that are still viable in that country. These arts are kept intact, for the time being, in technique and spirit, and passed on from teacher to student in a uniquely Japanese institution: the ryu.

Since their inception as a device for teaching and continuing on a tradition from one generation to the next, the ryu have protected and refined and conserved their teachings and methods, stubbornly resisting, in most cases (though regrettably, not all), any appreciable erosion or dilution. The oldest verifiable martial ryu date back to about the mid-fifteenth century. Ryu for other arts, tea ceremony, flower arranging, and so on, trace their origins from about the same time and can claim roughly the same success. The ryu then, is a remarkable achievement in maintaining traditions, in the correct transmission of an art.

It does not matter in the slightest whether the ryu is devoted to the tea ceremony, or calligraphy, or swordsmanship, in terms of how the teachings are presented and mastered. All have sustained the essence and viability of their arts in very much the same fashion. All ryu are characterized by a kind of discipline that is seemingly harsh and demanding, one that by its nature tends to weed out all but the most sincere disciples. Even to enter a ryu at its initiatory level was arduous. It always has been and must, if the integrity of the ryu is to be kept, remain so. Three times a week for over a month I had sought out instruction in the Shinkage-ryu, before I made it past even the front door of the house on the quiet street where my sensei had lived during his time in America. Once he agreed to teach me, I was still taught for a long time on an unexplained but quite real kind of probation. Fundamental techniques were only briefly explained, if at all. Sometimes Sensei would scarcely speak when he taught me. He would drill me in the basics or watch silently while I carved the air with a bokuto in the patterns he demonstrated. It was not for some years that I was taught the real meanings behind many of the techniques, the actual targets cleverly concealed within the movements of the kata. And there were many depths of the ryu, many unplumbed springs for which I had not yet been given the complete soundings. And will not, not for many years of study to come. The mirror of the bujutsu is in this sense like a lake. It is reflective at the surface, with a vast, unseen reservoir below.

Chiyoko, my teacher's wife's niece, had begun training in the Shinkage-ryu under Sensei. She was going through the same process as I had. She was probing into the teachings of the ryu, learning patiently the first measures of the soundings from an accomplished navigator of these waters, our teacher. Like many koryu exponents, Chiyoko entered into her study of these older arts through the more modern budo. She practiced kendo in high school, and iaido. After her graduation from college, she had come to live with her aunt and uncle. She worked now as an accountant for a local firm that sold tires for trucks and farming equipment. The rest of her time was spent as a student of the bujutsu. It is an avocation that places her in a minority in Japan. Some Westerners may have the idea that all Japanese today are knowledgeable about the martial arts of their country. In fact, Donn Draeger and other authorities have speculated that fewer than three percent of the Japanese alive today have ever even seen the koryu bujutsu. These arts are demonstrated occasionally in public. The Budokan in Tokyo holds an annual event where many of them are formally presented. And certain temples and shrines associated with various specific ryu sometimes host exhibitions that are actually, in many cases, part of religious ritual. But most of the audiences for these, unless they are connected with the ryu itself, have only a vague comprehension of what they are watching.

Many Japanese I spoke to in Japan were familiar with the name of the Yagyu Shinkage-ryu. Not because they recognized its historical or cultural significance. They knew it because a string of TV programs and samurai movies have featured plots centered around the doings of the Yagyu clan, nearly all of them fictional and wildly, romantically inaccurate. (In some, the Yagyu fight bravely and cunningly for the poor and downtrodden. In others, they are portrayed as evil spylords for the shogun.) Most Japanese are surprised to learn there are martial disciplines that predate kendo or judo. They are astonished too, to discover that these original feudal arts are still alive, some of them, still maintained in out-of-the-way places, still practiced by dedicated individuals who have inherited what they consider to be a precious tradition, and who have no desire to publicize or co-opt their arts for profit or attention. The bujutsu may be the mirror of the soul of Japan, as the innkeeper told me. If so, they are like the mirror at the innermost altar of a Shinto shrine: protected from ordinary view, kept out of sight except to the devout. They are a mirror hidden away, almost a myth to the modern Japanese, witnessed by only a few, appreciated for their true worth and value by even fewer.

"Uhhhh... here's the problem." Sensei grunted, crouched down on his hands and knees. He peered into the damp hole in the ground while Ito-san and I struggled to keep the bathtub-sized boulder of granite balanced on a teeter. "There's a tree root it's hung up on."

Sensei slid an iron pry bar into the gap we'd opened beneath the rock to lever the snaggling root away. Ito-san and I eased the boulder back down, then scrambled to steady it as it lurched forward another two feet across the slope. It thudded to a halt when it hit the pair of chockstones we'd set to catch it. In strictest fact it was not "our" rock. It belonged to Ito-san, my teacher's neighbor. He'd asked us to help him move it from where it looked to have been quite content to sit for the past couple of millennia or so, sporting a fuzzy hide of moss and warty lichens, half-buried just below the crest of a hill behind Ito-san's house.

"Look, can you see where I want it?" Ito-san had asked me after taking me inside his house, to the room where he and his wife ate each day. The shoji were open, the shutters racked in their compartments. We could look out the front of the house, onto an area of the yard bordered by a trio of small maples, their leaves toasted crimson and yellow, and across from them a thick screening stand of green bamboo. In the brief space between was a splendid view across the valley that included a horizon framed by Nara's gentle mountain ranges.

"You want the rock put just to the left of the middle of the open space there, lined up with the foot of that mountain," I'd guessed, when he asked me.

Ito-san nodded. "It needs perspective, this view," he told me. "Right now the leaves are turning, so the maples stand out next to the green bamboo. In winter, the bare branches look good against the bamboo, too. But for summer and spring, the view needs some perspective, something to set it off."

Ito-san was in the process of creating a *shakkei* style garden, a contained panorama, a living picture. For how long had he been sitting before the canvas of sky and earth he had to work with, framed as it was by the bamboo and maple and by the walls of this room that, slid open as they were much of the year, enclosed the space before us? "How long?" I asked.

"Well," he rubbed his chin. "My grandfather planted those maples when this was his house. My father started trimming them to that form." Ito-san paused. "I've just been watching them for a little while."

I sat and watched a little while more with him.

"Can't rush a garden like this," he said, "but I decided it needed a stone right there about a year ago. Your sensei's wife, Mrs. Kotaro, helped me pick one out."

I was impressed by the contemplation and care that had gone into this addition to his garden. I was fatalistic about his decision to relocate and settle a stone weighing several hundred pounds into a new location at exactly the time I had showed up to be enlisted into the sweaty task of helping to move it. More than anything, I was gratified to have been able to correctly estimate, when he'd asked me, how and where Ito-san wanted to position his rock. It satisfied me that all the effort Kaoru-san had spent on me hadn't gone entirely for naught. All the flopping down wet streambanks and battling chiggers had, in some small ways at least, accomplished her goal for me. It had taught me to "listen to the stones talk."

"Okay, which way does it want to go now?"

Ito-san was contemplating his boulder, bent over like an umpire, his legs spread wide, arms akimbo on his knees. Sensei and I maneuvered ourselves for the next push.

"Let's think about this a minute," I puffed. I glanced toward the downward fall line of the slope on which both we and the boulder were perched, eyeing it like a skier planning his run. It was a gentle grade for a few yards, then there was a sudden drop beyond, which pitched and became progressively steeper all the way to the roadway below. A long way below. I had a vision of the rest of the day being spent as one of a trio of Japanese Sisyphuses, shouldering our deadweight back up that near-vertical stretch of real estate. That was exactly what we'd be doing if we made an error in judgment here and the stone tumbled out of our control. Had this been in the city, Ito-san would have hired a backhoe to claw his rock out of the ground, hoist it as easily as Takeminakata had juggled those thousand-man boulders back in the days of deity yore, and plopped it right into place. But the backhoe hadn't been built that could lumber its way up and down terrain this rugged. So we were relocating Ito-san's stone the same way landscape gardeners had moved them in the feudal era—by sheer, brute cunning.

We analyzed the most direct course between the rock's original resting place and what we fondly hoped would be its new one. Ito-san had used a spade to excavate around one side of the rock. Our initial assault with a pair of pry bars had shivered the boulder and jerked it loose in stages and then we jabbed the bars more deeply under it to lift the stone. We looked a bit like Neanderthals, gang-spearing at the underbelly of a granite mammoth. It took nearly an hour before the boulder rose free and with a *whump!* that quivered the ground around us like a yard-sized earthquake, it tilted on its side and toppled over. The stone's exposed underside was smooth and cool, moist with clots of dirt that clung to it. Our mammoth had gone belly up and was ready to be carried away triumphantly… or rolled away, actually. It was a matter of cautiously and deliberately circling the subdued quarry, conferring at length, and finally getting down to the task of tilting it this way and that, rolling the boulder on a hesitant and erratic path towards the selected spot between the maples and the bamboo.

"We have to get it up this way and then let it fall around over in that direction," was Ito-san's rendered opinion. Since neither my teacher nor I had a better suggestion to offer at the time, we deployed ourselves under his direction. "Oh, and Dave-san," he added, "this time don't use your foot for a chock wedge. One of those little stones over there will work better, I bet."

I'd keep the advice in mind, I promised.

The formal shakkei style of garden Ito-san and his predecessors had created is not the sort of landscaping that results from a couple of Saturday afternoons puttering about. It is an art of astounding complexities and subtleties. All methods of Japanese gardening, including the shakkei style, have their own distinctive traditions, organizing philosophies, fundamentals, and prescribed aesthetic principles. They have schools, written texts, and secret teachings passed on from teacher to student, just as with any other traditional Japanese art. And as with every other art of that country, there are specializations within the craft of landscape gardening. One such specialty is *suiseki,* the art of "water and rocks," or, more prosaically, the craft of arranging rocks in the garden so they are transformed into mountains or seashores. Some suiseki landscapes are reduced to the dimensions of a tabletop. The suiseki aficionado will search out—studying vistas of real mountains and beaches—rocks that recreate the view around him. Presented on wooden stands carved specially for them or in shallow trays lined with powdery sand, these miniature suiseki are remarkable. Only a pinch of imagination when looking at them can conjure up fabulous sceneries. On occasion, a rock is found that closely resembles a particular landform that actually exists, a famous waterfall or mountain peak or, like the one discovered recently, a palm-sized likeness of the cone of Fuji-san, right down to streaks of milky quartz in the grain of the rock that resemble snow filled ravines. These extraordinary finds immediately achieve the status of fine and staggeringly expensive art.

On a larger scale, suiseki is employed in all of Japan's famous landscape gardens. "Before the planting of trees or the layout of the flora, consider first the placement of the stones," goes some advice from a scroll text on the principles of gardening. In some renowned temple gardens there are no flowers or trees or greenery of any kind at all, only groups of stones and flat seas and lakes of raked gravel. (The quintessential example is the garden beside the abbot's quarters at the Ryoanji temple, in Kyoto. It consists of three compositions of stones in clusters of seven, five, and three, placed upon a broad expanse of gray gravel.) In other forms of landscape gardening in Japan, the goal of the overall design is the creation of "borrowed scenery," as shakkei is best translated. Selected boulders and rocks are juxtaposed along with plantings of grasses and trees and objects such as stone lanterns, water basins, and so on.

Kaoru's father had been an authority in suiseki. He had taught her. She had exposed me to the fundamentals of the art. On weekend hikes along the streams and rivers of southwest Missouri, she explained to me that what to ordinary sight might be just another weathered boulder along the waterside actually had (or lacked) certain objective qualities. She pointed out in them characteristics by which the suiseki enthusiast can judge them: grain, balance, color, even a sense of "personality" they may possess. Moving them together or separating them into various compositions under her direction, I began to see how the rocks, or groupings of them arranged expertly, can achieve other, more subtle character still. An accumulation of stones could be arrayed, she showed me, so they seemed to leap and swim across a section of a brook like ducks at play. A tall, flat rock became the upraised wing of a crane in flight over a placid pool, and accompanying stones assembled before and behind the wing assumed the shapes of a gracefully extended neck, beaked head, and dangling wing. Other boulders have fixed and classic shapes that represent natural features. A long, horizontal stone situated beside a pond simulates fog hovering over the water at morning. Within the teachings of suiseki, too, are boulder compositions arranged to symbolize protective Buddhist deities or constellations with esoteric religious or spiritual connotations.

To recognize the qualities of a stone and to place it in a setting where its unique features are highlighted and yet blended in harmony with surrounding elements of the garden; this is a skill painstakingly learned. Kaoru used to interpret the technical details of the art to me with considerable patience. Much of her instruction went right over my adolescent head. Even worse, I have often had opportunity to regret in retrospect, I absorbed just enough to know when a rock in a Japanese style garden is placed correctly or incorrectly—but not enough to be able to explain to myself or to others *why*.

"Don't worry so much about the rules or the exact proportions," Kaoru had told me then. "I'm not really a sensei, so I can't teach you properly as a student anyway."

All Kaoru insisted she was doing was giving me an introduction, an overview of the various disciplines of suiseki. If ever I had the opportunity to apprentice with a master, she had urged, as I had been given in the arts of the sword under her husband, I should take advantage of it. Until then, she advised, I should concentrate on spending time with rocks in the places where they naturally belonged, along the streams and in the woods. And I should "listen to the stones speak," she said. To hear what they had to tell me about themselves and about me. I did. After Sensei and Kaoru returned to Japan I hiked out in the woods as often as I could and when I was at the shore or in the mountains, I made a habit of studying the rocks there and I tried always to "listen" to what they had to say. At times, the boulders and stones in those places were eloquent for me. At other times they remained mute. There were other occasions, I'm sure, when they may have been talking like hell but I was too busy doing something else to be a good listener. Ito-san's rock, for instance, may have been talking its moss off to me as we were moving it. But we were all making too much noise for me to hear it right then.

"That's it, that's it… we've got it rolling now," Ito-san shouted happily.

"*Matte, matte!*" Sensei warned, "Slow it down!"

We had tumbled the boulder onto level ground at last and with the momentum we had going we could trundle it along if not exactly swiftly, at least at a steadier pace. We got it right beside the hole Ito-san had dug earlier to receive it.

"One more roll," I gasped. "We ought to be right in the hole."

Sensei checked. "No, no. It'll go in on its side if we're not careful here."

A basic precept of suiseki is the appreciation of each stone's unique and individual physiognomy. In addition to its other features, a boulder has a "right" side or one facet that is the correct one to leave exposed. It has too, an underside, a base that is the part to be buried or at least to be against the ground. This is not a trivial matter in the making of a garden. There are tales of suiseki boulders and rocks that, ineptly positioned, their upper faces set clumsily, result in turmoil in the spirit of the gardener or the garden's owner. A poorly positioned boulder creates a sense of discombobulation in the lives of those around it. It must be righted, its balance, and in so doing, the balance of the entire garden is restored. We had to wrestle Ito-san's boulder before the final push, lurching it back and forth so that when we gave a final push, it tipped, paused, then thudded perfectly into the pit he'd prepared for it.

Ito-san could not have known what the contours of the rock's underground surfaces were; he had made a reasonably good guess, however. He had only to juggle and jostle the boulder with a pry bar for a moment or two before it settled. Some spadework would follow. A boulder in a garden cannot look as though it was just dropped on the ground. It must be set *into* the earth. With some boulders, the bulk of the stone is actually buried, like an iceberg. Only the tip is above the surface. All must appear at though it is completely natural, growing out of the earth as it would had the forces of nature placed it there.

Ito-san's boulder was what is termed in the technical parlance of suiseki a *kanseki,* a central or "Master Rock." The kanseki in an arrangement of stones is named because it is designated by the designer as the largest in the garden and because it is complemented by a grouping of "Vassal Rocks," or *shinseki,* around it that completes the scenery. The Master Rock also takes its title because it represents the master of the house where the garden is located. Accordingly, Ito-san's boulder had been situated in the northwest corner of the property, the most auspicious direction for such an important object, according to occult principles of suiseki, which are based upon very ancient Taoist configurations borrowed by Japan from China.

Ito-san had not made his decision for placing this boulder by whim nor by fortuitous chance, had he? I asked Kaoru, who had walked up the hill to join us in admiring our job.

"No, of course not," she said. She cast in my direction one of those looks as if to chide me into thinking everything she and Sensei had tried to teach me had been for naught. "Ito-san's grandfather consulted someone who knew about suiseki, I'm sure. Or maybe he practiced the art himself. He planned for the maples and the bamboo to be planted this way so they would eventually need a boulder over there for balance."

The late afternoon breeze stirred itself into motion from someplace far off. It rustled and twisted through the hills around us, trembling the colors of the elms and birches, and it brushed past us and struck the maples in Ito-san's garden. Bright golden leaves scattered and danced loose against the wind. Some of them fell onto the rock we'd moved and others drifted onto the damp, freshly shoveled earth around it. Ito-san's grandfather: had he planted the spindly maple seedlings with a day like this in mind? Did he envision a time when the shakkei he started would be ready to receive today's addition? And what work was left to be done here? There would be the attendant shinseki stones to be added to serve the master rock. Yet additions to any style of Japanese garden are strictly avoided unless they are absolutely necessary. Better to subtract, to abstract, to express beauty with the bare, almost severe minimum. That is the ideal.

Still, I wanted to know, what was next in the plan for this glimpse of the universe condensed into compositions of maples, bamboo, and quiet stone? I did not ask, though. I suspected the answer might lie in the mind and the aesthetic tendencies of a young man, a boy still in his junior high school years. He came often to the Ito house, I'd been told, on visits from Osaka with his parents… a boy who would inherit the house someday and who was taking an interest already in the shakkei garden beside it. It would be Ito-san's grandson who would continue to shape this space. A new generation confronting timeless patterns and principles of beauty.

The community dojo nearest Sensei's house was called the Genyokan. It was about four miles away by foot or car, along a narrow prefectural road, then another three-quarters of a mile after that by a seriously vertical hike. The first time I visited it, before I'd even reached the dojo itself I had already decided that if any martial artist came to Japan looking for the ideal training hall, the dojo of his dreams, there would be no way he could be disappointed in the Genyokan.

More gracefully rendered in Japanese than in an English translation, the kanji characters for Genyokan mean "the hall of the source of evening's twilight." It was an entirely appropriate name if ever there was one. I am certain that only the most determined or lucky or badly strayed beams of sunlight could ever have filtered their way through the evergreen canopy that enveloped the dojo. The forest around it was so intense that it was quite invisible from no more than fifty feet away from its front gate. At that distance, there were only the great round pillars of cryptomeria trunks, their piney scent tinting the shadowy, motionless air. The dojo was approached by a path of set stones that ran through the gate, its wood whitened with age. There was no fence, only this gate with its thick oak panels and above it, a Shinto torii arch. When the gates were closed, so was the dojo. Opened, they signaled that training was going on and members passed through them to the dojo structure itself.

The Genyokan was built in the *shindenzukuri* style of architecture, as are most traditional dojo in Japan. The walls were low, topped with wide-eaved roofs. The roof was hipped and fluted upward at the corners where it met the underhang. Roof tiles, once shiny blue were now a rich azure, which showed through here and there where the moss and fallen rusty cryptomeria needles had not completely covered it. The outer walls were creamy plaster and supported by a framework of dark, age-stained wood. There were no windows, just ventilation openings set high up on the walls and covered with wooden shutters. When the shutters were slid back, there were thin slats that protected the windows and kept birds out. These openings were also far up enough along the walls to frustrate any view in from the outside. In the old days, matters in the dojo were private. It would not do for an outsider, possibly a spy or an enemy, to learn the secrets of the arts being taught within. This concern for secrecy is reflected in the architecture of all traditional dojo.

Inside, the Genyokan had the typical appurtenances of the martial arts training hall: raised sections of tatami along side-walls, for those not training out on the floor to stay out of the way of the action; a dressing room and a rack for shoes near the door at the rear of the structure; an alcove centered up front. Upkeep of most community dojo like the Genyokan is funded in part with money from prefectural governments. For that reason, these dojo have been stripped of any of the Shinto or Buddhist regalia they may have had before the Second World War. (Occupation authorities pinpointed state-supported Shinto as a factor in Japan's wildly ethnocentric militarism. After Japan's surrender, occupying forces banned all government support for the religion, from major shrines like the Yasukuni Jinja in Tokyo to the small, shelf-top *kamiza* shrines in martial arts dojo. The traditional votive shrine in all prefecturally-funded training halls has been replaced by a Japanese flag hung in the alcove.) The Genyokan, though, did not receive any operating assistance from the prefecture. It was locally maintained; the land it sat on belonged to a Tendai Buddhist temple. So at the front of the dojo was both a Shinto shrine on one shelf and on another beside it, a small *butsuden,* a Buddhist altar. These reigned side by side over an expanse of training floor so polished by years and years, by generations of bare feet sliding and stomping and stepping that even in the near darkness it gleamed with a rich glow as if illuminated from within the planks of wood themselves.

The Genyokan was a wonderful place in which to train. Merely getting to it, though, was a kind of exercise and challenge in itself, as I discovered on my first visit.

"Time to leave for iaido practice," Chiyoko told me one afternoon not long before dusk. I assumed there was some dojo in the nearest town to which we would be driving. We drove all right, after packing our *keikogi* and hakama and getting the keys to Sensei's old Nissan. But Chiyo-san steered us even further away from civilization by my reckoning, on a road that was not quite wide enough for the only other car we met to get around us going in the opposite direction. Both vehicles had to ease off the pavement, putting our tires crunching into the soft berm. On my side of the car I tried not to notice that the mountainside plunged down hard as a ski slope. I tried not to imagine the spectacular crash we would make, the Nissan whirling over and over like a shuttle, down through the bamboo-studded ravine.

"Little close on this side, Chiyo-san." The other car crawled past us and the driver waved. He was close enough to have reached over and shook hands.

"Nah," Chiyoko dismissed my worries. "This is the wide part of the road. Wait 'til you see it up ahead where it gets tight."

She wasn't teasing. The next curve brought us around the flank of the mountain and on up it a few degrees. The ravine here was even more precipitous and any suggestion of a shoulder on the roadbed disappeared altogether. The only way we could have accommodated a car coming from the opposite direction now would have been if it or ours had a very good and reliable reverse gear. Any automobile manufacturer hoping to peddle his internal combustion wares in Japan should travel first along a few of the roads like this one, I thought, before going into the export business. Admittedly, this stretch of highway was narrow even by

Japanese standards. Still, except for major city streets and some of the arterial freeways, little driving in Japan is conducted on roadways as spacious as those found commonly in the u.s. (The historical reason for this is twofold. One, the use of wheeled vehicles in old Japan was limited to transportation for the emperor and a few other such exceptions. No oxcarts or wagons. Roads were built with the needs of horse and pedestrian traffic in mind. And two, narrow roads were easier to defend and to monitor and they hampered enemy troop movement. A feudal lord wisely kept his domain secure by making access to it difficult.) There are numerous thoroughfares, thousands of kilometers of them all over Japan, where the width is a little more than half that of a typical American two-lane street. Full-sized automobiles or pickup trucks from the West would never begin to safely navigate them.

We were not more than a few miles from Sensei's house where I had, up until that moment, considered the road to be sized, well, "quaintly." Now I was doubtful that even our compact Nissan was going to fit on the pavement. To my relief, a shoulder suddenly reappeared beside the road, broad enough for us to pull the car completely off on it, nosing the front end into the mountain. Chiyoko yanked on the emergency brake. Aside from three other cars parked beside us, there was nothing in sight but forest and mountains.

Chiyoko looked at me. "Now we start for the dojo," she said.

The series of steps we took up from where we'd parked the car were slabs of speckled granite, rough cut so long ago that by now they were worn so smooth they seemed to be bowed in the middle. The course they took zigged one way, then the other, but they always went up, right up the slope. Chiyoko led the way.

"Were these put in when the dojo was built?" I asked.

"No, this is the way that led up to the old temple," she told me. "Right up here," she said a moment later. We reached a stone landing and following her pointing finger, I made out an outline off in the twilight of the evening forest.

"That's it, what's left of it," Chiyoko said. "Looks like it's almost ready to collapse, doesn't it?"

It did. Even in the dying light I could see that the roof had lost most of its tiles. The framework rafters exposed beneath looked punky and rotted, even at a distance. The once-graceful lines of the roof sagged, giving in gradually to the demands of gravity.

"What happened?" I wanted to know.

"You'd have to ask someone from around here," Chiyoko said as we started along the path that led up and away from the shambling temple ruins. "Someone told me it was used for religious retreats by the Tendai monks once upon a time. The priest in charge of it died, I think, and the place was abandoned after that."

"That's odd."

"Yes, it is," Chiyo-san replied. "You should ask Sakunami-san. You'll meet him tonight at the dojo. He knows all about the history of this area." From over her shoulder, Chiyoko added, "Sakunami-san is the one who told me the temple is supposed to be haunted."

At just that moment, as if on cue, from the gloom behind us welled up a long and unearthly yowl. It was agonized, a tenor quaver that rose, held, then trailed off into a muttering, chuckling cough. It was horrible.

"Jeez!" I whirled around. My shoulders dropped and I flexed my knees, belly muscles tensed. Both hands wrapped into fists. I'm always surprised by this response in myself, that when I'm surprised and frightened on the inside by the unexpected, my outside prepares for battle. And then usually I am embarrassed because the noise turns out to be a skittering bit of street-corner litter, or branches scraping—the kind of adversaries my punches and kicks would scarcely intimidate at all. Arrayed against whatever was uttering this eerie shriek, I knew as soon as I'd readied them that the puny weapons of my body wouldn't have been much of a deterrent.

"Hear that?" Chiyoko said without looking back. "Gray owl. They're common in this part of Japan."

"Oh?" I packed my fists into my pockets and hunched my back, hoisting the bag my training clothes were in higher up on my shoulders—and I tried to loosen the skin of my scalp, which was still drawn and bristling my neck hair.

"Kind of spooky, isn't it?" Chiyo-san said.

"Kind of."

The remainder of the climb to the Genyokan, after the haunted temple and the Owl of Terror was scenic, but uneventful. Chiyoko and I had gone early to the night's practice, to spend some time working on the sword-drawing methods of the Shinkage-ryu. But there were already six others at the dojo when we arrived, moving about the floor, swinging their weapons in wide, chopping strokes to relax their shoulders and wrists. At the training hall in Suwa I had been a stranger and I had to prove myself to the group there. But here at the Genyokan, I was not a complete unknown. I was the *deshi* of Kotaro-san, the gaijin he'd taken on as a student during his time in America. Shyly at first, then with increasing enthusiasm, the dojo members came up to me, introduced themselves, and proceeded to have me smiling self-consciously at learning that they knew all about me.

"Chiyo-san," I pulled her aside after we'd dressed. "How come these people seem to know me?"

"Well, Sensei talks about you sometimes."

It was a revelation to me. I had grown up with an image of my teacher as a sort of walking definition of reticence. Only on the rarest of occasions had I seen even the slightest thaw in the icy reserve known in Japanese as *igen*, the outward manifestation of the inner stoical spirit of the samurai's cool discretion. Whatever affection or pride he may have had in me had always been demonstrated in the most oblique ways. Understatement was the preferred medium of his conversation. The distinction between approval and disgust was measured by him in the tonality of a grunt, nothing more. Sensei had talked about me? Told these people about my writing career and the modest foothills of success I'd scaled? This was information I wanted some time to sit with, to mull over and consider. The dojo, however, is not a place for musing. The senior member of the dojo, Suzuki-san, came onto the floor and we all gathered in lines before the kamiza. We bowed, then Suzuki-san spoke.

"We have a visitor from America with us tonight," he said. "This is Dave-san, the deshi that Kotaro-san had when he was living over there. He's come tonight to practice iaido with us, so let's not waste his time. Kotaro-san has asked us to correct as many of his weaknesses in iaido as possible and to show him some of the kata he may not have seen."

The members of Genyokan proceeded to follow his instructions with a generous spirit once the training session had begun. Unlike the dojo in Suwa, there was no single sensei in charge of practice or instruction. This kind of organization in a dojo might have been odd from the perspective of a Western martial arts practitioner. In budo dojo in the United States and elsewhere outside Japan, the term "sensei" or even "master" is used loosely. Often, the person leading the class during any given session or anyone who opens a school for studying the martial arts is referred to by students by one of those titles. In Japan, this aspect of the martial ways is subject to a more strict governance. In the art of iaido, a couple of national organizations oversee instruction and grading of exponents throughout Japan. They are stringent about the process for becoming a formally-recognized teacher of the art. Under their criteria, an *iaidoka* must have held the rank of fifth dan for at least three years before he is eligible for the title of *renshi,* the lowest level of instructor. For most practitioners, that means close to fifteen years spent in continuous training under high level masters are necessary before they can be considered knowledgeable enough to formally teach others. More than twenty-five years past that are the minimum that must be devoted to the art of the sword draw before the title of *hanshi* can be granted by one of the organizations, certifying a master of iaido.

At the Genyokan, the majority of the dozen or so iaidoka who practiced there had more than the requisite number of years necessary for reaching a teaching grade. A couple of them could have come close to qualifying for the level of master in terms of the years they'd spent in the dojo. But there are factors other than time spent learning and practicing to be considered in the awarding of teaching certificates. The Genyokan was a rural dojo. Members traveled to nearby Kyoto and to Nara for instruction under the senior teachers there on occasion. But they were not regularly enrolled in the big-city dojo and that placed them outside the mainstream of training and testing that went on in those places. This imposed some limitations on those practitioners unable to keep in close contact with the organizational bodies of the art.

If an iaido exponent misses the examination held in Kyoto for the fifth dan, for instance, it is another year before the test is given again. The organizations are also prone (too prone, many critics insist) to change requirements for the various grades. And since iaido, along with all the other modern budo, did not emerge as an identifiable art until modern times, it is still in a state of evolution. The final three kata of the basic forms of the art were not added to the curriculum until over ten years after a youngster like myself had started training. Other kata are still undergoing scrutiny by senior masters and teachers and some alterations in the exact methods of footwork and timing are still being instituted. At places like the Genyokan, these matters tend to be of little concern. As a result, no one at the dojo could or would properly be called a sensei. The most experienced members who took on the task of teaching were referred to, like everyone else, by the polite suffix of -*san*.

The Genyokan's lack of officially recognized sensei was proof of their respect for the ranking system that controls iaido. (And, given the contrary and independent spirit of many country folk in Japan, it was also a testament to their frequent disdain for matters concerning city people.) But it was in no way indicative of a lack of ability and skill in the dojo. I was delighted and intrigued by the iaido I'd seen in the Suwa Dojo. At the Genyokan, I was awed. Sato-san, a slightly-built fellow who looked to be in his sixties, came up out of a kneeling position and as he drew his katana horizontally, he reinforced the strike with a stamp of his foot that—*boom!*—shook, actually vibrated, the floor of the dojo. It was not mere physical strength, or the applied force of muscle alone; a man twice Sato-san's size could not have duplicated that stamp. His power came from a unified body, all parts working in harmony, relaxed, totally relaxed until the moment of focus, when the edge of the blade would have struck the target had there been a real one. At that instant, Sato-san turned his body to stone and then just as quickly relaxed it again as he slid forward in a shuffle to complete the action of the kata with another stroke, this time vertical, of his weapon. This was a demonstration at high level of *settsuku*, or "body connection," one of the mysterious qualities of the Japanese martial disciplines that make them so compelling and dynamic. The ninety-eight pounds of the proverbial weakling may seem trifling, yet imagine a weight of concrete equal to that catapulted into the middle of your chest. With settsuku of the caliber Sato-san was capable of generating, that would have been much the outcome.

All around me the members of the dojo began their practice, with the seniors keeping an eye on the newer practitioners, giving them advice and instruction. Sato-san's kata served as my example. I knelt, composed myself, then unsheathed and cut.

"No, no, no!"

A hand whapped me across my shoulder from behind. I jerked around to look directly into the galvanized gaze of Mrs. Koyomi. I was to feel both her hand and gaze on me several more times that night, and every other time I came to the Genyokan. Koyomi-san spoke only three words of English to me, well chosen ones. She had, in fact, just spoken them all. Falling back into Japanese, she unleashed a gush of correction that was interspersed with the same imperative.

In Japanese she said, "Your shoulders tight like this?" Then in English: "No, no, no!"

In Nihongo: "Your wrist that way?" and then back to English: "No, no, no!"

And so it went, Koyomi-san and I. She bounced me and prodded and pummeled my form and after twenty minutes I felt like I'd been on the receiving end of an enthusiastic massage. But I was improving my kata. I could feel it. Mrs. Koyomi's advice was precise. She found my weak points with a surgical accuracy and she corrected them without any wasted words or motions. From the corner of my eye I saw Chiyoko resheathe her blade, bow, and step off the floor. With such limited space as the Genyokan provided, there was not enough room for all of us to practice safely at once. Individuals then would take turns, periodically retreating to the sidelines to rest, observe, and allow others a chance to practice. There was no set limit on how much time one spent on the floor. But a pattern appeared to prevail and since Chiyoko and I had started at the same time, when she stopped, I did too. I followed her lead and started off the floor to sit for a while.

"Ahh, Dave-san." It was Sato-sempai, tugging at my sleeve. "Something I'd like to show you that might be of interest."

He lowered himself, not in the heels-to-buttocks posture of *seiza*, the position from which most of the basic forms of iaido commence, but in an older method of sitting I recognized. He was crouching now, on the balls of his feet. I understood the meaning. The position was much more aggressive than seiza. He was moving from the discipline of iaido back into the more classical combative art of iaijutsu. The kata of iaido are distilled and adapted from this much older art. Iaido has among its primary goals the development of an aesthetically beautiful form, and combative reality often takes a back seat. Iaijutsu is beautiful too, in its own way. But its techniques are rooted in lethal practicality. They are tricks, stratagems, bold and cunning, intended to kill a man or to provoke him into a fatal mistake so he can then be dispatched. It is an art of killing, of spilling blood, and even though it survives only as an historical oddity, the performance of iaijutsu nonetheless has about it an air of sobriety and the scent of death.

"This is the first kata of the Kaji-ha Itto ryu," Sato-san said, after showing me the fundamentals by which the swordsman from this particular school grasped his blade, kept its sheath in his obi with a twist of the cord looped and tied to the scabbard. There were, in the feudal era, over seven thousand ryu devoted to swordsmanship in Japan. Each school had its own techniques. Most included special training in the art of iaijutsu, an art which allowed the swordsman a considerable advantage in a fight. To be shown some of these ancient techniques was a rare privilege. I watched and began to follow the form he demonstrated, suffering once again the pleasure and pain of one who has been presented with more wealth than he can possibly hold. I would not remember a tenth of his instruction, I knew. Once I left the dojo I would not even be able to practice what he had demonstrated for me.

"That's good," Sato-san said, watching while I copied the movements he performed, repeating them when I stumbled or forgot. "Next time we'll go on to the next kata."

I bowed gratefully to him and he turned away to supervise a younger junior, Nishiyaki-san, who was learning the basics of timing in one of the fundamental forms. Without much grace I lumbered to my feet, slowly stretching legs that were quivering from the efforts of crouching for so long. I started again for the side of the dojo and the haven of rest it promised. This time is was Sakunami-san who intercepted me, another senior who had been watching and came over to touch my sleeve, his smile bright.

"Dave-san, I saw you practicing the second level of the kata earlier tonight. You know, there are some variations in them you might not have seen. Could I show you some you might want to try?"

I remembered the dreams I'd had in Suwa after a session at the iaido dojo, my subconscious trying to sort out all I had seen and tried to learn. They were the kind of dreams I'd be having tonight, I was sure, if I wasn't too tired to dream.

What had been long shadows in the dusk on the hike up to the Genyokan had lengthened and deepened and now all around on the walk back down the mountain were barely distinguishable shades of dark forest black. I walked between Chiyoko and Sato-san, her behind, him in front, and I depended on the sounds of their footsteps to keep me on the trail. To have strayed, even by the width of a pace or two, would have gotten me down that part of the mountain much, much faster than I wanted to go. The angle of the slope was that severe, and I drained off the last dregs of the adrenaline I'd distilled during training on the walk back to the car. Once we reached it and started home, whatever roller coaster ride adventures we may have encountered on the narrow roadway were lost on me. I was dozing in my seat before Chiyo-san even had the Nissan into reverse and headed back around the side of the mountain.

I roused as we were parking on the berm below Sensei's house. Compared to the alpine ascent to the dojo, the steps up the hillside to the house did not seem nearly so daunting. Halfway up, I paused to glance over to the Ito's place across the road. A single light twinkled, no more than the glow of a firefly in the blanket of dark that had been pulled up over the countryside. I thought it was a yard lamp at first. Then I remembered a stone lantern that was set low amongst a planting of cotoneaster shrubbery. It was the lantern's candle sending out an amber spark. Someone at the Ito's must have been up and about there. I looked up from the lantern's puny illumination. The outer shutters in one room were open. It was Ito-san. I could tell by his silhouette. He was sitting on the tatami in the room, contemplating by the light of the lantern his shakkei garden and the stone we had added to it.

8
Touchstones...

$\mathcal{S}$ensei's house, for the most part, was built at the turn of the century. It had been constructed, though, around an original house that was much older, the home during the final years of the feudal era of a samurai turned farmer. Some of the original architecture of that time remained, incorporated into the newer parts of the structure that had been added on. Along a hallway below the staircase leading to the second floor was tucked a cozy, six-mat room that had been altered to include bookshelves along all the walls. The original tokonoma space had been left untouched, however. It was arranged typically, with a hanging scroll that got changed regularly with the season, and a Shigaraki earthenware bowl that held fresh flowers that were changed more often than that. And most uncharacteristically, for the tokonoma is virtually a shrine to aesthetic brevity, there was a katana in its scabbard, propped against the back corner of the alcove. This odd place for keeping a sword was uncommon too, because a katana belongs properly on a horizontal or vertical rack with carved arms designed to cradle the weapon, keeping it safe from damage and ready to be used quickly. There was no shortage of these racks in Sensei's house; how come none was used for this katana? When I asked, Sensei produced a scroll that he untied, rolling open its tale out onto the tatami between us.

In the waning years of the Kamakura period (1185-1333), a descendant of the eighth generation of the Ogasawara clan was granted land by his father in the district of Miyoshi, in Awa Province. Awa was a rugged promontory on the eastern side of the most diminutive of the Japanese main island chain, Shikoku. The Ogasawara were a celebrated samurai family, a *buke*, as they are called in Japanese. The Ogasawara could trace their family's line all the way back to the Seiwa-Genji, the elite coterie of clans that were collectively known by the name Minamoto, a name they had been given by the emperor Seiwa in the ninth century. Many of the most renowned buke could trace their pedigree back to the Seiwa-Genji; still, the Ogasawara were a particularly illustrious example. Ogasawara Nagahide is the warrior who taught mounted archery to the shogun Yoshimitsu. Nagahide was, in fact, the founder of the Ogasawara-ryu of archery and he fostered as well a related tradition of the same name that delineated and defined the warrior's code of manners and etiquette. Both traditions, the archery and the etiquette, are still alive today (both headed by direct descendants of Ogasawara Nagahide), just one legacy of the Seiwa-Genji heritage.

It was another Ogasawara, Ogasawara Nagayuki, who settled in the Miyoshi district, and in time he took the name of that wild and beautiful place as his own. He did not, however, change his profession, nor did his descendants. The Miyoshi were stalwart retainers of the Hosokawa, the clan that ruled all of the island of Shikoku. In 1509, an inter-family quarrel sparked between the two sons of Hosokawa Masatomo, Sumiyuki and Sumitomo. The quarrel broke out after the father died and history does not record exactly what it was over. Whatever it was, it culminated in a battle that took place south of Kyoto, in a hilly, verdant region famous for its tea and sake manufacturing. The Miyoshi were caught between the two brothers in their loyalties to the Hosokawa family. In the end, led by the patriarch of the Miyoshi, Miyoshi Nagateru, the clan sided with the brother Sumitomo. Miyoshi Nagateru commanded both his *bushi* and those of the Hosokawa and during the fight he wielded a sword he'd had made for himself, a modest "working" blade, forged by a minor craftsman of the Bizen tradition of smithery. Nagateru was victorious in the battle. He saw to it that his lord Sumitomo was named regent of the city of Kyoto and of the surrounding province, as that was the title that belonged to the rightful—or at least the ruling—head of the Hosokawa clan.

Sumitomo may have been, thanks to Miyoshi Nagateru's battle skills, the rightful head of the clan. But his reign was by no means undisputed. It lasted, in fact, less than a year. The shogun Yoshitane launched an assault on Kyoto, forcing Sumitomo and his vassal, Miyoshi Nagateru, to scurry ignobly back to the Hosokawa lands in Awa Province. It was the ancestral home of the Miyoshi, yet it was also a kind of exile for Nagateru. He did not take the defeat in Kyoto complacently. For nearly a decade he committed himself to the rigorous practice of the martial arts and to the strategies of heiho. Nagateru also immersed himself in the esoteric rituals of *mikkyo,* a mysterious sect of Buddhism. In 1519, his head tonsured like a priest's, Nagateru adopted the religious name of Kiun. He returned to Kyoto then, intent on reinstating his lord Hosokawa Sumitomo to the office of regent. It is not a matter of record (nor of any real interest to history), but we can assume Nagateru gave his Bizen blade to his son, Miyoshi Nagamoto, before he embarked on this campaign.

A battle simmered, conch shells trumpeting and silk clan standards fluttering listlessly in the heat of the Kyoto summer. Then, as a punishing sun rose, the fight came to the boiling stage. Nagateru's plan depended upon the aid of his lord Sumitomo. Sumitomo was to charge from the east at a critical moment, encircling the enemy shogun's forces in a pincer. For all his study of heiho, though, Nagateru neglected to consider the effects of seasonal rains, just ended. The Kamo River, which ran between Sumitomo's army and Kyoto, was swollen at full flood stage. Sumitomo's planned advance, crucial to Nagateru's plan, was completely stymied. Surrounded and outnumbered by his enemies in the northeast part of Kyoto, Nagateru retreated to Chionin, a principal shrine of the Jodo denomination of Buddhism. In a gravel courtyard beneath the broad eaves of the Chionin, Nagateru composed himself and took up a sharp dagger, the length of its blade wrapped in paper. He turned the tip inward and thrust, dying as he had lived, a proud Miyoshi samurai.

The heir to the head of the Miyoshi family, Miyoshi Nagamoto, must have inherited more from his father than Nagateru's sword. In 1520, inflamed by the same determination to take back Kyoto, he too attacked the capital city, in the service of the same faction of the Hosokawa family. Unlike his father, however, Nagamoto was successful in the venture. He routed Kyoto's occupiers and restored his daimyo, Hosokawa Harumoto, to the post of regent. An interlude of calm followed for the Miyoshi samurai and then: who knows? Perhaps Nagamoto became restless. Maybe it was disgruntlement as he came to believe that his military conquests for his daimyo were not fully appreciated. More likely, given the convoluted plotting and counter-plotting of politics during that era, the Hosokawa regent suspected his Miyoshi vassal was scheming against him. Hosokawa Harumoto accused Nagamoto of treachery. The leader of the Miyoshi clan was ordered to commit suicide. Nagamoto complied; in protest, seventy-five of his warriors followed him with their own bloody *oibara*, the form of disembowelment that was intended to demonstrate one's ultimate loyalty to his master.

Whatever wrath or suspected treason might have brought about Miyoshi Nagamoto's death sentence, it did not extend to his son. Miyoshi Norinaga was the eldest offspring of Nagamoto and to him fell the role of leadership for the Miyoshi clan. Not only was young Norinaga's life spared, he was expected to continue to serve Hosokawa Harumoto, the same daimyo who had commanded Norinaga's father to kill himself. (Why would Nagamoto's samurai commit *seppuku* to honor their leader's death while at the same time his own son could not is the obvious question here. The answer lies in the harsh, sometimes nearly inhuman code demanded of the samurai. So long as his lord was alive, the life of the bushi was not his own. He belonged, body, sword, and soul, to the daimyo he served. And if he chose the path of honorable disembowelment for some reason, without asking his lord's permission first, it was no different than if he had deserted or been otherwise unfaithful. He was beyond punishment for this transgression, of course. But his family could be banished or even executed. Worse still, his family name could be put through the legal process of *kaieki*, his crime noted in deeds of record, his reputation forever tarnished. Nagamoto's own warriors were free to protest his death with their own, since technically and legally, they no longer had a lord to obey. Nagamoto's son, however, was bound directly to the Hosokawa clan. The obligation of the son did not end just because his lord had ordered the death of the father.)

Norinaga accepted the burden his service to the Hosokawa demanded. In fact, he appears in historical accounts to have fulfilled his duties almost from childhood with distinction and martial ardor. In the annals of the Miyoshi clan, there is a mention that Norinaga was a disciple of one branch of the Shinkage-ryu. In his training, he almost certainly would have used the Bizen katana that had been handed down to him upon the death of his father.

Shortly before his eighteenth birthday, Norinaga led his bushi into the provinces west of Kyoto to do battle with the daimyo in power there. He was accompanied by the armies of two of his relatives, one a close cousin, the Matsunaga; the other more distant, the Masanaga. (While these names share a phonetic similarity, they are genealogically unrelated.) In an attack on a fortress in Izumi, Masanaga refused to carry out one of Norinaga's orders. He insisted that a flanking movement Norinaga planned would needlessly expose Masanaga's troops to a raking enfilade of arrows from the enemy castle. Furious at Masanaga's disobedience, Norinaga retreated, returned to Kyoto, and reported Masanaga's insubordination to the regent. To his surprise, though, and his subsequent rage, the Hosokawa regent supported Masanaga in the dispute.

Considering the political climate of the late Muromachi era, one of quick and shifting alliances and treacheries that were almost regular occurrences, Norinaga's reaction to all of this was not remarkably inconsistent. The leader of the Miyoshi turned on his relative and ally. He attacked Masanaga and then, citing his regent's failure to back him in his disagreement with Masanaga as proof of Hosokawa infidelity to their retainers, Norinaga also struck out with vehemence at his daimyo. He attacked the Hosokawa castle in Miyake. Hosokawa Harumoto's stronghold was overrun by a combined force of the Miyoshi and the warriors of Matsunaga Hisahide, Norinaga's other relative and an ally who had remained (for the time being, anyway) faithful to the Miyoshi.

The defeated Hosokawa regent limped away in retreat, abandoning Kyoto, to the province of Omi. Norinaga took possession of Kyoto and declared himself *shobanshu,* a title below that of shogun. In gratitude for the alliance of Matsunaga Hisahide, Norinaga presented Hisahide with a number of gifts of land, rice, armor, and weaponry. Included in the latter, according to a notation in Matsunaga family records, was a "deeply curved Bizen blade with a clove blossom temper line forged into the cutting edge." The record indicated too, that this sword had been shortened from its original length, as was common when warfare in old Japan switched from a predominant reliance upon fighting from horseback to combat on foot, and that it had "long been an heirloom of the Miyoshi clan."

His outrage mollified, Miyoshi Norinaga turned his attention from Kyoto to the fertile lands of the Kinai, the provinces west of the capital. Within the space of a few years, he conquered them one by one, at the same time repelling attempts by the family of his old daimyo, the Hosokawa, to destroy him. Judged by the success of these military exploits, the constellation of Norinaga's power seemed to be in ascendancy in the last half of the 1560s. He had subjugated a considerable area of south-central Japan and had kept at bay more than a half-dozen serious enemies, most of them affiliated with the Hosokawa, who sought to return to Kyoto. But across the winter skies in the tenth year of Eiroku (1568), two comets burned their way, one right after the other. They were portents, as it turned out, for the approach of twin tragedies for the leader of the Miyoshi.

Norinaga had it demonstrated to him by his onetime comrade, Masanaga, that enemies can materialize from the most unexpected angles. He had proven it himself, turning on his daimyo to avenge the mistreatment he believed he'd suffered from Hosokawa Masatomo. His first warning that his stars were imperiled came when his son Yoshioki died following a lingering and, at first, inexplicable illness. Suspicious, Norinaga had his servants questioned about any unusual activity in his castle. A maid confessed. She was having a romantic liaison with a handsome young priest who had visited her in the middle of the night regularly, right up until the time of Yoshioki's death. The "priest" was found, arrested and tortured. It soon became evident that he was not from any religious sect at all. His allegiance was to a *kumi,* a league of ninja terrorists that specialized in assassination. He had manipulated a romance with the maid to gain access to the Miyoshi castle and to Yoshioki's food. He brewed a slow-acting poison distilled from the gall bladder of a weasel and added the concoction to Yoshioki's meal. A little extra coercion from his captors prompted him to admit still more. (We can imagine what kind of persuasion was used—but would probably rather not, considering that interrogations at that time in Japan included the dislocation of every bone in the hands and some bizarre strangulation techniques of which Torquemada never even dreamed.) The ninja confessed that he had killed Yoshioki under the orders of none other than Matsunaga Hisahide.

The irony of betrayal was bitter as tannin. The son of Norinaga had been murdered by Hisahide, Norinaga's ally and co-conspirator since the very beginning of Norinaga's career—the same Hisahide to whom Norinaga had presented the Bizen sword after the defeat of the Hosokawa.

In an earlier time, Norinaga might have sought to even the score against his betrayer. But as foretold by the arc of the second comet, another misfortune appeared on Norinaga's horizon. At the height of his political and military power, the leader of the Miyoshi began to fail physically. He was afflicted, probably with some form of tuberculosis. His battlefield changed. His opponent in life and death was now within himself; lesser enemies could no longer occupy his full attention and energies. Weakened by the disease and unable to attend to the defense of his realm, he failed to retaliate against Hisahide then, or a few years later when Hisahide struck again, having Norinaga's brother executed. In another passing of the seasons, Norinaga would be dead as well, frustrated to the end, no doubt, at his inability to avenge his family. Yet he must have taken some measure of contentment, too, in dying not by the steel of a foe but rather by an opponent against which no warrior's strategy is infinitely successful.

Matsunaga family history exonerates Hisahide of perfidy in his murderous actions against the Miyoshi. Their personal annals reveal a dark secret, actually: decades before, when Norinaga set out to control the provinces of the Kinai, he had initially been unable to convince his relatives, the Matsunaga, to accompany him. They joined the Miyoshi on the expedition only after one branch of the family was slaughtered, their mansion burned to the ground while many of them were still in it. Norinaga presented evidence to the surviving Matsunaga, seeming to prove that the massacre was at the hands of one of the daimyo he planned to attack. Not until years later did Matsunaga Hisahide discover that it was actually Norinaga who had engineered the whole plot, a scheme to enlist the aid of the Matsunaga in his fight.

Whether Hisahide's depredations against the Miyoshi was a cunning, long-planned and cold-blooded act of revenge or not, it was the basis for Hisahide's own rise in power. Establishing a center of command in a mountainside castle in Kawachi

Province, Matsunaga Hisahide spun a web of political intrigues. Battles were won, lost, fought to indecision. The shogun Yoshiteru granted Hisahide an official post in the government. After Miyoshi Norinaga died, Hisahide petitioned the shogun to be appointed to the higher office of *Kyoto kanryo,* a prime minister, of sorts, to the shogun. By tradition and law, the kanryo could be selected from one of only three families. Hisahide based his right to claim the title upon a tenuous family connection to one of them, the Hosokawa. (Yes, the same Hosokawa against whom Miyoshi Norinaga, with Hisahide's help, had turned upon. Commingle the plot lines of four or five TV soap operas. Give characters names that sound very much alike. Add a code of warfare that applauded certain treacheries and double-dealing. Mix in a generous dollop of generations-old rivalries with an absolute passion for revenge, and you have a good basis for understanding the strategies and machinations of feudal Japan.)

The shogun Yoshiteru refused Hisahide's request for appointment to the office of kanryo. Hisahide responded by advancing his troops to the villa of the shogun, the castle at Nijo, in Kyoto. Hisahide demolished much of the villa and forced the shogun to kill himself. Hisahide appointed his own shogun, a toddler with the necessary familial connection to the Seiwa-Genji and was thus able, for all practical purposes, to take the mantle for himself. Hisahide and his son, Matsunaga Hisamichi, ruled the whole region of the Kinai then, including the capital city of Kyoto and the strategically vital province of Yamato. Yet at the peak of his triumphs, Hisahide too, had sowed the seeds of his eventual destruction.

Miyoshi Norinaga was dead, but a successor, Miyoshi Yoshitsugu, wanted revenge for Hisahide's treason. The Miyoshi declared war on the Matsunaga. In the winter of 1563, Hisahide accepted their challenge. He unleashed his own strike against an army of pro-Miyoshi warrior-monks at Tonomine, a monastery in Yamato. Hisahide was joined by a young warrior who had his own reasons for extracting a quantity of Miyoshi blood. His name was

Yagyu Munetoshi. Twenty years before, an alliance of Miyoshi and Tsutsui samurai had besieged Munetoshi's village of Yagyu-zato, razing it. Matsunaga and Munetoshi joined to defeat the monks, even though Munetoshi's fist was struck by an arrow during the fight. Shortly thereafter, though, Hisahide found himself under attack by the Sasaki clan, one of the families Hisahide had forced from Kyoto years earlier.

Assailed on two fronts, Hisahide arranged a peaceful alliance with the Miyoshi. Having consolidated his problems in this way, he stayed the threat that was posed by the Sasaki, too. In 1568, he was appointed governor of the provinces of the Kinai. His appointment was through Oda Nobunaga, who was at the same time busily bringing Japan under his despotic control and ruthlessly exterminating all who opposed him.

Hisahide was pleased with his promotion to the governorship. He soon chafed, though, under the administrative yoke Nobunaga had harnessed upon him. Before long, he was plotting with his ally/nemesis/ally/nemesis/ally, the Miyoshi clan. Together with Miyoshi Yoshitsugu, he defied Nobunaga's authority, refusing to pay the taxes levied on his lands. A firecracker string of minor skirmishes followed, during which the Miyoshi family was decimated and Matsunaga put on the defensive. Hisahide and his son continued their feud with Nobunaga until 1577, when Nobunaga's troops, under the command of his son Nobutada, poised a thrust at the Matsunaga castle at Shiki, in Kawachi Province. Forewarned of the attack, Hisahide sent a contingent of samurai with his own son, Hisamichi, at their lead, out from the castle to intercept the Nobunaga incursion. Hisamichi hoped to lay a trap for the invaders at a valley where the Kamo and Katsura rivers join, below a mountain called Kasumigane (The Mist Peak).

Both Matsunagas, Hisahide and his son Hisamichi, were clever strategists of the first order. But against the nefarious Nobunaga they were playing well out of their league. Spies had informed Nobutada of Hisamichi's advancing columns and he dispatched a unit under Tsutsui Junkei to intercept Hisamichi's interception. Nobutada's main advance then, bypassed the Kasumigane valley and Hisamichi, drawn reluctantly into battle by Tsutsui's diversionary troops, was unable to halt it. A quick march brought the enemy to the Matsunaga fortress and for three days the sloped stone walls there trembled under the full force of Nobutada's battalions. On the fourth, they crumbled and gave way. Hisahide's samurai were courageous, but their struggle was without hope. The head of the Matsunaga clan was able to perform seppuku in a room at the top of a corner tower just moments before the enemy burst in to find that Hisahide's own dagger had cheated them of their objective.

Hisahide's son Hisamichi, fled, taking refuge with relatives near Kyoto. Those warriors with him scattered. One of them, a cousin of Hisamichi's named Matsunaga Fuyuyori, hiked to the secluded mountain fiefdom of the Yagyu clan north of Nara, to petition the clan to be accepted as a retainer. With him went the Bizen sword, which his cousin Hisamichi had inherited and which he had, in turn, given to Fuyuyori. Yagyu Munetoshi accepted Fuyuyori as one of his vassals and in time, he became a trusted samurai within the clan. He married, and his wife bore him eight daughters and three sons. At the battle of Sekigahara in 1600, he fought alongside the warriors Yagyu Munetoshi recruited from neighboring clans to assist Tokugawa Ieyasu in this great decisive conflict that laid the foundations for the three-hundred-year unification of Japan under Tokugawa rule.

The Bizen blade was not carried or used at Sekigahara. It had been handed down by then to Fuyuyori's eldest son, Fuyuyoshi, who also served the Yagyu clan, so faithfully that he was buried just outside the Yagyu family cemetery, on a bamboo forested hillside in Yagyu village.

The sword went to Fuyuyoshi's son, and then to his son; then to that son's nephew, another Matsunaga bushi who was apparently bisexual and balanced a home life as the father of three daughters with a homosexual relationship with a famous Noh actor that continued until he died in 1728. His nephew inherited the sword, and for the first time a record is made of its having been used in combat. Matsunaga Taisuke fought a duel, using it to kill a samurai of the Tanabe clan in 1752.

Taisuke passed the Bizen sword to his son, who gave it to his nephew in 1793. The nephew, who had both a wooden leg and four wives in his lifetime, died of smallpox in 1829. His son inherited the sword and continued to carry it long after swords and samurai were outlawed, each in their own way, after the fall of the last Tokugawa shogun in 1867. He wore the sword as his ancestors had for centuries, cutting edge up in its saya and thrust through his obi, until a police official from Nara threatened to arrest him for the act. He then carried the weapon concealed in a walking stick that served as a scabbard. Upon his death in 1894, Matsunaga Nobuyuki, his nephew, inherited it.

Nobuyuki, according to Matsunaga family lore, never quite forgave his karma for delaying his admission into the world until 1868, a year after samurai privileges and feudalism were abolished. Nobuyuki grew up keenly aware of his warrior heritage and all his life he conducted himself as though he was a living part of it. He studied Confucian philosophy, wore a hakama and formal kimono regularly, and practiced the Omori-ryu of iaido and the Ichien-ryu of traditional bujutsu. He also learned Western mathematics, however, and taught it to the sons of wealthy Nara merchants in a private academy.

Nobuyuki had scant patience or empathy with the modernization that brought Japan into the twentieth century. In 1918, when socialist-backed unions were striking and rioting in many Japanese cities, the aristocratic Nobuyuki crossed paths with four union members on a Nara street corner. It was a period of nationwide and frequently violent unrest in Japan. Many citizens habitually carried weapons, daggers and sword canes, or even pistols, with them when they were out. Nobuyuki used the excuse of his iaido practice to have a reason for arming himself with the Bizen katana on his way to and from the academy where he taught. It was in his grasp then, when the union toughs spotted him leaving the school. Despite the weapon, they assumed him to be an effete intellectual, useful to their cause as one who might be intimidated into publicly supporting unionism. They cornered Nobuyuki and started bullying him. Nobuyuki did not bother to reason or argue. He punched the scabbarded tip of the katana squarely into the face of the leader, pulverizing his nose. The tough staggered, his face a spout of blood. The others, their geta clattering on the pavement, vanished as quickly as they could.

On a late autumn afternoon, early winter really, when the woods near his home turned dark and gray and lacy fringes of ice wrinkled the quiet pools of stone-shouldered brooks, Nobuyuki had been training with his sword. His practice spot was a clearing on the other side of the mountain from the Genyokan. His walk home took him past a neighbor's, who came rushing out as Nobuyuki strode by, feverish with excitement. The Imperial Navy, it had just been reported on the radio news from Kyoto, had attacked an American military base. An island in the Pacific Ocean. The nation of Japan was at war.

The radio report had to be wrong, Nobuyuki insisted. He was a widely read man, knowledgeable about Western civilization, and he had a friend in Nara whose son had been to college in America and had spoken often of its immense wealth and resources. Japan could never hope to win a war against a power like the United States, he knew, contrary to the bombastic propaganda emanating from Tokyo ever since Japanese troops had invaded China. He hurried home. At seventy-three, he was still a bachelor and his youngest sister and her husband lived with him, cooking and tending to his house. They listened to the news broadcasts from Kyoto. They would have the story correct, he was sure. When he arrived, however, his sister confirmed the neighbor's account. Japan had declared war, not only against the British and the Dutch now, but against the most powerful nation in the West. Her fate was sealed, disastrously. Japan's destruction would come at the hands of military leaders and pompous politicians who were, in Nobuyuki's estimation, little more than glorified peasants. Japan's martial spirit had been perverted, warped to justify a monstrous evil.

Without a word, according to his sister's recollection, Nobuyuki went to a small room under the stairs and cleaned the Bizen katana, wiping away smudges with *uchiko* powder and spreading a film of fragrant clove oil over the steel. He propped it in a corner of the alcove and never touched it, nor did he practice iai again.

Matsunaga Nobuyuki died of pneumonia in the spring of 1943. At the time, his country home was filled with refugee relatives who had fled wartime shortages in the cities of Japan. One of them was a quiet, teenaged girl who studied the tea ceremony and wore her ebon hair in twin glossy braids that hung straight down her back.

Matsunaga Nobuyuki's nephew inherited the house. He died in 1973, leaving it and its contents to that girl who was by then a woman, living for a time in the United States with her husband. The woman, of course, was Kaoru-san, my sensei's wife.

Kaoru was descended from two buke warrior families. The Yoshioka were on her mother's side, the Matsunaga on her father's. She had told me stories when I was young, about her ancestors. She told me too, about the uncle she remembered, a kind man but remote and haughty. Yes, she said, he was a swordsman. But when she had stayed at his home during the last year of his life he no longer practiced the art. His katana, though, was in a tokonoma at his house, still there for all she knew. It was, her elders had told her, a very old one. A Matsunaga family treasure, really, an heirloom.

…a touchstone.

9
Obligations

Sensei and I were close. Less than a finger's length separated the tips of our bokuto. Without altering the distance, my teacher switched his stance. He lowered his weapon, dipping it swiftly and then flipping it up again, his arms crossed at the elbows so the bokuto was poised close to his body. I moved my bokuto, cocked at my shoulder, and struck. I aimed for the left side of his body, where he appeared to have left it exposed and vulnerable when changing his stance. Yet no sooner was I fully committed to my attack than Sensei twitched. Catching my timing perfectly, his weapon flicked mine aside. He sliced a cut right down the center of me. I stepped back in a hurry, lifting my wooden blade above my head, threatening another strike, but he followed, his step thumping into the bare earth. He drove his bokuto forward, a thrust that would have killed me even if his initial riposte had not.

Chotan ichimi—"long and short the same"—was the name of the movement, a difficult one to translate (as are virtually all kata, the language and the concepts they express being so intimately bound). According to the *Heiho Kadensho,* the family scrolls of instruction written by the early masters of the Shinkage-ryu, one meaning of chotan ichimi is to be able to respond to an opponent whether his attack is up close or from a distance. But the scrolls are notoriously and deliberately vague. These records of methods, called *makimono* ("wrapped things"), usually copied from originals by one's sensei and presented in sections as he progresses in the ryu, are not intended to be step-by-step textbooks. References are often oblique, information fragmented and couched in cabalistic aphorisms within the scrolls. To someone without an introduction into the strategies and tactics of the ryu, these makimono would be nearly meaningless. They are more a shorthand series of notes, decipherable only to the initiated.

Makimono serve as a written record of the kata and principles of the ryu. But instruction must come as well, from the teacher himself. This personal aspect of the bugeisha's learning is the *kuden*, literally the "oral teachings" that cannot be found in any scroll or text. The kata chotan ichimi is a good example of the importance of the kuden as they apply to kenjutsu, the art of the sword. Nothing in the written makimono mentions the significance of the shift in stance at the onset of the kata. The switch, changing from a right leg forward posture to one with the left leg leading and lowering the sword at the same time, seems to be a weakening of the defense that might have been afforded by the *kamae*, the physical carriage of readiness taken by the swordsman. In a way, I had learned through Sensei's kuden, there is a weakness of sorts in the position. The kamae, often misunderstood as postures meant to display strength, to make the body impregnable, are often quite often just the opposite. Many kamae are a ruse, a combative invitation, a deliberate attempt to "sucker" an opponent, making him go for an obvious opening offered in your posture.

When I was first under his tutelage, Sensei had instructed me in the basics of the kamae. Now, in a fallow field under a warm autumn sky streaked with carded wool clouds, he explained further. (Actually, the term "kamae" is not used in the Shinkage-ryu. Combative postures are referred to as *kurai*, a term with several layers of meaning but which, in ordinary practice, serves in the same sense as other martial arts schools might use the word kamae. Likewise, the word "kata" is not used in the ryu; instead, the forms of movement involving attack and defense are called *seiho*. I use the more common terms here since they are far better known in Western martial arts circles.)

"You're in this position," he demonstrated, taking the same posture as before, arms crossed, sword in front of him as if it were a shield for his body. "Okay," he said, "where's the opening?"

What he meant was, where was the *suki*, the gap, the weakness in his kamae where an enemy would be drawn to attack. There were several points against which I could have struck, but in selecting his target the bugeisha must consider first of all, all the possibilities of multiple opponents. In a fight, he could not have wasted his time hoping to inflict a series of wounds that might eventually do the job, a strategy that was often employed in European-style sabre fencing. There was too great a chance that, squared off against one enemy and concentrating entirely on engaging him, another might slip up from an unexpected angle. The fight, in most instances, had to be quick. The bugeisha had to concentrate on those vital spots where death or a nearly immediate incapacitation would be the result. And just as importantly, he had to consider the matter of his opponent's armor.

"My target is behind the peak of your shoulder," I replied. I motioned to where the broad protective plates that fit over the biceps would have been fastened to the rest of the armor that covered the upper trunk.

Sensei grunted in agreement. "But look," he said. "Notice how this part of my leg is also exposed. Maybe the opponent knows I'm trying to trick him to go after my shoulder, so instead this part of my leg is what he chooses to go after instead. Go ahead; try to cut there."

The theatrical swiping slashes of the samurai hero's film duels are choreographed with an eye towards entertainment, not historical accuracy. Anyone trying the form of swordsmanship seen in Japanese "samurai" movies against a well-trained swordsman from a classical ryu would be dead in short order. The wide, windmill strikes and baseball swing follow-throughs would present a smorgasbord of suki, gaps galore. The blows exercised by kendo practitioners are likewise unrelated to the kenjutsu of the koryu. The center of the forehead, wrists, flanks, and throat—all the prescribed points where kendoka can hit to win a match in the modern sport, were well sheathed by the bushi's armor. Targets for the exponent of kenjutsu are aimed at weaknesses that are more assailable, places where, because the armor must articulate to allow movement, are unprotected and vulnerable.

I hitched my bokuto up to my shoulder and directed another strike, this time at the back of Sensei's leg. The front of the thighs are protected with what are called *haidate,* an apron-like covering of mail or lacquered leather with plates that fit over each leg. The fleshy hamstrings behind, however, are exposed. A quick cut there, even a shallow one, will sever tendons and cripple the most determined opponent. Under my teacher's direction, I was altering my role as the *teki,* the "enemy" in the movements of chotan ichimi. But he used the same technique of the kata to show me how it could cope with this variation as well. His bokuto wheeled over and slapped through my offense, settling in an eyeblink, with its tip focused again right at my hands.

We ran through the kamae to be found in the formal movements of the Shinkage-ryu. Sensei explained the suki that each revealed, the methods inherent in them to riposte the attacks they would elicit. There are some kamae shared by nearly all ryu that involve the use of the sword (although their names may differ from school to school). *Chudan kamae,* with the sword held pointed out at the opponent's throat, seems almost to curve up like a steel extension of the *hara,* the body center that is located physically a few inches below the navel. When the gripping fists push the sword out a little further, the tip's aim moves from throat to eyes, into *seigan kamae.* With the weapon held vertically in front of the shoulder, the swordsman is in the stance called *hasso kamae,* significant in duels or in battle because it draws the lower, left hand across the body so the arm protects the chest and heart. A kamae with fists lowered and the sword stretching out beside the body, tip extended to the rear, is more dangerous for the swordsman who adopts it. The sword seems to be casually dangling, yet it is once again an enticement to an attack. This posture is referred to as *sha*, or "wheel," in the Shinkage-ryu; some other schools refer to it as a "dragon's tail kamae," because the length of the weapon trails out behind the swordsman like an appendage—and it can lash too, like the coiled tail of that mythical beast.

Other kamae are exclusive to a ryu, almost a signature that is recognizable immediately when they are assumed, if one has a knowledge of their ryu. Instead of the typical middle level posture, or chudan kamae, in the Shinkage-ryu the sword is characteristically canted slightly to the swordsman's right, his shoulders twisted marginally as well. The combative advantages this modification offers are not to be found, for the most part, within the teachings of the makimono. They are passed along from teacher to student, a careful transmission through the kuden, the oral traditions of the art.

Neither a ryu's scrolls nor a master's verbal and physical instruction are a guarantee that the ryu will remain viable. There were thousands of thriving schools of martial science during the age of the bushi. Only hundreds remain today. Of those still extant, many are incomplete. Components of their curriculum have vanished along the way. In some koryu, tragically, the last generations are practicing. They have no students, no one to whom they can pass on the knowledge of their unique arts. The reasons for these extinctions and deteriorations are the same as may account for the loss or razing of any art or collective artistic skills and tradition of any country or culture. A catastrophe like a protracted war might have wiped out the entire tradition of a ryu; more likely the knowledge of the school was forfeited through less dramatic, more ordinary, neglect. The end of feudalism meant an end to the need for the bujutsu in a real, practical sense, and their very antiquarian nature led to an inevitable decline. Then too, the traditional bujutsu were representative of an undeniably unique aspect of the Japanese character. They were, as the innkeeper I'd met in Nara had called them, the mirror of Japan's soul. And as with all peoples at certain times in their history, the Japanese were not always content with the reflection they saw in that mirror. The bujutsu were ancient. They were classical; anti-egalitarian by their very essence. They were the exclusive domain of the aristocrat (though not necessarily, it is important to note, of the aristocracy). The era of Meiji Japan, though, occurring at the very beginning of the twentieth century, was a time when the Japanese craved to see the reflection of modern technology when they peered into the mirror—Western dress, literature, and art. They wanted to see the leveling face of populism, the blandish elevation of the medio-cre. With an enthusiasm propelled by an undercurrent of self-loathing, the country abandoned two thousand years of its past, in a very significant way, to embrace the contemporary world.

In the new Japan, traditional folkways like the tea ceremony and flower-arranging were popularly ridiculed and neglected, but while they had a musty odor of quaintness about them, at least the ritual of tea and flower-arranging could be dismissed by the sophisticated as merely old-fashioned. The bujutsu, however, were a different matter. These were energetic arts, unrepentantly elitist, integrally bound to classical values. The bujutsu were vigorously scorned by the intellectual classes in Japan after the age of feu-dalism. That some of them were actually preserved is due almost entirely to the fact that many koryu were headquartered in rural backwaters, away from the eye of many of their harshest critics. A clearing in a field served as a dojo. A headmaster of a ryu who earned his living as a farmer gathered some students who were neighbors or family and taught them in his home. Many ryu had been spawned far from cities, originating in sparsely populated districts. They were at home there, where the twentieth century penetrated slowly, its effects softened by enduring patterns of country life that did not easily change.

Survival for the bujutsu has been precarious, though. World War II decimated the ranks of exponents of the martial arts who were of military enlistment age. Wartime privations in Japan killed hundreds of old masters. Makimono, precious resources of the ryu, were burnt to ashes in Allied firebombings, along with dojo that were generations old. After the war, Occupation authorities did not make it easier for the bujutsu when they summarily banned all budo practice. The ban did not specifically mention the koryu. It was directed at the modern forms of kendo, judo, and karatedo that the American military knew about.

"The Occupation forces wouldn't have known Shinkage-ryu from kendo, of course," Sensei told me with a rueful smile when I asked him about those years. "But if they had seen my sensei and me practicing, I'm not sure the military police would have taken the time to entertain our explanations of the finer points of distinction between the two."

Like most other bugeisha, my teacher and his teacher were reduced to training furtively, often at night, after work. They were always in the countryside, as far as possible from anyone who might be watching them. Some classical martial arts exponents hid their swords rather than turning them in, as the law required, and they substituted trimmed tree branches for weapons in their practice.

"The Allied authorities never got out into our part of the country," Sensei explained to me. But he added that his fellow Japanese might have reported any martial arts training to the police themselves. Having just suffered a nightmare of war and a pair of nuclear sunsets, they were not entirely enthusiastic about anything even remotely martial in those days.

Today, the koryu bujutsu are healthier than in that dark period after World War II. Even so, their future is by no means assured. Some ryu have fewer than ten active members. At one of the annual demonstrations of koryu bujutsu given each February in Tokyo, a gathering of old men tottered out to demonstrate their particular tradition. An observer commented, just realizing it with dread, that a local calamity, an earthquake, for instance, could well mean that an entire four-hundred-year-old lineage could be wiped out and ended in seconds. Every living member of the ryu was there at one time under the roof of the Budokan.

Yet it need not be anything so dramatic as a cataclysm to extinguish the flame of a koryu. It will not be anything that spectacular for one ryu in the Kyoto area. There the end will come quietly, if it has not already, in the form of heart failure or some cancer or another, and a matriarch, the last headmistress of a school of naginata that was already venerable two centuries ago, will be gone. With her passing will vanish the ryu. She has no students who have inherited the entire tradition.

Still, all is not so bleak for the classical Japanese bujutsu. Some koryu have been declared Intangible Cultural Properties by the prefectures where they were founded. Some headmasters are being recognized as valuable living bonds with the past. In some koryu, where segments of the original curriculum have disappeared, senior masters have gone to other, related koryu to try to piece together known remnants of techniques and kata, in an effort to recreate their own. The Kashima Shinto-ryu, which traces its ancestry back to the Katori Shinto-ryu, for example, is involved in a study of the latter school's methods of iaijutsu. Somewhere in the nineteenth century, the sword drawing techniques of the Kashima-ryu vanished with the death of a master who did not pass all of them on. Other leaders of the ryu died, taking their fragmentary knowledge with them. So plans are now to reconcile what little was transmitted to current practitioners and what instructions are written in the Kashima-ryu makimono, with the iaijutsu kata of the Katori-ryu. The wine and its vineyard, in the case of Kashima-ryu iaijutsu, are gone. But the variety of grape is known, and something of the particulars of its vinification, and there are vintages of a similar provenance to compare. With persistence and luck, the Kashima-ryu may rediscover at least a taste of their original iaijutsu, flavors and aromas long lost.

Brightly too, young people in Japan, a few of them anyway, are seeking out the old koryu, sensing in these traditions some values and worth that are lacking in the modern world. Gaijin are among them, foreigners training in the bujutsu in Japan. Some Westerners have been practicing there long enough to have become respected, senior trainees in the koryu. Almost without exception, they are individuals of high caliber, knowledgeable about Japanese culture, sensitive to traditional ways. They are the very antithesis of the Ugly American.

"The arts of traditional Japan have already been willed to the next generation," the master potter Shoji Hamada said in 1978. "We of the last one must make sure they are passed down in as good a shape as possible." Kodomo tame ni. For the sake of the next generation. And as children of that generation, our task is to ensure that our inheritance is one we fully understand, perfectly appreciate, completely deserve.

A couple of children of that generation who are inheriting the koryu, Chiyoko and I, took the bus to Nara to perform an obeisance to a part of our inheritance — and to be tourists.

It had been drizzling when I was in Nara before. Chiyoko-san and I returned under an azure sky that held puffy pillows of fair weather clouds, a glorious autumn day.

"We need directions to get to the cemetery," Chiyoko said.

"No problem. Last time I was here a beautiful damsel appeared in the middle of the night and took me right to where I wanted to go. Let's wait here a second and see if another one shows up."

Chiyo-san snorted. "First, that word you used for a 'young girl' hasn't been in vogue in Japanese since the thirties. And second, I think we'll get directions a little faster if we ask at the Tourist Information Center across the street."

I acknowledged her point. But the bespectacled retired fellow behind the information desk I did not find nearly so entertaining or helpful as the schoolgirl I'd encountered my first evening in the city. I let Chiyo-san ask him which intra-city bus we needed.

"Get off at the Daibutsu stop, right by the Tamukeyama Hachiman Shrine," the information guide informed us. He pointed it out on a multicolored map under the glass atop the counter.

"Hachiman?" I asked.

"Yes, he is a Buddhist deity. The god of war. Have you heard of him?"

I nodded. Asking a bugeisha if he knows of Hachiman is like asking an Irish Catholic if he knows of St. Patrick.

"We'll be sure to go see the shrine," I said.

The bus was packed. We stood. Visitors come to Nara in every season, drawn to its remarkable collection of historical sites, specifically to its sacred real estate. If the cathedral at Chartes, Westminster Abbey, Angkor Wat, and the churches and synagogues of Seville, Moscow, and half a dozen European cities were all stuck in an area a bit more than twice the size of New York's Central Park, the result would approximate Nara. The temples and shrines I glimpsed, ducking down and looking out the bus windows, were too many to count in the fifteen-minute ride we took through Nara Park. Directional signs pointed to dozens more.

The city of Nara became the religious center of Japan in the eighth century. That's when Chinese priests came there at the invitation of Emperor Shomu.

The fortunes of Nara rose and fell across those early centuries, always wedded to the fate of Buddhism. When a government, emperor, or military leader embraced the religion or promoted it for one reason or another, the city and its shrines prospered. Enormous sums were spent constructing temples of fabulous design and in sizes that staggered imaginations. When a ruler or regime felt a threat from the political influences of Buddhism, those same holy structures were promptly razed. Different sects of the faith had their own moments of glory and dissolution, official blessings and condemnation as well: the Tendai, the Jodo, the Nichiren — all left their architectural mark on Nara. Political authority eventually shifted north to Kyoto, then to Edo in the east. But the shrines and temples remained. Today, especially in the older half of the city, one is rarely out of sight of one or another of them.

The cemetery we sought was one near the Tamukeyama Hachiman Shrine, wedged in between a neighborhood Shinto reliquary and a noisy grade school. The smooth, brown dome of Mt. Wakakusa dominated the horizon above us, its grassy slopes tan and sere in this part of the year.

"Gaijin! Gaijin!" A flock of primary school kids in navy shorts and starched white blouses came chattering across their asphalt playground to take in the extraordinary—or at least temporarily distracting—sight I presented. The introduction of Buddhism to Japan brought not just a new faith to compete with native Shinto practices. The priests from China arrived with a cornucopia of learning and culture. In the full bloom of Nara's spring, a historical growing season between 700 and 800 A.D., the Buddhist temples of that city included medical clinics, libraries, and schools, available to all. In this century, the Japanese government has taken over these responsibilities. The school was a public one, not parochial. Yet given its proximity to the shrine, it was built, no doubt, on the site of an earlier academy where monks had taught children the strokes of the writing brush, the clattering calculations of the abacus, and the sutras of the Compassionate Buddha. The teachers of the children now were young women in blue warm-up suits with healthy, athletic faces and bodies, who shooed the shouting little scholars back to the center of the playground. Chiyoko and I went through the gate the school shared with the cemetery.

"This is it. Can't be too hard to find the grave."

"Nope," Chiyoko agreed. "The place isn't that big."

It wasn't. The gravesite we were looking for was in one corner, blessedly far from the cacophony of the recess in the playground. An entire plot of perhaps ten graves was lifted a couple of feet above the surface of the concrete pathways that crisscrossed the cemetery. In the center of the plot was a triple-tiered stone, a square column of polished granite that looked like the *ihai* mortuary tablets on a household family shrine. The kanji for the family name of Iwakura were chiseled on the face. Chiyoko and I stood in front of the marker, one as tall as I am. The scent of the cemetery's cedar trees was as sharp as a freshly opened clothes closet.

"Did Sensei ever tell you about Iwakura Sensei's 'one-tooth geta training'?" Chiyo-san asked me.

"Yes. About the time he turned blue?"

Our sensei's sensei. We had both heard so many tales about him from Sensei, we could talk as if we'd known him ourselves. He had become even more real to me now that we had come to do *o-hakamairi,* to visit his grave and tend to some of the rituals of its care. Inside the cemetery's confines was a cypress maintenance shed and pavilion, with shelves of scoops and buckets and a water trough with a drippling spigot. While I drew water, Chiyoko brushed the raised area around the gravesite, sweeping it clear of twigs and leaves, using a whisk that was kept in the shed.

Iwakura Sensei had been a landowner, the proprietor of a modest tea plantation. He was almost able to make ends meet with his tea. In the winters when the tea harvest was in and his tea bush yards were leafless and dormant, he supplemented his income by working for a cloth dyer who lived near him. Iwakura was an accomplished bugeisha. In addition to the Shinkage-ryu, he practiced a method of spearmanship. He was utterly diligent, my Sensei remembered, about developing a balance to all his skills and so he worked incessantly at perfecting his ambidexterity.

"He would use his chopsticks in his right hand one night at dinner and in his left the next," Sensei had told me. It was more difficult than it sounds. A proper Japanese table setting is situated entirely with the chopsticks meant to be used in the right hand. The rice bowl is on the left, soup bowl on the right, with other dishes arranged in front of them. "When my sensei was using his left hand, I had to remember to set the table the opposite way," Sensei told me, when describing his days as a student of Iwakura's.

Iwakura never missed a chance to train with both sides of his body. Pruning his tea bushes, he would switch the knife in his hand back and forth as he worked his way through the terraced rows of tea, shifting his stance at the same time. "I think that's why he liked the spear as much as he did," Sensei said of Iwakura. "Because it's used with the left hand leading, the opposite of other weapons."

Iwakura made every effort to employ daily activities as a part of his training. That's how his "one-tooth geta swims" came about. The old fashioned way of setting a natural dye in handwoven fabric was to wash the cloth in cold, running water. A source for the water was conveniently near the dyer's house where Iwakura worked, a cold brook that came directly from a spring. Bolts of the freshly dyed fabric were sunk in the stream, unrolled, and let flowing out by the current of the brook where they floated until the dye was set. In the winter, this was obviously a miserable task. The dyers had to wade up to their knees into the brook to drag the long banners of soaking cloth, heavy with water, up from the stream to wring them out. To practice his balance, however, Iwakura would volunteer to retrieve the fabric. To make the chore more challenging, he wore a pair of geta clogs into the brook, a pair that, unlike the normal clogs with their two teeth, had only one, right in the middle of the sole. Noh actors still use these odd contraptions to polish their theatrical poise. Iwakura was not an actor and the dyeing brook was no smooth, flat theater stage.

"Sensei took a lot of impromptu swims before he was good enough to judge the current and the slipperiness of the rocks in the streambed," my teacher said. "One time he slipped and got tangled in a big sheet of fabric as he was spreading it out. By the time he got out of the water and unwrapped from the cloth, the dye had gotten all over him. His arms and face were bright indigo. It was weeks before his skin looked normal again."

I ladled a scoop of water over the grave of my teacher's teacher and that of his wife's. Hers was a rectangular stone to the left of the family marker; his a semi-circular natural rock sheered flat on one side with a bas-relief of Jizo, the bodhisattva and savior of lost souls, carved into it.

Iwakura Yoshinori took pride in what he called "being remarkable in his ordinariness." Even though he was related distantly to Iwakura Tomomi, a famous political figure of the late Tokugawa period, he lived a life of studied and contented anonymity.

"Sensei was a great believer in the adage 'the nail that sticks up will get hammered down,'" my sensei told me. But I think it was something more than just modesty and a preference for his privacy that galvanized Iwakura. It was a passion, I suspect, for the aesthetics of *shibui,* the understated, the quiet, the reflective, hidden beauty of contemplation. What was your teacher like? I had asked Sensei when I was still a schoolboy and had not for long been training with him. Sensei had answered, "My sensei was a man of shibui." It was probably the first time I encountered that most Japanese of concepts. But it was not to be the last. I believe it was an affinity Iwakura passed on to his disciple, for many times I would see in my own sensei's actions and preferences the quality of shibui. Years later, I would find myself describing my teacher exactly as he had described his. And hoping that someday, I might be worthy of being described in the same way.

The opening salvos of the Second World War moved Matsunaga Nobuyuki to put his sword to rest forever, propping it in the corner of the alcove in his home near Nara. The horrifying climax of that same conflict drew Iwakura Sensei into it—and for an awful and frightening few days, it threatened to separate him from his carefully cultivated lifestyle of shibui.

"The town's mayor had the only radio near where we lived," Sensei began the story. "It was in front of his house that Iwakura Sensei and I heard the broadcast that a terrible bomb had been dropped on Hiroshima. We heard too, that an Allied invasion was coming to Japan." Japan, the rumor spread, was to be plundered; children slaughtered, women violated. "We were told to prepare for it and there was a lot of talk about fighting to the end, 'until the bullets were spent, then until the knives were broken, then until the bamboo for spears ran out,'" Sensei said.

A day after the broadcast about Hiroshima, Iwakura Sensei was visited by the captain of the local police, and the commander of the Home Guard. The Guard, a militia of old men, wounded veterans, and others too badly handicapped to be drafted, was to be augmented, the two visitors informed Iwakura. The women and children were to join the ranks of Japan's last-ditch defenders. Japan was so lacking in matériel that normal arms, rifles and pistols, were out of the question. The country was to be protected in the end with spears of sharpened bamboo. What had been braggadocio, propaganda sloganeering, was to become a desperate reality.

"The officials approached Sensei because he practiced the art of the spear," my teacher said. "They wanted him to conduct public classes to teach people to use the sharp bamboo poles against the coming invaders."

In order to get the measure of Iwakura Sensei, one must understand the social and political weather of those times. The war, the destiny of Japan, and the wishes of its military leaders had all acquired the mantle of cultish fanaticism. Japan would unite the whole of Asia, the orthodoxy held, and become as its divinely-inspired history had foretold—propaganda explained it—the center of all culture and the world's dominant political force. The average Japanese believed in Japan's invincibility and righteousness so thoroughly that most of them could no more have conceived of its defeat in the war than they would have considered the possibility of the sun rising in the West. Patriotism was heated to a level so white-hot that even wondering aloud about the war concluding with anything but a complete Japanese victory was reason enough to bring about questioning or even an arrest by the Kempeitai, Japan's wartime equivalent of the Gestapo. Patriotism was so rabid and absolute that even after the actual surrender had become fact, schoolteachers who brought the news of the defeat to their high school classes were jeered, assaulted, and in some extreme cases, were actually murdered by their disbelieving students. That was the spirit of the age in Japan during the war.

"I was shocked when Sensei politely refused the request by the authorities to teach the spear," my sensei recalled. "Those were the kind of government officials you did not say 'no' to. Ever. But I remember that Iwakura Sensei said that the martial arts were not meant for civilians. They were for warriors, he said, and to try to teach them to others would be pointless."

Iwakura's refusal was not merely a matter of his opinion conflicting with that of the local government's. He was informed that if he did not comply with the "request," he would be arrested. Given the hysteria of the country at the time, with American B-29s soaring unchallenged over Japanese skies and an alien army massing to the south, set to invade, it was not at all beyond the realm of possibility that Iwakura's arrest would be followed by a pistol shot to the back of the head in some lonely place, his disappearance as easily explained as it would have been for anyone who dared to undercut the control of the government.

"I very much believed my teacher would be executed if he was arrested and taken away," Sensei said. "No one could defy the military and police and expect to get away with it at that time." But, Sensei went on, his teacher was adamant. "It was a side of him I'd never seen before. It was like he was displaying, for once, something that had been hidden away inside him for so long. I think back on it now and I am reminded of a rounded wooden *shirasaya* [a plain scabbard of white wood in which a sword is stored when not in frequent use]. All of a sudden, I was seeing that inside the smooth, soft-looking wood of the case was a sharp steel blade."

Nearly frantic with worry, my teacher could do nothing to change his sensei's mind. So he continued to train with Iwakura every day, never knowing if this lesson would be the last. It was not until many years later that my sensei discovered how close his worst fears had come to being realized.

"Maybe twenty years after the war, I was talking to an old fellow who had been a lieutenant in the prefecture's police during that time. We got to talking about the war and I told him the story about my sensei's defiance.

"'Oh, yeah, you mean the sword teacher they wanted to teach martial arts to get ready for the invasion,' this guy said. 'That crazy man escaped by a fox hair. We'd processed orders to arrest him, but the captain didn't want to drive all the way out to where he lived to pick him up. He wanted to put it off until the end of the week.'"

By the end of the week, though, the authorities could have been excused for having forgotten all about a martial artist, tea grower, and part-time cloth dyer in some prefectural outback. The second atomic bomb had fallen over Nagasaki. Japan sued for peace.

"Maybe if the war had gone on another week, I would have lost my sensei," my teacher told me. But the arrest orders were never carried out. The bamboo spears to protect the homeland were never sharpened. And Iwakura Sensei lived on for another twenty, healthy years. The nail stuck out. What fates converged—President Truman, the Manhattan Project, an Imperial war machine finally unable to ignore the sufferings of a nation, what happened so that, at least in this case, the nail sticking out did not get hammered back down?

Chiyoko arranged a ceramic bowl with some oranges we'd brought. It was an offering to the spirits of Iwakura Sensei and his wife. We ignited twigs of incense. There were other visitors to the cemetery, attending to the graves of their loved ones with the same rituals. The smoky perfume of their tapers mingled and swirled in plumes, drifting among the stone markers and cedar trees and the slim fingers of *stupa* that poked up beside the graves, flat sticks like unpainted picket fence posts and decorated with Sanskrit. The fragrance of the incense, acrid and pungent, lazed in circles in the air around us and floated up into the endless blue of the Nara sky as we stood before the grave of Iwakura Sensei.

The lemon trees at Tamukeyama Hachimangu had already been wrapped for winter. They were sheathed in cloaks of rice straw to protect them from the cold and they looked like weird gaunt scarecrows as we strolled through them. Chiyo-san and I paused at one of the outbuildings of the shrine complex, a treasure repository near the center of the grounds. The repository was built in the *azekura* style; it looked like a pioneer's log cabin, topped with a sloping pagoda roof. About the size of a single stall garage, the architecture of the repository was fascinatingly clever. No nails were used to build it; the logs were notched and so the wood shrunk and expanded according to the levels of humidity that fluctuate through the seasons. When the air was cold and dry, the logs contracted, allowing air to circulate into the interior of the structure. When it was muggy and hot, the logs expanded, squeezing off the ventilation, and so the religious treasures inside, precious lacquerware, scrolls, and other delicate objects, were constantly as well protected as if they had been in stored in the most sophisticated museum facilities.

The shrine itself is dedicated to a central deity of warfare and martial art, Hachiman. In his historical incarnation, Hachiman was the Emperor Ojin, who ruled Japan around 200 A.D. After his death, Ojin became deified as an enlightened being, one who needed but a single lifetime to attain buddhahood—a bodhisattva, or, in Japanese, a *daibosatsu*. His mother was the Empress Jingu, a Japanese Valkyrie who led personally an invasion of Korea (Jingu, pregnant at the time with the future daibosatsu, allegedly wedged a stone into her belt to prevent Ojin's birth until the invasionary expedition could be completed.) Not long after the Emperor Ojin's enshrinement and the assignment of his divine title, Hachiman, he was adopted as the patron saint and protector of the Minamoto clan. The Minamoto were a multi-branched family who provided many of the great bushi and shogun who steered the military course of Japanese history from the ninth century to the thirteenth.

Because of his status as the personal kami of the Minamoto, Hachiman eventually came to be revered by the warrior class in general in Japan. "The noble samurai had always prayed to Hachiman for success in glorious battle and relied on his spirit to guide them courageously in their exploits" is the way a brochure at the shrine put it in several different languages. Of Hachiman, the average Japanese knows little more than the information contained in the brochure. Rare is the Japanese or foreigner who has even an inkling of the cryptic connection the classical bugeisha had with Buddhism, one that is still maintained in the koryu. But Chiyoko, a native, and I, a foreigner, had at least that, at least an inkling of Hachiman's importance to the martial arts. That is why, after wandering at Tamukeyama Hachimangu, we walked to the temple, the imposing roofs of which I had seen from my ryokan room my first evening in Nara: the great temple Todaiji.

10
The Sound, the Sign, the Symbol

en.

Few discussions of the spiritual aspects of the Japanese martial arts will progress very far at all without Zen being mentioned. No more so than you could talk about the history of rock music without mentioning Chuck Berry. The very pronunciation of the word (Zen that is, not Chuck) smacks of a mysterious Orientalism in general, and specifically, of the exotic arts and disciplines of the East. It is a word widely misunderstood. More widely still, it is misemployed. It was most famously bastardized, along with its trappings and nomenclature, when Zen became a gobbledygook of catch-phrases and clichés for the Beats of the early sixties. They used Zen the way a TV evangelist uses Christianity: to justify their self-indulgences. They interpreted it as they wished, to disguise their lack of profundity and the shallow and rather pedestrian philosophies they espoused, which without the mantle of "Zen" would have been revealed as just another ordinary version of egotism.

The methods, teachings, and the vocabulary of Zen have in particular become firmly wedded to the Western (and to a certain extent the Eastern as well) conceptions of the Japanese martial ways. Even those who have never stepped onto a dojo floor are familiar with the precepts that link Zen to karate, judo, and the other fighting arts. "Make the mind reflective as the moon shining off the water," or "Have the mind of no-mind." Those who engage in the practice of any of the modern budo soon become acquainted with the concepts embodied in these phrases and in their applications in meeting and overcoming an opponent. In the same way, they learn to strive to attain a state of "Zen calm" in meditation periods before and after their practice. Along with the general public, the kendoka and judoka and karateka have come to accept that Zen and the martial culture of Japan have a long and intimate relationship. In their training, these budoka believe themselves to be the inheritors of a venerable samurai tradition, that their ancestors, the warrior elite of old Japan, counted the philosophy of Zen as instrumental to their craft as they would their swords or armor. This is, to a considerable degree, quite a foundless notion.

Here is what happened: Zen came into its position of dominance in the philosophy of the modern Japanese martial ways because it exerted first its influences upon one koryu during the feudal age. Yagyu Munenori, the second headmaster of the Yagyu Shinkage-ryu, had himself a master. While Yagyu was a fencing teacher to Tokugawa Ieyasu, the first of the Tokugawa shoguns, he was a student too, of the eccentric priest of the Rinzai sect of Zen, Takuan Soho. In a series of lectures and letters to Munenori, Takuan interpreted Zen Buddhism in terms of battle and of strategy and of the arts of the sword. He explained it in a way that was readily grasped by a warrior like Munenori.

The Yagyu Shinkage-ryu incorporated in its oral and written teachings much of Takuan's terminology. His anecdotes and analogies became a part of the ryu's lore and curriculum. Because the Shinkage-ryu under the Yagyu family had a tremendous stature and influence during much of the latter half of the feudal period in Japan, Takuan's ideas about Zen eventually found their way into those forms of the budo that evolved after the modernization of Japan. However—and this is important—while Zen philosophy looms imposingly in the spiritual education of today's budoka, Zen and its doctrines in their formal sense played a relatively minor role in the daily life and in the combative practices of the bugeisha. He did not think or act in terms of Zen in his martial arts training or on the battlefield. Even those bugeisha like Munenori who were influenced by Zen by no means utilized it as their sole or primary source of spiritual exercise. Nor were the bujutsu lacking the religious influences of Buddhism as a whole before the sect of Zen itself was introduced to Japan. Zen, of course, is only one of several sects of Buddhism. Long before Zen was imported to Japan from China during the Kamakura era (ca. 1200-1400 AD), the Japanese fighting man was reliant upon the incantations and secret rites of another form of Buddhism, one called mikkyo.

Mikkyo, or "secret teachings," might be described as Buddhism at its most esoteric. The sources of mikkyo, as with all forms of Buddhism, are to be found in India. They go so far back that the illuminating experiences of the Buddha that later became the doctrine of the faith he founded were still in their infancy when mikkyo originated. Buddhism was just a quirky offshoot, at the time, of the hoary trunk of Hinduism. As with all the different forms of Buddhism too, mikkyo teachings are based upon the belief that mankind's sufferings are the result of his illusions about the nature of reality. Perceive reality for what it is, the Buddha taught. Strip away the facades of ego and desire and fear and all other such impediments to the truth, he preached, and you will attain perfect understanding and peace. Ah, but parting the many layers in the curtain of those facades is no simple feat. Orthodox Hinduism maintains that only through the fantastically long process of samsara, death and rebirth repeated again and again in a cosmic cycle too vast to be fully contemplated by the puny human mind, could the many pitfalls of illusion be transcended, the curtains parted, truth revealed. The Buddha taught that enlightenment was closer at hand. It could be reached, he explained, through a sincere attention to his precepts concerning daily life: righteous thoughts and deeds, piety, humility, and so on. From his original teachings were derived scores of varied sects and schisms. All of them advocated their own methods for following the Buddha's path. Some relied upon prayers for divine intervention, or the recitation of chants. Others depended upon the performance of virtuous works or on meditation or devotional activities. All were aimed at burning away (and that is what nirvana, the original Sanskrit word for "enlightenment" means, "to burn away") the layers of illusion that cloud one's perception of existence.

The path of the mikkyo faith of Buddhism leads towards enlightenment through a series of esoteric rituals. In this sense, it has much in common with the tantric Buddhist practices of Tibet and Nepal. Mikkyo worship revolves around sacred symbolism, around meditation upon icons, and around a complex canonical liturgy. The faith relies principally upon the doctrine of a supreme being considered by adherents to be the personification of the whole universe. The personification of the "Supreme Unity," or Dainichi Nyorai, is seated at the center of mikkyo cosmology, surrounded by a pantheon of deities. Mikkyo saints, in tempestuous contrast to the placid and beatific Dainichi Nyorai, are a riotous lot. They are portrayed vividly in votive paintings and sculptures of the sect's art: fierce jockeys astride galloping wild boars or floating on ethereal thunderheads. They brandish swords, flaming pikes, tridents and other weapons, sometimes carrying them in multiple, spidery arms. They are a scowling, frightful crew of unearthly pirates, flames sizzling in their hair, with their demon enemies trampled howling and cursing beneath their feet. The phantasms populating the paintings of Bosch or Goya look like a meeting of the Kiwanis Club in Iowa by comparison.

It is the power of these passionate monster-gods upon which the mikkyo devotee relies. He does not seek to accumulate such mythic energies for himself. More accurately, he invokes their spirits, seeking to burn away all that binds him from breaking free to grasp the essential nature of reality. In mikkyo ceremony and rite, the conscious self of the practitioner is sublimated by the essence of the deities. The result is supposed to be a profound and encompassing wisdom that allows access into the very heart of life, to the final stages of enlightenment. The process is summarized in the *Dainichi-kyo*, a principal sutra of the faith: "The enlightened mind is the goal. Infinite compassion is the motivation. Skillful methods are the way."

The main body of mikkyo teachings were introduced to Japan by the ascetic Kukai, better known by his posthumous title, Kobo Daishi. Ordained as a priest in the ninth century at the Todai temple — I could see its roofs at the inn where I had stayed in Nara — Kukai traveled to China to be initiated into mikkyo esotery. Because its dogma is recondite and must be transmitted only from a master teacher to a disciple thoroughly qualified to receive it, mikkyo had little appeal to the masses in Japan. But the warrior caste, emerging as an elite during the Kamakura period three hundred years after Kukai's introduction of it, adopted this occult form of Buddhism enthusiastically.

The attraction of mikkyo for the samurai is easily understood, considering their extraordinary lifestyles. For long periods of Japan's history, warfare or the threat of it was almost a daily concern for these men. Even in times of comparative peace, treachery and the spirit of professional warriorship demanded of the bushi an emotional, philosophical, and physical state of readiness. He had to respond to action — to die if necessary, without a second thought, and he had to be willing to do so at any time. He was required to smother his own desires and sense of self in an instant, for if he harbored the slightest regard for his own safety or needs, he risked failing to serve his lord. Zen promised a method by which this approach to life and death could be reached, true. But the satori enlightenment of Zen came at the end of a long, demanding journey of meditation and introspection. The results of the way of Zen were an effective process to overcome the self. It was a path too far to walk, however, to serve the immediate needs of the warrior who knew he might face lethal danger not in a few years but in a few days. His quandary was unique. The search for equanimity in the narrow chasm that brought life and death close together for him often forced the samurai to confront his own mortality. This was a search that was better addressed by the rituals and teachings of mikkyo.

In the beginning was the Word, wrote the apostle John. Logos. The Word. The most elemental utterance of conscious and coherent sound. Words, as intonations of the holy and sacred, play a significant role in all religions. They are particularly vital to faiths of a cabalistic inclination, of which mikkyo is a good example. In mikkyo thought, vocalizations embody sacred as well as protective attributes. They offer protection even against the snake that tempted our kind not long after that beginning about which John wrote, as I was reminded one afternoon in Japan.

Ito-san, my sensei's neighbor, and I were crossing an open, fallow field bordered by a lush, two-story tall hedge of bamboo. We followed a beaten trail through the bamboo thicket and Ito-san pointed to where earlier in the summer he had spotted a snake sunning itself, larger than his arm, he said, and nearly as big around.

"Abura un ken so waka," I recited. Ito-san chuckled.

"Yes, I haven't heard that in years," he said. "Some of the old-timers would chant that to keep the snakes away when I was a kid."

The incantation I'd repeated was from mikkyo lore. It was meant not to keep snakes at bay specifically, but to protect oneself against them. It was one of a number of similar chants. Others are directed at easing childbirth, for instance, or conjuring rain during dry spells, or keeping a traveler safe in dangerous climes. Mikkyo is more generically referred to as Shingon-shu. "Shingon" means literally "True Word," and much importance is attached in its teachings to invocations and chants. In Sanskrit, these are called mantra, a concept familiar to many Western enthusiasts of certain Indian religions or philosophical systems. The Japanese pronunciation of mantra is *myo*. The recitation of myo takes two forms in mikkyo practice. One may be thought of as akin to the mental trick of counting sheep to fall asleep. Myo can be used to focus the mind or to distract it, from pain or fear or extraneous stresses that need to be ignored for the moment. In this employment of myo, the actual words or syllables that comprise it are relatively inessential, just as it hardly matters what exactly we choose to count—sheep or cows or tollbooth jumpers at the subway—to lull ourselves to sleep. But in other usages, the myo are actual requests or prayers or the repetition of deity names or titles, and they are chanted to assist in merging the practitioner's consciousness with that of the individual deity. These myo, like the prayers of the Roman Catholic to patron saints for particular favors, are directed at gods who grant composure against danger or sharpen perceptions or permit to the devotee some ability he seeks.

The myo is the first pillar of the bushi's mikkyo practice. The second is *ingei*, the gestures. In Sanskrit, ingei are known as mudra. The ingei are the physical manifestations of mikkyo deities. Typically, they take the form of gestures made with the hands, clasped or gripped in various configurations. Each signifies distinct attributes or attitudes assigned to individual deities of mikkyo worship. The posture of *gassho*, the prayerlike clasping of the open hands palm to palm often seen in religious statuary in Asia, for example, is an ingei. So is the gesture of the Daibutsu, the enormous Buddha who sits in the main hall of Todaiji in Nara, his right palm extended skyward, fingers of his left hand held out horizontally. This ingei is named *segan semui-in*, a symbol of fearlessness because it was used by the Buddha, tradition has it, to stop a maddened elephant charging at him.

As with nearly all tenets of mikkyo, there are strata of meaning within the ingei, and more strata layered atop those. The fingers of the left hand in most ingei represent (among other things) the five elements of earth, water, fire, wind, and the void. Those of the right denominate the five senses of reality: form, perception, thought, will, and consciousness. Sometimes a single, static gesture of the hands constitutes a full ingei. Others are completed by an interweaving of hands and fingers in predetermined patterns. All are runes that are, in a (forgive the pun) handy and always accessible way, a means of access to the powers of the mikkyo forces. (The notion of ingei is not entirely unknown in Western religions, of course. We see it in the most common forms of Christian prayer, with palms pressed together or with the fingers interlocked. Christ is often depicted with his arms outstretched or with one hand held fingers pointing upward. Scholars have established an influence of ancient Greek art on Indian statues of the Buddha and other, Hindu deities. The relationship is a fascinating one, yet to be fully explored.)

The third pillar of mikkyo is the *mandara*, the visualization of the sect's deities. Mandara—the Japanese pronunciation of the original Sanskrit term, *manda*, known better in the West by the Chinese pronunciation mandala—usually take the form of scroll paintings or supplemental decorations surrounding mikkyo statues. They are often fantastic, wildly colorful, dream-like renditions of the gods encircled by their seraphic attendants, by billowing gouts of flame, or other such dramatic and mystical symbolism. A mandara may consist of a written or painted symbol, such as a single character in Sanskrit like *A* or *Un*. These connote the elemental expansion and contraction of the universe, the throbbing of cosmic energy. Sometimes mandara are painted to cover the entire floor or walls of a temple. In India, the mandala began as an earthen platform, ritually prepared and sanctified for use by worshippers in rituals or in meditation practices. Japanese mandara used in mikkyo became less elaborate over time; they are two-dimensional in most cases. (One exception is in a place that may seem totally incongruous: the packed dirt mound and the ring atop it that are used in sumo. A number of aspects of the construction of this structure, from its dimensions and layout to the ornamentation on the Shinto style roof that covers it inside the arena have elements, intermixed with Taoism and native Shinto, of mikkyo.) Yet just as his Indian counterpart placed himself physically within the mandala, the mikkyo acolyte sought to do the same, to join with the deity depicted in the mandara in order to attain the higher realm of consciousness that is at the heart of all mikkyo worship.

Myo, ingei, mandara: the word, the sign, the visualization. All are synthesized into the ceremonies of mikkyo. All were implemented by the bugeisha in his mental and spiritual training and of the koryu that still exist today, the majority continue to incorporate some kind of each of these three mikkyo exercises in their traditions. Examples of all three are to be found at the Great Eastern Temple, Todaiji, in Nara. As inheritors of a koryu in which mikkyo plays no small role, it was natural that Todaiji was the first place to which Chiyoko took me when we went to spend a day sightseeing in Nara.

The complex of temples and shrines that make up the whole of Todaiji sprawl over the southwestern foot and lower slopes of Mt. Wakakusa. At the center of the complex is the Daibutsuden, the Hall of the Great Buddha. As Nakanishi-san had pointed out the night I spent in his inn, it is the largest wooden structure in the world. Its dimensions, nearly two hundred feet long, wide, and tall, appear even more impressive under the two immense roofs that cover it, one stacked above the other, spread like vast wings. Tourists mill about on the expansive walkways leading up from the main gate to the Daibutsuden, careful not to tramp on the manicured lawns. Inside, the Daibutsu, the Great Buddha, holds court. He sits in a pose of perfect calm, legs crossed. His gilt and bronze skin is nearly incandescent in the light of votive candles that surround him. Near the base where he sits, the tips of lit incense twinkle like hundreds of eyes of yellow coal. The right hand of the Buddha, making the ingei of imperturbability, is taller than a standing man. Ranked alongside him and surrounding the rest of the hall are his attendants and lesser divinities, visible through a fog of incense.

There are over fifty halls and sub-temples at Todaiji. It is, like the city of Nara itself, almost an embarrassment of cultural riches. Begin as the guided tours of the place do, with the Daibutsuden and before you have covered a tenth of the precincts of the temple complex, its art and architecture will have started to blur for you. It is too much to take in at one time. Chiyoko and I traipsed to Sangatsudo, a sub-temple much smaller than the center hall, one situated off to its east. Way back in the seventh century when Todaiji was merely a provincial temple of little importance, scholars believe, the Sangatsudo ("Third Month Hall") was the primary worship site there. Sangatsudo is a post-and-lintel building, perhaps the oldest one still standing among the halls that make up Todaiji. Intricately jigsawn timbers fastened with frame joinery hold it together, a child's giant wooden puzzle. The wood in its main timbers are sooty black. They stand out in angular contrast to plastered walls the color of beach sand. A quartet of the herds of tame deer that live on the grounds of Todaiji cantered past us, having scented some children approaching and suspecting the possibility of food.

Inside the Sangatsudo, the brightness of the day blinked out as abruptly as if the sun had been turned off. It was a place of ancient shadows, incense mists. There was in the hall too the sensation of electricity. I stood still and felt it, felt the fingers of an atavistic voltage reach out and touch me. It was that acute. It stirred, like the atmosphere before an afternoon thunderstorm, and the longer we stood there, just inside the door, the more strongly I felt it. It crackled and roped through the still air. Power. Accumulating energy. Later on, I would go to Kuramadera, the Buddhist shrine perched on a secluded mountaintop outside Kyoto. Kurama is where the samurai hero Yoshitsune learned martial strategy from goblins. It is a place of magic, almost a Japanese Stonehenge in its aura. At Kurama, I sensed an energy similar to what I felt at Sangatsudo, yet different. At Kuramadera, the power was muffled and quiescent, like a volcano long inactive though threatening still, muttering and rumbling beneath the surface. At the Sangatsudo, the Third Month Hall at Todaiji, the energy of the place sparked. It glowed like the frothy orange mouths of fire at Kilauea, undulating with strength and potency.

The source of the mysterious amperage at the Sangatsudo seemed to come from a gathering of statues that dominated the space within it. They were arranged as if each member was parading across a celestial stage in acknowledgment of an encore. I recognized most of them. They were the ministering deities of mikkyo. They are frozen now, caught in dry lacquer and clay. But the figures, each of them, saints and guardians of the Buddhist faith, look as if they might spring to life at any second. Their eyes, glowering, glaring, bulging wide on some faces and nearly closed in ecstatic contemplation on others, had such a glint of animation within them that I caught myself staring, half expecting them to blink.

The diva of the group was Fukukensaku Kannon, with her eight arms available to assist the faithful in time of need. *Fuku-kensaku* means "the encircling rope that is never empty." *Kannon* is a title indicating that she is one incarnation of the Buddhist goddess of mercy. The Fukukensaku Kannon wears her rope like a surplice draped over her arms, a snare that will be thrown to rescue those who stray from the trail towards enlightenment and risk stumbling into the seas of illusion. She and the Sun and Moon bodhisattva who flank her all wear expressions of tranquility, although it is a haughty and baleful tranquility to be sure, and they are at the center of the tableau of statues in the Sangatsudo. The rest of her company have faces and poses that are ferocious. They may be called "saints," but mostly for lack of a better word. They would be more than slightly out of place cavorting with St. Francis among the bunny rabbits and fawns or sitting in a rude hermitage in the wilderness like St. Anthony during his temptation. More likely, the mikkyo crew of the Third Month Hall would have been mistaken for some of those fiends who were tempting Anthony. As Chiyoko put it when we first approached, "They look like looters in search of a riot."

The laws of Buddhism are protected throughout the reaches of the universe, mikkyo doctrine teaches, by four tutelaries. Each of them is assigned a post at one point of the compass. Sculptures of each of these four gods are on duty at Sangatsudo, each with its own particular niche in the rituals of the sect. Dressed up in a full sheath of fish scale armor is Zochoten, his spear gripped in both his fists as if to twirl it before him. He keeps watch over the south. Tamonten, decked out in armor as well, balances on his palms a long-necked flask, an ewer to be specific, that contains the elixir of universal principles. He guards the north. Jikokuten, protector of the east, brandishes his spear in a resting position, his left hand at his side in exactly the position a swordsman would keep his left hand to hold his scabbard from slipping around in his belt. Komokuten keeps a vigil over the west, standing with flinty resolution, his straight sword pointing to heaven. It was an odd experience to see them all. There were chants and hand-signs to conjure the assistance of each of them that I had been taught, but the religion from which they sprung was not my own. They had never been more to me than lessons learned. They were the object of arcane spells and incantations that I committed to memory because they were a part of a tradition I was receiving and so, important for me to know and respect. Now, in the presence of their representations I heard their chants reverberating from within me and it was as if I was seeing photographs of some ancestors I had only heard about before.

Other mikkyo deities I recognized stood watch at the altar at Sangatsudo. The pugilistic pair Misshaku Kongo and Naraen Kongo, the sinews of their forearms taut as stretched leather, their abdominal muscles corrugated, are situated as they are in all temples, with Misshaku to the left and Naraen on the right of the main doors—watchgods. Inevitably, there was Fudo the Indomitable, appearing as if in the very midst of a fiery holocaust, his razor sharp sword and rope clenched before him to defend and rescue the righteous. Before Chiyoko and me were assembled a convocation of mikkyo's gods, the spiritual agents of this cultish sect, the protectors of warriors and the source of their strength. I looked at the mob of intimidating divines and tried to imagine how the classical bugeisha who preceded me would have looked upon them, these same statues in this same temple. I was separated from them by time and race and religious faith. But the connection was there, nonetheless. The connection could not be broken.

"Skillful methods are the way," the *Dainichi-kyo* puts it. The skillful methods of mikkyo are in the implementation of myo, mandara, and ingei. When the bugeisha seeks to enter into the solace of mikkyo contemplation, the realm of higher consciousness it affords him, the state of mind honed to an edge to slash through the curtains of illusion, he begins by interweaving the word and the visualization and the sign in a coherent pattern. As with the combative methods of an individual ryu, each martial school had its own rituals of mikkyo. Some were quite rudimentary, others were more complex. It is almost an infallible hallmark of the koryu, however, that it has some bond with esoteric Buddhism. (This is an important distinction the koryu have from the modern budo forms.) And it is as universal within the various classical ryu that members are taught the details of mikkyo practice only after they have proven themselves worthy and devoted to the ryu. The mikkyo rituals of a koryu may be thought of, in some ways, as their vital force. They are still preserved and transmitted carefully, once the student has proven his integrity and willingness to loyalty to the ryu.

The bugeisha initiates the *shuho,* the ritual, (also called *goshin-ho,* or "protective methods") by metaphorically emptying himself. The process might begin, as it does in the practice of many koryu, with the visualization of Tamonten, the guardian of the north who carries a *hobyo* flask in his hands. The bottle symbolizes, in part, the willing emptiness of the spirit. It represents a void opened in the soul of the practitioner that becomes a receptacle ready to be filled with wisdom and insight. To reinforce this image, the bugeisha weaves his fingers into the ingei specific to Tamonten. In the "here's the church, here's the steeple" finger game of children, make the steeple with the middle fingers, the other fingers interlocked, palms pressed together: this is the ingei for the hobyo, resembling the long neck and round body of Tamonten's bottle. Along with the ingei, the bugeisha recites an incantation, *"Om bai shira manta ya so waka."* Then he continues on, knitting the signs with his fingers, bringing to mind the images, and repeating the chants for the prescribed assortment of other mikkyo protectors as taught by his ryu.

(My description of mikkyo practice here may be misleading. The classical warrior was not the only kind of person who may have engaged in mikkyo. Of course, historically and at present, while mikkyo Buddhism is small in comparison with other sects of the religion, it has adherents other than those of a martial arts background. Japanese of every class, like the old folks Ito-san remembered who warded off snakes with a mikkyo chant, are aware of at least some aspects of mikkyo ritual, just as even non-Catholics in the West would recognize a "Hail Mary." But the mysticism of mikkyo, impenetrable to all but the dedicated, and mikkyo's doctrinal insistence upon a direct transmission of its catechism, has always limited its numbers in Japan. Those very qualities, however, were a primary draw for those who were attracted to mikkyo. The ascetic priests of *shugendo* included mikkyo ceremonies in their worship of Buddhism. So did the black-cloaked ninja, the terrorist-assassins of the feudal era. They used mikkyo as an occult form of self-hypnosis to assist them in carrying out their nefarious and clandestine activities.)

The bugeisha completed the ritual of shuho usually by summoning the image of Zochoten, guardian of the south, and by executing the appropriate ingei, the left palm held in front of the right, thumbs touching. The ingei of Zochoten evokes a spirit of intense concentration, of a breakthrough into the realm of the inner self and of reality. The chant accompanying it is *"O ara-ba sha no-o wo so waka."* Both the chant and the ingei, thumbs touching to form a circle, signify the completion of the ritual, the unity of the practitioner with the sovereign deity of mikkyo worship, the Dainichi Nyorai.

There are fascinating variations in the bugeisha's implementation of mikkyo within different ryu, reflecting his special needs. Some mikkyo incantations follow the ingei gestures along with the drawing of kanji characters. The characters may be written with a brush and ink on paper if circumstances permitted. In an emergency, they could simply be traced in the palm of one's hand with a fingertip. Emergencies, as might be expected, were not an infrequent occurrence for a professional warrior living in the sort of world in which the samurai lived. The manipulation of a series of ingei and myo taught in a typical koryu could usually be performed in less than half a minute, a ceremony to be conducted before training or prior to going into battle. But there were not always thirty seconds to be spared for such prayer. A bugeisha was awakened in the middle of the night, for example, by the sound of a shutter in his house stealthily being slid open. As he came awake, the bugeisha was already resorting to the protective devices of mikkyo. He bypassed the entire ritual (which, in most ryu, consisted of the making of the gestures, chants, and visualizations of either seven or nine deities). Instead, he called specifically upon the tutelary Shosanze Kongo who, with his thunderbolt double-spiked truncheon in his fist, symbolizes focused strength and the mental intensity necessary for the battlefield. Shosanze Kongo's ingei has the fists of both arms crossed at the wrists, the backs of the hands held facing in. It takes less than a second to make the sign, as it does to complete the chant, and his sleepiness flushed away by the process, the bugeisha would be charged with a spurt of energy. Readied, he is able to snatch up his weapon and rush to investigate the disturbance.

In some situations to which the warrior had to respond, there was not enough time for him to perform even an abbreviated form of the ritual. Danger then, as now, often gave no overt warning signs. Outwardly innocuous, a passerby on the road or a traitor in one's own clan could be harboring murderous intent, searching for a weakness at which to launch a sudden attack. (The detection of mortal danger, called *satsui o kanjiru* or *sakki no miyaburu*, was an art in itself. The bugeisha constantly worked to develop skills designed to strengthen the powers of intuition—"putting one's feelers out"—and this ability too, was believed to be enhanced through mikkyo.) When he had time to prepare, the bugeisha might resort to an energy represented by the deity Komokuten, the divine sentry of the west. The incantation for Komokuten is spoken, the gesture is made with the left fist closed, its forefinger extended so the fingers of the right hand may be gripped around it. This is the ingei of the "diamond sword," capable of cutting away all the shadows surrounding the consciousness, sharpening the spirit for immediate action. Yet for threats posed on the roadway, a murderer calmly passing by and then planning to turn and strike in an eyeblink when the opportunity presented itself, there was not time for the warrior for even a single complete ingei or chant. In such cases, he could apply a *shuji*, a "seed syllable" taken from the full incantation, which conveyed for his purposes the essence of the whole ritual. He might verbalize or speak to himself the syllable, which gave him the concentration and attitude to meet the danger. Fortified by a thorough mastery of esoteric ritual and by a familiarity with their shorthand versions, the bugeisha could avail himself of either the entire process or just a critical piece of it, a sort of "instant mikkyo" that afforded him the equanimity and perception to deal with difficult, even lethal, circumstances.

The classical fighting man of feudal Japan synthesized mikkyo into many spheres of his everyday activities as well as employing it for battle. Mikkyo symbols appear on pieces of his armor (as decoration to some extent, but also as important talismans) and engraved on the steel of his weapons. Atop the crown of some styles of helmets worn by the samurai, for example, are openings about the size of a quarter. To the armorer, they were known as *tehen*. The tehen provided air circulation. It also permitted the wearer to run silk cords up through the bowl of the helmet where they could be knotted at the tehen in such a way that they took the weight of the helmet off the head. These knots were the *shiten musubi-me,* the "four knots of the guardian mikkyo kings." From some of those same helmets sprouted horned spikes which, at first glance appear nothing more than fanciful adornment. They are not. They are simulacrum of the *chiken,* the straight, double-edged sword brandished by Fudo, the immovable paladin of the Buddha who embodies the never-changing, never-relenting permanence of virtue and rectitude.

The signs of mikkyo's importance to the bugeisha are not hard to find. Etched into the side of the warrior's sword at the weapon's strongest point, just above where the blade fits into the handle, were often carved depictions of Fudo's blade or other related symbols. On some katana can be found renderings of the shuji, the seed syllables of the chants. These typically appear in their original Sanskrit form. Another ornamentation carved into sword blades are the *kongosho,* fist-length batons capped on both ends with twin claws or spiked tips. Kongosho were wielded by certain warrior gods in mikkyo hagiography, while real examples of this odd instrument (variations occur throughout all of Asia) were actually used by the mikkyo priesthood as a sort of ceremonial caduceus — and also as a formidable weapon.

The use of mikkyo symbology was not limited to the warrior's personal effects. In the foundations of some castles in Japan, and in the mansions and houses of the samurai that have survived into modern times can be found characters, grid patterns, and other hieroglyphics, inscribed on stone blocks. These are mikkyo signs, like the farmer's horseshoe nailed above the barn lintel or Amish country hex signs, that ensured no harm would befall the structure.

Some bujutsu ryu incorporated ingredients of mikkyo directly into their training. They began their practice by adopting preparatory postures or by taking kamae during the sequence of the kata that, while combatively effective to be sure, were also physically evocative of Komokuten or Jikokuten or Fudo or other mikkyo figures. The koryu exponent becomes, with his entire body an ingei, an expression of mikkyo precepts, even in the desperate struggle of hand-to-hand warfare.

In his armament, his aesthetics, his surroundings, the bugeisha constructed a complex matrix of psychological and spiritual protections about himself. The strands of esoteric Buddhism provided for him a security that made it invaluable to him (so much so, in fact, that in many cases, the historical authenticity of a koryu can be established through an examination of the mikkyo rites contained within its traditions). Mikkyo furnished the martial artist with a sense that, in his precarious calling he had some control over his destiny. It afforded comfort, lent reassurance that he could rely upon forces greater than himself in times of trouble or need. He may have acquainted himself with the philosophies of Zen, may have even worshipped in the temples of other Buddhist sects. And many members of the samurai class actually converted to Christianity at different periods in Japanese history. But in times of crisis, when the moment came to take up the sword, the bugeisha turned to the mystical rituals of mikkyo and to the powers it generated within him.

In straggles and knots, tourists came into the shadowed halls of Sangatsudo and stood near me and Chiyoko. They studied the signs describing the deities there, and looked up at the Fukukensaku Kannon and the rest of the mikkyo pantheon. More than a few of them, I could sense, were looking with some interest at the young Japanese woman and me, the gaijin with her. And their curiosity led some to eavesdrop onto our conversation, one full of what must have sounded like mumbling, full of nonsensical syllables, and punctuated by gestures that looked like the sign language of mutes from some alien world.

The principal mikkyo worthy revered by the Shinkage-ryu is Marishiten, the Goddess of the North Star. Mikkyo sometimes merges with Taoist astrology and prognostication, beliefs and occult sciences also brought to Japan from China. So while she is represented in statue and mandara form in temples and paintings, in a tradition borrowed from ancient Taoist mythology

Marishiten is to be found too, in her stellar abode. In the teachings of the Shinkage-ryu, she is a part of the constellation of the Great Bear.

In the cabal of esoteric Buddhism's exotic denizens, Marishiten more than holds her own for pure weirdness. She is often depicted as having three faces. Her preferred means of transport is to balance on the back of a charging boar. She sprang into existence, according to the mythology of Hinduism where she first appeared, from the loins of the Goddess of Light. She herself has children, who dwell in the constellation known to the West as Sagittarius. In many depictions of her, Marishiten has eight arms. In their hands they grip the sun and the moon, a sword, a spear, a bow and arrow, and a war fan. She is a restless deity. She roams the limits of the universe, according to the sutra devoted to her, the *Marishiten-gyo*, "endlessly passing before the gods of sun and moon," traveling at such speeds that she is quite invisible. "Mortals cannot perceive her, cannot capture or bind her. She cannot be injured or deceived."

Mikkyo lore has Marishiten residing in a pivotal star of the Big Dipper. Her star, in turn, revolves around the fulcrum of Polaris, traveling indeed, as the sutra observes, "before the gods of sun and moon" at least in an astronomical sense. To the bugeisha of the Shinkage-ryu, this is the "star of martial destruction," which acts as a galactic mandara painted in the night sky. The ingei for Marishiten is called the *inyogyo-in,* the "gesture of concealing form." To make it, the left hand is curled into an empty fist, held with the thumb facing the chest. The right hand is open, palm above the left fist and covering it. The myo, the incantations spoken in the rituals of Marishiten (there are more than one, some meant to be spoken aloud, others chanted silently) are a secret of the ryu's original teaching, dating back well into the fifteenth century and perhaps even earlier. No one knows for certain. All of the myo for her, however, contain the shuji or seed syllable, *in.* In, in this instance, is the Japanese pronunciation of the Chinese Taoist yin, the darkened half of the swirl of yin and yang. In is the shadowed, the obscure. The concealed.

Despite her striking form, Marishiten whirls across the heavens with such rapidity that, as the sutra reminds, she cannot be detected. It is this attribute that is the most significant to the exponent of the Shinkage tradition. Marishiten's gift of invisibility, the ability invoked by her devotees to render undetectable the self—or more importantly, one's thoughts or strategies or intentions or personal weaknesses—makes her an integral part of the character of the ryu as well as a force for cultivating the character of each of its members.

"In the matter of swordsmanship, always train and discipline yourself. But do not display this. *Hide it...*" So wrote Yagyu Munetoshi, the first headmaster of the Yagyu Shinkage-ryu. To reveal nothing, to reflect back only the opponent's own stratagems while concealing your own; this is the fundamental principal of the Shinkage style. It is as well, for the bugeisha trained within the ryu, a master plan for life itself.

"It is not that you should wish to be without feelings," Kaoru had told me years before, after I'd become upset about something and showed my anger. "It is only that you must cultivate your feelings in private." For the samurai in Japan, *enryo*, the sense of reserve and dignity, was always to be nurtured and refined and treasured. It was a mark of the stoicism their way of life demanded. It demonstrated too, the special niche the warrior occupied in the social order of Japan, a class apart from the rest of society. But the self-effacement and passion for modesty and unpretentiousness represented by Marishiten went further for the bugeisha of the Shinkage-ryu than a mere disposition of impassivity. As a member of the ryu, he was expected to forge for himself through his training a personality that disdained aggrandizement or attention of any kind. He constructed in his demeanor a barrier of privacy between himself and the rest of the world, a spirit of reticence that could easily be mistaken for aloofness. Yet his goal was to exemplify the attributes of Marishiten.

Marishiten has always held a position of high esteem for the swordsmen of this particular ryu, and in this esteem there is both irony and paradox. That members of such an illustrious tradition would venerate the qualities of anonymity and restraint seems contradictory in light of even a brief look at the history of the ryu. The Yagyu Shinkage-ryu was the best known school of martial strategy of the entire feudal period of Japan. Munenori, the son of the first headmaster, was a confidant of the shogun Ieyasu as well as his fencing teacher. Munenori's son, in turn, became the teacher of Ieyasu's son, and so it went. Every shogun of the Tokugawa lineage placed themselves under the tutelage of masters of the Yagyu Shinkage school of combat. Swordsmen of the school hobnobbed with the cream of society throughout much of almost two centuries. In addition to their posts as instructors in the arts of warfare, the Yagyu clan and swordsmen of their ryu moved easily in the social circles of the highest-ranked daimyo, government officials, priests, and poets. While other martial arts masters came and went, their fortunes and privilege fluctuating with time and circumstance, only the Shinkage-ryu retained its position of power and favor for so long and so steadily. And so, the paradox. A renowned institution with reticence its inspiration. Yet perhaps this duality was the secret of success for the Shinkage-ryu. No matter how lofty their positions and reputations, the bugeisha of the ryu never forgot the image of Marishiten.

Whatever the reason, from the earliest inception of the school, Marishiten has been a central figure within it. The "Shin" of Shinkage means "new" or "revised," and it indicates an older source of combative tradition. Indeed, its methods are based upon a system of swordsmanship and martial strategy that go back to at least the fifteenth century. The original was the Kage-ryu ("Shadow Tradition"). Marishiten, it can be ascertained from old documents and scrolls of the ryu (which is all that remains, for the Kage-ryu has been extinct for several hundred years), played an important role in the occult practices of the Kage school. Her lore figured prominently in the art, from both a philosophical and a psychological point of view. In the formative era of the Shinkage-ryu, the mid-sixteenth century, the mikkyo deity of invisibility remained the dominant Buddhist figure, forming one half of a duo. The other half of the ryu's cosmological center was the Shinto god Takeminakata-no-Kami, he of the thousand-man rock dead-lift and the frosted handshake. Members of the ryu who were taught the deepest secrets of it were initiated first before an altar dedicated to Marishiten. When Tokugawa Ieyasu wrote a letter requesting admittance into the school, he promised formally and soberly that should he break the vow of secrecy required of all members, that he would accept the punishment of vengeful gods "great and small," he wrote, "and particularly of Marishiten."

Just as the Shinkage-ryu began flowing from the spring of the older Kage style of swordsmanship, in time it too, gave birth to other derivative ryu. A number of them, actually. More than a dozen systems of martial art owe their inspiration and formation to the teachings of the Shinkage-ryu. Some of these descendant schools have maintained a firm link with the mikkyo rituals surrounding Marishiten. Others retain some of the esoteric rites devoted to her, taught in a desultory, fragmented way. Still others have abandoned Marishiten altogether. It was a matter my sensei and I had often discussed, whenever the subject of the many variations of the Shinkage-ryu came up. His lineage of the ryu had branched off through his master's family from the mainline Shinkage school, but he knew a great deal about the histories of the different, related ryu. He would never disparage any of them, although I knew from my own research that some had allowed their practice and their curriculum to weaken and some were combatively impotent, empty exercises devoid of real meaning. Instead, he taught me the mikkyo shuho, the rituals of Marishiten. And he told me more than once that "those who neglect Marishiten will soon lose the true spirit of the Shinkage tradition. Without her, the meaning at the heart of the ryu is gone. Without Marishiten, there is no Shinkage-ryu."

Chiyoko and I took the bus home from Nara, arriving back at the house in time to help with supper preparations. We took handfuls of vegetables out to the side porch to clean them: carrots, chunky pale daikon radishes, and *gobo,* or burdock root, with their dirty brown skins and crispy snow white hearts. We sat on round rush cushions on the porch beneath the eaves to start scraping and cutting. "Porch" is a poor description of where we were. Traditional Japanese homes have an *engawa,* what might be called in other parts of the world a veranda or a lanai. It is a wide space between the house and the outside, raised off the ground. It forms a buffer between the inner, private area of the home, and the outer area surrounding it. The engawa is protected from the extremes of weather by the eaves. It is the perfect place during all but the most severe periods of cold to socialize with visitors or just to sit, as Chiyoko and I were, doing chores.

The sky was clear. The mountain air was brisk and a coldness was settling in as fast as the sunlight weakened and faded. We had spent a day as tourists and we were still in the mood—in no hurry to get anything done. We talked about mikkyo some more, about how its influences upon us were different for me, a Christian, than they were for a Buddhist like Chiyoko. We talked about the future, when Sensei and his wife might not be able to care for themselves, much as someday, we knew, our parents might need assistance from us. As our conversation ran on and we whittled the skins from the vegetables in our laps, an autumn moon pushed up between a couple of hills, brimming full and rich as amber. This side of the house looked down over a narrow valley. At the bottom it was just wide enough for a few skinny plats of rice fields to be squeezed in. They were stubble-shaven now, and dry, and already they were covered with a gloaming of fog. I heard a rustle from down there, though it was a few seconds later that my eyes, adjusted to the dark, caught the movement. A pair of foxes poured themselves from the side of one of the hills. They slipped out of the bamboo and pine forest, russet slivers of motion. They chased one another across a field of stubble. They scrambled and lunged in play, snapping and boxing with their front paws. Then both paused abruptly, both glancing up at the same time towards the full moon. They lifted their slim heads and yipped and then gave forth with long howls. Then, in a blink, they had vanished.

"Kishikawa-san wrote that an autumn moon makes all the creatures under it lonely for something," Chiyo-san said after the foxes had disappeared and we were both left wondering if they had been wisps of our imaginations.

"Who?"

"Kishikawa, I think," she replied. "Maybe it was what's-her-name." Chiyoko had spent the previous summer reading a number of short story anthologies of modern women writers in Japan. She'd read so many she was starting to confuse them.

The foxes and Chiyo-san had both had their say about the moonrise, so I added mine, working in a poetic reference about the *oboro tsukiyo*, "the moon shining faintly through the misty clouds" that I remembered reading in a haiku by Buson. Or maybe it was Shiki.

"Your Japanese is *so* dated," Chiyoko sighed.

"It's not dated," I said. "It's quaint."

Sensei returned home from some errand. He and Kaoru came out and sat with us on the wide planks of the engawa. Dinner was late that night. By the time we all retreated inside to get away from the cold, the round moon had cleared the crest of the tallest of the hills around us. Polaris emerged in the blue-black sky. Below it, circling endlessly in the night was the warrior's star of martial destruction, the mandara star of Marishiten.

11
The Bamboo's Suppleness, the Hardness of a Rock

*T*here's something I've noticed about your sensei when he's around the house," Dr. Young told me one day. Dr. Young was a professor at the university near the house on the quiet street where my sensei had lived during his years in America. The professor's wife was Japanese; he knew my teacher and most other expatriate Japanese in the area and he was one of the frequent visitors at the house on the quiet street.

"I'm not sure what you mean," I said. I was sixteen. I had been training long enough with Sensei to have an idea of just how much there was about many things I did not yet know. I didn't try to bluff the professor.

Dr. Young smoothed his bushy red mustache. He had no background in the bujutsu or even in the modern martial ways. But he would, on occasion, watch Sensei and me during our training and his ignorance gave him some objective insights.

"Watch your teacher and take note of what's always close by him," he said.

So I did. It did not take long at all for me to see what the professor had been talking about. Unlike most martial arts enthusiasts who go to a dojo as part of a class, I was with my teacher not just for lessons but in other situations as well. Puttering in the house with him, reading while he worked in his study, visiting with his friends. And after being alerted by Dr. Young, I began to notice that whenever Sensei was occupied, whatever he was doing, he was never more than arm's length from a weapon. Or something that could be used as a weapon. There were racks that held katana in the dining room and living room. In the corners of other parts of the house would be bokuto leaned against the wall. Outside, there was invariably a rake or a hoe or a screwdriver nearby—and having watched him plunge a sharpened iron spike into the trunk of a sycamore, throwing the spike from more than eight yards away and sticking it so deeply into the trunk that I couldn't pull it out—I knew what kind of weapon an ordinary tool like a screwdriver could be in his grasp. An orthodox weapon like a sword, or a tool that could be pressed into service in an emergency—there was always an implement close at hand. In another person, perhaps, the habit might have come across as a self-conscious affectation. But it was never obvious enough to be affected, too natural in his daily habits to be self-conscious. In all the time I spent training with him, I certainly never knew my teacher to have any use for violence outside of training. It was simply a facet of his behavior to keep a weapon around him, something he had inherited from his teacher, making a certain standard of vigilance a regular habit.

"To my mind, the master is the one who can simultaneously give the effect of simplicity and restraint—yet you can go right up to it and explore it endlessly with the greatest joy." That is how the artist Andrew Wyeth described the soundings of the master's personality and his art. During my time with him in the United States, I saw the surface of the canvas upon which my sensei, my master, had painted his own life. I saw the simplicity and restraint that Wyeth spoke of, and on occasions that were both infrequent and cherished in my memory, I glimpsed the implications that were brushed into the background, adding depth. To train with him again, in Japan, was to renew the perceptions I had gained into a master's persona. In his homeland, within the country and culture that gave birth to his art, I had the opportunity to contemplate not only my perceptions of my teacher, but their varied shades and gradations as well.

To practice kata, we went down to a wide spot of trail that passed along the flank of a hill below Sensei's house. On one side of the trail, the forest rose up along with the slope. The canopy of maples over us were losing the vivid hues of their foliage; the leaves faded and the giant ferns on the ground below them that had been vibrantly green yesterday had already started to dry and curl up like brown skeletons. On the other side of our practice spot, the hill dropped and we had a spectacular view of the valley. The air was musty with the scents of autumn. Damp earth and leaf mold, woodsmoke, and pollen dust hung on in sneezy motes suspended in an unstirred haze.

Crack! crack-*Crack!*

Bokuto, Sensei's and my own, jumped together, negative and positive charges of electricity, poised, then thwacked again. The oval handles of our weapons where we gripped them were stained wet, several shades darker than the rest of the pale white oak of which they were carved. I was going all out. Sensei was not, but he was still working hard, the tempo kept by his bokuto was furious. The folds of our hakama snapped and popped as we moved, and they flared wide, like crinoline skirts whenever one of us paused suddenly. With only a few exceptions, the formal exercises of the Shinkage-ryu do not employ any kind of vocalized kiai, the shout used to unify (*ai*) the spirit (*ki*), which can also unsettle the most sanguine of opponents when it is released at the right time and in the right way. Nor was there any of the glaring machismo associated in popular imagination with the facial expressions of deadly combat. Nothing but the sounds of our strained breathing and the sharp echoes of our weapons as they clashed. And yet, as any bugeisha who has survived it on a regular basis will aver, the kata of a koryu are as physically challenging, and most likely more so, than any other activities he may pursue. They are beautiful inevitably, graceful, and stimulating to watch and to perform. But they are also frightening as hell.

The kata of the koryu are not difficult or taxing in the same way as, say, an obstacle course would be. They are not frightening in the way that a real fight or an actual battle might be. Because of this, critics observing them from what anthropologists call the etic position, the detached view of one who has never involved himself in them, are sometimes skeptical of kata. The practitioner of the modern budo, in particular, has reservations about the efficacy of the kata as a learning method. This is understandable. Judo, karatedo, kendo—all have their free practice or "sparring" that allow the exchange of techniques in a spontaneous way and these practices figure prominently in the teachings of these combative forms. Budoka have a hard time believing that the pre-arranged, precisely choreographed exercises that comprise the kata of the Shinkage-ryu and other classical schools have any relevance to the extemporaneous demands of a true fight.

In part, the budoka is correct in his assessment of kata. The kata do have scant application in the confines of the sporting facets of fighting arts, in the tournament ring. They are only marginally more applicable in resolving a subway holdup or an alleyway rape. The kata, however, were not evolved to meet the needs of the sporting arena. They were never intended, either, to foil a mugger or robber or any other of the pathogens roaming our landscape today. The kata of the koryu provide the framework for the traditional martial arts of feudal Japan. They met the particular needs of the professional man-at-arms of that age, needs that are beyond the realm of sport, outside the concerns of modern society's requirements for a street-effective "self-defense." When my teacher, or any training partner, uncorked a strike as it is called for in the performance of a specific kata, I could be certain the kata would also call for me to be exposed and in a vulnerable position. In competitive environs such as might be found at a tournament, I would be able to shift away from the attack, to adjust my position to keep myself safe. Much of the freestyle practice of judo, karatedo, and kendo is given to this activity, to shifting, jockeying for position, evading an aggressive attack until you can set up for your own. In the kata of the bujutsu, though, there is no such freedom. True, there are pauses in the offensive and defensive sequences and stratagems that provide an escape from an attack. But the majority of these are only ellipses in the action. They do not dissipate the tension of the kata or drain off the intensity of the moment. In fact, these pauses usually serve to heighten the intensity. Sensei could hold a pause in a kata, delaying the next move that I had to respond to, and in the horrible stillness of those seconds he would seem to grow before my eyes, his posture generating a kind of power until I fairly shook with the desire to get on with it. For the most part, though, the participant must leave himself in the danger zone, receiving the attack in some kata with the bokuto as a shield, in others simply freezing, trusting that his partner in the kata will stop his blow within a hairsbreadth of contact—theoretically the coup de grace that would terminate the exercise fatally if it was not just an exercise but an actual duel.

When it is his bokuto that absorbs the strike from his opponent's weapon in the kata, the concussion can jolt a shock wave from the grain of the bokuto's wood that shivers all the way into the muscle and bone of the bugeisha. There is an overwhelming, almost instinctive urge to flinch. Those kata that call for the exponent to accept a partner's strike coming in to within centimeters of its target are even more likely to draw a wince. In the Shinkage-ryu, a favorite objective is to cut at the wrists of an enemy. Sometimes, the kata call for contact to actually be made against these targets, in the form of firm "taps." Even under the most careful of circumstances, a practitioner's wrists in these kata tend to field hits that are more than merely firm and much more than just taps. It doesn't take too many vigorous whacks before one's wrists are bruised and throbbing. The urge to flinch away from every strike that comes in anywhere near them is almost irresistible.

"Biko tomo shinai!" ("Don't flinch!")

I had heard it in my training with Sensei—how many times? So often that eventually Sensei did not need to voice the admonition; I didn't need to hear it. All he had to do was to give me a certain disapproving glance. I could feel the message: I had just flinched while performing the kata. And I shouldn't do it any more.

Competition, the element of sport, molds a particular kind of personality. The exigencies of the various methods of self-defense currently taught in schools and dojo around the world now produce their own mentality, too. In both, the consideration of avoidance is implied or advocated. Within the tournament ring, a contestant almost always has the option to move away from the encounter, to regather his wind or rethink his strategy. The practitioner of self-defense skills seeks consistently to avoid conflict altogether, to cross the street rather than risk an encounter with the gang lurking on the corner ahead, to check in the back seat of the car before getting in against the possibility of a bad guy concealed there. The bujutsu contain some notion of both these concepts. The bugeisha whose personality and attitudes are sculpted by the koryu has in his kata, as I mentioned, movements that could be categorized as readjusting his space from an opponent, in some ways similar to those used in a sporting contest. And in his ethos are unquestionably the strictures of preventative vigilance against an unexpected attack that are central to ideas of modern self-defense. The classical warrior, however, did not seek the public accolades of sport. His attention to self-defense as that term is used by martial artists today was inconsequential. His métier was in protecting and furthering the interests of his daimyo and his clan. The options of his profession were not so broad as to include the conveniences of the competitor's arena. No on-deck or warm-up swings. No weight divisions. No free sparring that permitted him to take a step back and reorganize himself. He could not always avoid confrontation, either. Often, if it was advantageous to his lord, in fact, he had to precipitate the confrontation. And if it came down to a choice between defending himself or defending his daimyo or clan, there was no choice at all for him.

"Cut my skin, I cut your flesh. Cut my flesh, I cut your bones. Cut my bones, I kill you," was a cautionary precept for the feudal bushi. It was a reminder that in joining a fight, he must be willing to escalate it to whatever level of lethality was necessary to achieve his aim without flinching. The ultimate objective of classical bujutsu training is little more than this: hitting the mark without hesitation.

In a world where the combative talents of the bugeisha are every bit as antiquated as are the arms and armor of old Japan used in learning them, though, what exactly is the target to be hit? That is a question all of those who keep these arts alive today must eventually ask ourselves, an important one for us if the bujutsu are to have any meaning beyond the confines of the practice place. My sensei had asked it of himself, I knew. While still in his teens, he had left his rural hometown to take advantage of a chance to study at a university in Tokyo. It would have been a trying passage for anyone, even under the best of circumstances. For my teacher, it was more than that. It was almost a test of survival. While he was attending the university, wartime shortages were still the norm throughout all of Japan. His college days were lean ones. He had described them to me as a period of constant hunger. A couple of mouthfuls of cheap brown rice with barley mixed in as a stretcher. Bits of stale vegetables scrounged from market stalls. In the unheated, ramshackle lodgings he shared with four other students, one of them kept all the others awake through the winter nights with a tubercular cough. Another died of pneumonia he contracted as the result of the starvation diet and the sheer physical exhaustion brought on by his studies.

Sensei took a job as an architectural engineer after graduation from the university. Like most of his generation, he was virtually adopted by the firm that hired him, guaranteed a lifetime of employment. The major chunk of his career as an engineer, over thirty years, he spent with the firm. Sensei rose in the company to the managerial ranks. Among the projects he helped design were some of the facilities constructed for the Tokyo Olympics in 1964.

A few years afterward, he applied for a program sponsored by the Japanese government, one that would send him to the United States to work under the supervision of engineering professionals there. (u.s. law prevented any engineer from working independently without a degree from a university or college in this country. For that reason, his experience and accomplishments in Japan would carry little weight. During his time in America, Sensei worked purely in an advisory capacity for u.s. engineering firms. It was a point he would later bring up to me in the discussion we had when I was in Japan with him, about the trade restrictions Japan had in its dealings with the u.s.)

To go to the United States cost Sensei much of his seniority in his company. It came at an age when most of his colleagues were entertaining their first thoughts of retirement. Yet when he was accepted into the program, he took the opportunity without hesitation and moved himself and his wife across the world.

When I met Sensei, he was in his fifties. Middle-aged, a white collar professional, at home with concepts of skyscraper construction and sophisticated architectural design. He was essentially, though, a member of the generation that had grown up before the war and who suffered the privations that came after. When he first arrived in America, Sensei could remember every night he'd slept in a frame bed. He had never driven a car with the steering wheel on the left side. He struggled with the basics of English and its tortuous foreign neologisms. He tackled the manipulation of cutlery and other Western exotica. Frustrated and discouraged though I knew he became after arriving here, I never heard my teacher complain. If he was homesick, it did not reveal itself. In the dojo at the house on the quiet street one day, I slipped during a practice session with him. (I slipped many times after that, to be honest, but this was the first one.) My bokuto caught him hard, clipping him right above his ear. Sensei shook his head; the tip of his bokuto never wavered, still directed at me, right where it was supposed to be. I bowed quickly in an apology. He nodded. We took up the kata sequence where we'd left off. It occurred to me in retrospect that his reaction to my accident was the same as his reaction to all of the adversities that I saw him endure. All were met with impassivity and an air of confidence. My sensei's manner invariably affirmed, no matter what the opposition, an unshakable belief in himself and in his aim.

In the sixties, when my teacher began guiding me into the bujutsu with its timeless values and profound traditions, there were plenty of examples of people who had precious little regard for either. They were, in many ways, human weather vanes, unresisting to whatever currents of fashion or politics or social trends that were blowing at the moment. Individuals like Sensei, who remained as imperturbable and steadfast as a rock against the capricious squalls of all the change and adversity gusting at them, were not so common. What it was that energized others who maintained such a stable conservatism in the face of the social tempests that blew during the Age of Aquarius, I could not guess. With Sensei, a considerable part of his ability to remain steady had to do with the tempering of his spirit and body, I think, through the teachings and training of the Shinkage-ryu. They imbued him with a character capable of steering through the superfluous, the ornamental, the shallows upon which much of modern affairs tend to float. The classical bujutsu magnetized a compass needle within that pointed unerringly true. The course it set was his life. To be with him again in Japan was to be reminded that he navigated that course in a way, without flinching, that I deeply admired.

The spirit of the bugeisha is one that does not countenance indecision or a flinching from the path. Yet that is not to say that the bugeisha is rigid and never yields. Quite the opposite. Take-minakata-no-Kami did just that—yielded when there was no other reasonable action to be taken against the heavenly kami who sought to deliver mythic Japan from chaos. In doing so, he served as a model for the bugeisha, a paradigm for a side of the warrior opposite the flinty constancy that a warrior needed to persevere. Yielding was the *yo* (yang, in Chinese) or "lightness" to the corresponding "darkness" of his *in* (yin). The juxtaposing of such opposites is not unique to the bugeisha, of course. Duality pervades all of Asian philosophy. To be firm without a complementary flexibility is to be a corpse. Conservative self-confidence without a liberal broad-mindedness becomes chauvinism, pedantry. My sensei taught me the value of the rock's obduracy. He provided too, the example of the fluidity of the sea that flows around the rock…

With another firecracker explosion, our bokuto barked together once more, then again, this time in the midst of a different kata of the Shinkage-ryu and this time I did not freeze my movement to accept the attack Sensei unleashed. I did not absorb the strike with my bokuto either, with an immovable spirit. Instead, I flowed with the force of the blow, which was aimed at my temple, and used the energy of it to whirl my own weapon around, arcing it at the side of Sensei's forehead. The movement is known generically in Japanese swordsmanship as *utte gaeshi*—to "snap back" or to make a "reversal strike." (In the Shinkage-ryu, it is referred to more poetically as the "shrugging of a cicada's wing.") But the term describing the principle behind the snap back blow is *yawara*, or more simply, *ju*.

Judo and jujutsu are usually translated as "gentle way" and "gentle art," odd descriptions once one has seen a brawny judoka slamming his partner to the mat with a resounding thud, or an exponent of jujutsu wrenching an opponent's joints with a kind of surgical wickedness. This is gentle? Actually, ju connotes a concept that lacks a single word equivalent in English: flexibility, suppleness, pliancy; ju is all of these. It is the ability to bend against pressure in an advantageous way, to bow rather than break, so one may then snap back again.

Ju is most aptly approached through analogy. A stroll through the rural districts of any prefecture in Japan provides natural examples for it. An upright stand of bamboo—notice how beneath the load of winter's wet snow the stalks bend, bend, droop at such an acute parabola they practically double back on themselves. And then, as the topmost leaves touch the ground, the whole stand shivers, the snow plops off. The bamboo springs back up again. The plant survives, surrounded by the shattered boughs of maple and other hardwoods that cracked and split beneath the weight of the snow. The willow, or *yanagi*, also has the quality of ju. Observe how, when the typhoons roar up out of the South China Sea across Japan, the willow gives against them. Its limbs twist and flex, no matter how violent the gale or from what direction it blows. And when the storm howls itself out, the willow shrugs and straightens, while the oak, stiff and resistant to the onslaught, has been broken or uprooted by it.

Ju yoku go o seisuru. The supple overcomes the brittle. Flexibility endures over rigidity. Ambitiously, these and similar axioms have been offered as a kind of Japanese version of the Biblical promise that the meek are due controlling stock in the planet. It is ecumenical notion. But the quality of ju is not synonymous with meekness or weakness. To give or bend is not necessarily to capitulate or to want for power. The enrollee in popular classes taught to defend against rape or other crimes may also make this misassumption, supposing that the mechanics of ju are a quasi-magical sleight-of-hand that will enable a person to fling assailants hither and yon with nothing more strenuous than the flick of a wrist. That isn't ju. That is a dangerous myth. The application of ju does not discount power. For all its elasticity, the fibers of the bamboo are phenomenally strong. The willow is pliant, but its roots are deep and tenacious. Ju is, in its own way, strength. It is a supple, flexible strength that, like the bamboo pressed down by its load of snow, snaps back all with all the more energy that comes from its ductility.

In the trailside clearing below Sensei's house we had completed several kata. My muscles felt tuned and oiled. My stances grabbed the earth solidly. I flew over the ground when I moved and while my arms were burning with exertion and my lungs were pulling like deep bellows, I felt good. Sensei grunted.

"Empi no tachi, mo ikkai," he said.

Empi no tachi is a series of six separate kata which are strung together and performed as a single set. They date all the way back to the Kage-ryu, the school of swordsmanship from the fifteenth century that was the predecessor to the Shinkage-ryu. The Kage-ryu is extinct now and has been for centuries. All that remains of it are a few kata, including the set of empi no tachi, a series that takes its name and inspiration from the cavorting antics of monkeys at play. Empi no tachi is extraordinarily difficult to do correctly. It features quick changes in positioning, numerous attacks that originate from odd angles, and many different kinds of timing. It takes less than a minute to complete; in that brief time, the two partners doing the kata exchange more than forty attacks and counters. I was confident enough to go through the movements at full speed and with the correct rhythm and power. On the other hand, I was not yet at a level where I was going to perform them in my sleep. Then too, much of the safety factor in performing kata full out is an understanding of one's partner's idiosyncrasies. It had been more than a decade since I had practiced the movements of empi no tachi with anyone.

We began. Sensei was taking the role of *uchidachi*, the "striking sword" who initiates most of the sequences of the kata. I was *shidachi*, the "responding sword." There are several offensive techniques, ripostes and counters; after a spiraling thrust at his face, I followed Sensei, who stepped back briskly, as if I was chasing an enemy I'd wounded, to finish him off with a crippling strike to his wrists. He avoided my second cut and then, gripping his bokuto with one hand, he cut for my own extended fists. Twice the kata called for strokes aimed at the side of his head. These he defeated by stretching out his bokuto horizontally to catch my strike, reinforcing the move by snatching his left hand off the handle and using it as a prop to steady the block, bracing the curved spine of the bokuto's cutting edge along his open left palm. It's a tactic common to many koryu. In empi no tachi is a specific tactic for countering this counter. As soon as he caught my attack on the length of his weapon, I bounced mine away, twitched it up and snapped it back down in a diagonal slash that would have, if the blades had been real, severed his left thumb. Sensei was supposed to jerk his exposed left hand away to avoid my cut, then drop back to gain distance for his next attack. Still grasping his bokuto with only his right hand, he would finally cock it at his hips and then fling it like a javelin at me. The katana is not balanced or built to be a missile. To throw it is a truly desperate stratagem, a last-ditch maneuver. My role in empi no tachi was to parry the sword in mid-air and to dodge simultaneously, dropping to one knee to complete the kata. I was supposed to parry because Sensei was supposed to heave his weapon at me. But he didn't.

Sensei switched, moving from empi no tachi to another set of kata. As I made my cut at his head, instead of receiving it on his bokuto, he flipped his wooden sword around my cut and drove the point at my throat. It was a vicious technique, one taken from the kata *ranken,* which means the "sword of chaos" or the "turbulent blade."

To change from one kata to another without warning or prior instruction is a device used by a sensei for a particular purpose in training his student. Once the student has learned the sequence of the kata or can perform it without conscious thought, the student can quickly become complacent about the whole process. He knows what movement will come at him and when and how, and how to handle it according to the model set by the kata itself. He knows the offensive actions he must take and is relatively sure his partner will respond appropriately and as expected. The kata, in other words, become a dance. The practitioner loses his sense of alertness, his awareness of danger. His zanshin becomes lax. He is faltering and, worse still, satisfied by his mechanical ability to reproduce the kata physically, he is not even aware of his predicament. The sensei steps in at this point. He may take the deshi into the kata at full speed and then, when there is a pause in the movements called for in the kata, he will take the pause — and hold it. He remains a statue. If the student has been dancing his way through the form, he will keep right on going, blocking a cut that hasn't come or striking out at a target that isn't there. Often, in fact, he will find he has impaled himself, or would have, if the sensei's sword had been steel, since the student will move himself right into it as his teacher holds still rather than moving as the student expected. Even with the blunt oak tip of the bokuto, these blunders can hurt. They are always embarrassing. I know.

The sensei may also take the opposite tack in altering the rhythm of the kata. He may suddenly speed up, feinting what is supposed to be a fully committed strike and zipping right into the next technique. The student counters empty air and is caught unprepared for the follow-up. Still another tactic for nudging the bugeisha trainee back on to the correct course set out by the kata is to, as my teacher did, change from the pattern set by one kata into that of another, in mid-performance. It requires a far greater presence of mind to deal with this apparently extemporaneous modification of things than it does to cope with a mere change in the kata's pace. In the complete catalog of the swordsmanship of the Shinkage-ryu are about fifty kata. In an instant, the exponent of the ryu must recognize which one his teacher has switched to and adapt his own responses accordingly. It's sort of an armed version of "Simon Says."

I responded to the change Sensei implemented. I wheeled away from the thrust to my throat, using the force of my half-pirouette to bring my bokuto down in a chopping action directed at his leg. It was a technique taken from another of the empi no tachi kata. Was it the correct response? I studied Sensei's face as he lowered his weapon and backed away. But as usual when he taught me, he was expressionless. He might take me through the form again or he might go on to another, leaving me to contemplate the encounter. (In this, rather moderately advanced form of training, the kata become almost like the Zen disciple's koan, the puzzling riddles such as "What was your face before you were born?" The "correct" answer may be as obscure as the question: only the disciple's master knows by the response given him whether the disciple is making progress.)

To change the order of the kata's form, to switch to another without warning or to throw in an unexpected variation is known in the nomenclature of the Shinkage-ryu as *hensei* ("odd form"). More generically, it might be thought of in martial arts terminology as *oyo-waza*. Oyo-waza refers to those sequences of attack and defense which, when thoroughly understood and polished, can be implemented at will to defeat an opponent. Oyo-waza are the embodiment of ju, demonstrating perfectly the principles of flexibility and infinite spontaneity. In some very critical ways, the oyo-waza elevate the kata beyond the level of simple exercise or mnemonic device, bringing them to the mature stage of development for which they were so cleverly designed: cutting down an opponent, no matter what methods he might use against you, no matter under what circumstances you might meet him.

The martial artist who engages primarily in the practice of free sparring or training for a sporting event will have, inevitably, a limited grasp of the applications of ju. His opponents, free to use whatever techniques they like, will nearly always fall back on their favorites if they have the choice. He may learn then, through his own efforts in training, how to deal with these techniques. Yet he would have to face hundreds of opponents over decades of battle in order to deal with the wide variety of methods that can be demonstrated against him by one partner in kata, in a single practice session.

Surprisingly—or perhaps not, considering the flexibility they must have in approaching the kata and the oyo-waza that supplement the kata—masters of the ardently conservative koryu tend to be among the most engagingly open-minded of individuals... At the dinner table, for instance.

Mealtimes in most Japanese homes are quiet, in comparison with the average supper at a Western table. Dinner conversations consist usually of grunts by men and murmurs by women. There may be the intrusive blare of the television in the background, but as a rule, only the kids chatter at the table. At the table of my sensei and Kaoru-san while they were living in the u.s., I was that kid. Growing up in my parents' home with two brothers, the evening meal was as much an occasion for talking as for eating. We all had friends who would drop by and take a seat at the table, not to eat necessarily, but to get their place in the discussions. When I began to eat at the house on the quiet street, I assumed a similar enthusiasm. I would ask questions, bumble through attempts at my elementary Japanese, review Sensei and Kaoru-san on the particulars of my school day, and while they were both initially askance at all my talking, it was only one of the more minor accommodations they made in having me around. And it was infectious, apparently. Gradually, maybe just to shut me up a little, they both began to talk at mealtimes, too. During the course of my training, Sensei and Kaoru came to hold their own conversationally at the table, so much so that when in Japan the subject of Chiyoko-san came up in a chat he and I were having, Sensei told me how he and his wife had looked forward to Chiyoko's moving in with them after her graduation from college.

"With just the two of us, it was too quiet at mealtimes," he said. "For the first few months she was around here, though, she wouldn't say hardly a word. We started calling her Mokko-san — 'Miss Silent Thoughts'."

"Well, Sensei," I said, "you must understand how the Japanese are." My tone was a kind of smarmy sageness. This was a bit of impromptu improvisational theater he and I had long ago perfected between us: the Sincere Young Gaijin explaining Japan to the Japanese. "The Japanese, you see," I lectured him, "don't talk much at dinner."

"Well, they should, " Sensei replied, his tone in keeping with the bit. Yet even though he was kidding along, the table at my teacher's house *was* the center of some lively conversations in Japan, as it had been during his time in America. Sensei was a traditional Japanese man of his generation — and in more ways than one, a Japanese man of far earlier generations. But he was of a spirit of such flexibility that when he was exposed to what he saw as a better way — exchanging opinions and experiences and ideas over the rice bowls instead of the "traditional" grunts, hums, and TV blather—he adapted to the better way cheerfully. He had learned tricks of the engineering trade in the U.S. that made him even more valuable in his profession when he returned to Japan, bringing with him new ideas and technology he might not have known about had he insisted upon a rigid and fixed attitude to his work. Roots sunk deep in a culture ancient, he simultaneously flexed with the adaptable springiness of the bamboo.

Adherence to established values, an affinity to creativity. Perseverance and innovation. The dualities of a hardness like stone and the pliancy of the wind-bent bamboo, these twin qualities flux and twine through the persona of the master and give him the presence and personality by which we know him. Their influences provide all the depths that lie beneath the "simplicity and restraint" of which the artist Wyeth spoke. To merely "explore it" as the artist aspires to do, however, is not enough for the student of a master of the koryu. He admires the qualities that constitute the personality of the master; more, he seeks to reproduce them within himself. That was why I had placed myself in the shadow of my teacher's form. While I had a long road still ahead of me, my reunion twelve years after I had begun the journey with him made me realize that in ways—admittedly odd and unexpected ways—the shadow was coming closer to the form.

The big columns of cumulus clouds that had been holding up the canopy of fair sky for the past few days had lowered. The clouds seemed to curdle. Rain fell in indifferent, intermittent spits. *Potsu–potsu* is the Japanese expression for such rain, "here and there." Gusts tore about in jagged fits that vanished as quickly as they came. Sensei asked me to help bundle up and store the bamboo screens that had protected delicate flower beds from the summer sun. Sakunami-san, one of the senior members from the Genyokan Dojo, came by for a visit and volunteered to join us. We wound the bulky, eight-foot screens into rolls. I squatted at one end of a bundle of them, knotting a cord around it while Sensei did the same at the other end. Sakunami-san knelt at the middle of the roll, keeping it tight and compacted while we tied it off. It was a pleasant chore. Sakunami-san and I were barefoot and we could feel the coolness of the earth in our toes, along with the textures of dried grasses and pine needles. Sensei wore thin zori sandals, khaki trousers, and a pullover shirt. But as always, he moved like he was dressed in the hakama and cotton jacket he used in training.

A rumble of distant thunder trembled from some place off south of the mountains around us. We all stopped our work and looked up, searching the sky as if we could see from where the sound was coming. While I looked, I scrubbed my head with the palm of my hand, an unconscious gesture. It is a habit of long standing, one I find myself doing when I am tired or bored or perplexed. I happened to glance over at my sensei, who was still crouched over the screen bundle opposite me. He was staring up at the muddy gray sky and he scoured his scalp with his hand in exactly the same way I had. Sakunami-san saw him do it, as he'd seen me. He grinned.

"Donguri no seikurabe," he said with a laugh. It is a regional colloquialism, one that implies that we, my teacher and I, were as indistinguishable as a couple of acorns fallen from the same oak.

A gesture, a habit, a subtle mannerism. Of such as these are shadows drawn between a sensei and a deshi. Of such moments are mirrored something of what it is that connects them to one another.

12
Noodles and the Art of the Slurp

I ate.

At noodle stalls, and *o–bento* stands, in *sushiya,* and sweet shops; in specialty restaurants that offered delicacies like eel innards and—when someone else was picking up the hefty tab for it—paper-thin fillets of *fugu,* the deadly blowfish that is delicious if not terminal, I ate.

The joyful measure of my gluttony in Japan reached its fullest expression in once again shoveling a pair of chopsticks into *furusato ryori,* the "home-style cooking" of everyday fare, the Japanese equivalent of meatloaf, tuna casserole, and three-bean salad. *Ochazuke* is typical of this homey cuisine, a meal rarely found in restaurants. It consists of steamed rice with a pot of hot, barley tea poured over it; perhaps a slice of grilled salmon or tuna layered on top, with a thumb of fiery horseradish wasabi, a couple of tears of sesame seed oil, and a flurry of roasted seaweed flakes. Delicious.

Kaoru-san had taught me a lot about cooking while I was her husband's deshi. In the years since they'd returned to Japan, I had many an occasion to regret not having written down her recipes or not having asked her for others. It was an oversight I did not intend to commit again, which is why, as soon as the fuss of my arrival had quieted—well, actually, within about an hour after I'd gotten to Sensei's house outside Nara—I started to nag Kaoru for her recipe for *kakejiru.* Kakejiru is indispensable in the alchemy

of a favorite dish of mine, *tempura soba*. Tempura soba is simple
to prepare for the most part; tempura-fried delectables are put in
a bowl full of hearty buckwheat *soba* noodles. Both the tempura
and the noodles loll in a salty sea of broth. Kakejiru is that broth.
There are variations to the dish, but the standard (if anything
about tempura soba could be considered standard) is prawns
and eggplant slices fried in tempura batter and placed over the
noodles. It's good. By which I mean to say that if Japan produced
nothing else in the course of its civilization, I think tempura soba
could still rank it as one of the world's great cultures. Tempura
soba is served for dinner, but it is a popular lunch in Japan, available in little shops that specialize in it. It is easy enough to make
at home, though, and so it is representative too, of Japanese home-
style cooking. Every Japanese cook worth his or her soy sauce
takes immense pride in the quality of their own kakejiru broth.

The Itos, Sensei's next-door neighbors, were coming to dinner, along with Horiguchi-san, a retired woman who lived alone
a few houses down, and Kaoru-san was making tempura soba. I
followed her into the kitchen to help put the meal together and I
made notes so I could reproduce it myself when I returned home.
Despite the sprawling size of the old house, the kitchen was as
tiny as in the majority of Japanese homes. A refrigerator small
as a clothes dryer, glass-fronted cases keeping the assortment of
plates and platters, variously sized bowls and dishes needed in
presenting a proper Japanese meal, and a two-burner gas range;
in contrast to the spareness of other rooms, Japanese kitchens are
crowded and cramped. I was alert to help and watch and to stay
out of the way.

Kakejiru begins with an infusion of *kombu*, seaweed dried to
the consistency of brittle cardboard. The kombu is simmered in
a pot of water, then plucked out to be replaced with a handful of
dried, flaked bonito called *katsuobushi*. Katsuobushi is a propi-
tious ingredient to use in Japanese cooking. Written with different
characters but ones which are pronounced the same way, it can

mean "the warrior's victory." It has a smoky aroma and the look and feel of wood plane shavings.

"Now look. How long you let the katsuobushi steep is going to determine the saltiness of the broth," Kaoru-san instructed me. She showed me how to judge the time the flakes needed in the pot by the level at which they were floating in the water there. The bonito shavings were removed too, and she added measures of soy sauce and *mirin*, a sweet cooking sake. The mixture, dark and savory, was set on the fire to season while the noodles were prepared.

Soba are noodles of buckwheat flour, pale brown, with a reputation for controlling cholesterol. Dried soba is boiled and cooled repeatedly in a pot to cook it al dente, then rinsed.

When the soba is cooked, the broth ready, then at the last minute the tempura is fried. The water in which the dry ingredients for the tempura batter are stirred must be icy, the oil for the frying so hot as to be just this side of bursting into flame. Good tempura is not "cooked" so much as it is flash-combusted to a golden lacy crispness. The prawns and eggplant circles were dropped into the batter and then into the smoldering oil. In seconds, they came out lightly breaded with a crackling skin. As Kaoru placed them on paper towels to drain, Chiyo-san and I lifted them off with long chopsticks and arranged them over bowlfuls of noodles. We poured on the kakejiru and then carried the bowls into be served and eaten immediately. Tempura soba is Zen cooking; it must be eaten here and now, before the noodles cool and the tempura is sodden. You cannot hesitate, and there is no need to, not with a culinary satori at the other end of your chopsticks waiting for you.

Mrs. Ito passed me the bottle of *shichimi togarashi*, a peppery spice I sprinkled lightly over my bowl. I inhaled the fragrance of the tempura, admired the rich, shimmering kakejiru, the secrets of which I now possessed, and readied myself to dig in. Then I noticed that all three visitors around the table were poised, motionless above their own bowls, watching me. The silence was so complete I could hear the chirp of the crickets outside. The room was taut with expectation. It was like the climactic moment of a spaghetti Western, just before the big shoot-out. Only it was a noodle Eastern, and the townsfolk were anticipating the big *slurp-out*.

Just as tempura soba is a unique, home-style dish, so too, the manner in which it and many other noodle dishes are eaten in Japan. In a word, that manner is—noisily. Soba is slurped, inhaled along with a lot of air. Those who contemplate such things insist the air helps cool the steaming noodles, and contributes to their taste. Miss Manners might blanch and hyperventilate at hearing the Japanese burp. She'd be twitching in apoplexy at their soba-slurping. It is mildly remarkable if you have never experienced the phenomenon. A noodle restaurant at high noon sounds like a chorus of vacuum cleaners on a wet, deep-pile carpet, all of them going in varying pitches and at full voice. Much as the Japanese enjoy their slurping, they are aware that—like mixed bathing—slurping is not one of those habits universally appreciated or indulged. That's why the Itos and Horiguchi-san were waiting.

"They want to see if you'll slurp," Sensei said. Kaoru-san put a hand over her mouth, her eyes rolling with laughter. Chiyo-san bent her head over her bowl, but her shoulders shook as she laughed, too.

I shrugged. "I am not a complete barbarian," I said. And I slurped a mouthful of dripping soba with a satisfying whoosh that ended only when the tips of the noodles whipped against my chin with a splashy flick and disappeared. Having been thus relieved of their anticipation and curiosity, our guests all poked chopsticks into a dinner meant to be savored *and* heard from.

When the lip-smacking meal was completed and I was delightfully bloated, Chiyo-san reminded me that it was time to leave for iaido practice. Groaning at the thought of enduring one of Mrs. Koyomi's "No, no, no" pummelings on a painfully distended stomach, I staggered to my feet. Going upstairs slowly to my room to get my training clothes, I overheard Horiguchi-san.

"He's very Japanese in some ways, isn't he?" she said to Sensei. "You must be very proud of him."

"Why yes," chimed in Ito-san. "The way he eats soba is just like a Japanese." Ito-san's wife agreed. Brightly she said, with real admiration in her voice, "He really sucks!"

13
Withered and Chill

I went to Kyoto because I want to be a man of *okuyukashii*.

A person of okuyukashii is an individual of rare perception and depth, one who sees things deeply—*oku,* in Japanese—and broadly—*yu.* Specifically, the word refers to a person who has an affinity to the tastes and nuances of the aesthetics of traditional Japan, aesthetics that are broad in that they apply—or their principles do—to virtually every aspect of life and experience, and deep in that comprehending their meanings and subtleties is far beyond the resources of the average, the mediocre, the majority. Sensei was a man of okuyukashii. To my immense pleasure, a woman, a teacher of the tea ceremony in Nagano Prefecture, had used the word in conjunction with me. I caught my breath when she did, and held it in my embarrassment when she told me, "It is not easy for even a master to produce a student who has the correct attitude of okuyukashii; yours must be extraordinary."

I did not mention this compliment to my sensei because I was not yet a person of okuyukashii, not by any means. I am still not. But in going to visit Kyoto, dropped off at the bus stop by Chiyoko-san on her way to work, I was taking one step closer to my goal.

Can you get to be a man of okuyukashii without seeing what is in Kyoto? I had asked Sensei when I was his student. You don't "get to be" a person of okuyukashii, he said. He did not qualify a trip to Kyoto as a requisite, either. But when he would try to explain to a teenaged American boy the intricacies of words like shibui, and *mono no aware*, and *sabi* and all the other verbal approximations of those aesthetic qualities that are, by their nature, beyond words, he would very often sigh and say simply, "You must see Kyoto someday."

"Someday" for me was one of those fleeting days in October that at first blush would appear to have been lifted right out of August. The gusts and drizzle that had been coming and going the whole week were in intermission. It was bright and clear under clouds of drifted mashed potatoes. The appearance of days like that can deceive, though. The slant of light in October is different from that of August's. Its texture is not the same. At least, not in Kyoto. The sunlight came obliquely and, no longer filtered by the lushness of summer, it fell with long shadows through the bare, rattling branches of an old plum on one side of the path before me, fell without warmth on the rustling tan hedge of dead pampas grass on the other. The breezes of August are humid. They bring the smell of growing things with them. The breeze that day in Kyoto was dry as husks of rice. When it rattled the plum and rustled the grass, it also started piling clouds before the sun. Suddenly the air was chilly. *Withered and chill...*

The path was one of the dozens that connect the temples, the monk's quarters, the gardens and all the rest of Daitokuji, the "Temple of Great Virtue." In a city that is a living repository of more than a thousand years of culture and beauty, Daitokuji is a few square blocks at the heart of it that is Kyoto in a concentrated form. Its artistic, architectural, and spiritual treasures would take a lifetime to appreciate. Some remarkable men and women have done just that. The list of Daitokuji's patrons includes many of the most famous names in Japan's history. Yet for most of us, the only way to gain perspective on Daitokuji—or Kyoto itself, for that matter—is to slice it into small pieces that are digestible, and to savor them. A piece I'd cut for myself lay at the end of the path at the center of Daitokuji's compound. It was a sub-temple, Jukoin.

In the tea room within it, Sen no Rikyu had performed a tea ceremony for the last time. Afterwards, on the orders of his master, Rikyu cut open his belly and died.

On my way to the Jukoin, I passed the Daisenin, another subtemple with two of the most photographed gardens in Japan adjacent to it. The Daisenin, or "Retreat of the Sages," has to its east a landscape tucked close by the eaves of its main hall. Mountains, a gushing stream, even a tall-prowed ferryboat are all reproduced in green-gray stones assembled in the second decade of the sixteenth century. Looking at it, one is reminded of a Chinese ink landscape painting, of misty peaks and fairyland gorges. The similarity is not coincidental. The East Garden is built upon Sung Dynasty principles of Chinese decorative gardening, principles imported to Japan. I paused to listen to a tour guide outlining the history of the garden, explaining it to a busload of tourists from Tokyo. Then I doubled back to skirt along the border of Daisenin's other garden.

The South Garden of Daisenin is in stark contrast to the florid extravagance of the Sung style landscape of the East Garden. A rectangular lawn of fine white gravel stretches out, raked in swirling waves and contained by low stucco walls. The expanse of the white is broken only by collections of scattered boulders set low into the ground and a pair of gravel mounds. The rocks are buried so that nothing more than a few mossy inches of their girth is left exposed. The gravel mounds are scooped into perfect cones. About them is a mystery. Do they represent mountain ranges? Streams of moonlight? Or are they, as some suggest, merely piles of spare gravel, left by attendant gardeners centuries ago, left so long they have become an institutionalized feature of the place? They are the subject of much conjecture, yet, as with the rest of the South Garden, their beauty is, from the point of view of okuyukashii, intentionally incomplete. They require the perception and imagination of the observer to invest meaning into them. The sere understatement of the South Garden affords no distractions, no contrived diversions, to catch the attention of the visitor. It offers nothing, really, except that which one brings to it—which is why most of the time tour groups pause long enough only to expose a few frames of film at the South Garden, before moving along to something "prettier," and it is why Daitokuji's monks, martial artists from all over, craftsmen—people of okuyukashii of all persuasions—sit in contemplation before the garden, sometimes for hours at a time.

The austerity of the South Garden was perfect to prepare me for the Kanin tea room that is contained in the small sub-temple of Jukoin. Even within the atmosphere of rustic and stark simplicity that dominates the preferences of taste of those who pursue the way of tea, the three-mat space of Kanin is startling. Kanin means "The Hall of Tranquil Living." I suspect, however, that one unsympathetic to the tastes of okuyukashii might be tempted to describe the room as reminiscent of a cell from some gulag. Its plainness is almost intimidating. The tatami and the walls are the same soft color of old straw. The tree trunk that forms one upright of the tokonoma frame and the hand-polished lumber that makes up the rest of the alcove are smoked nearly black with age. A rush and bamboo splint ceiling echo the same color scheme; the hues are flaxen and umber. A scroll hung in the tokonoma, the calligraphy so abstract that from the airy, grass-swept strokes of ink I could make out only two words I recognized, the kanji for "calm" and the one for "solitude." If the sixteenth-century tea master Rikyu, who had created this room, had stepped into the Kanin, he would have found nothing to add except for maybe a sprig of greenery and a blossom arranged and placed on the floor of the tokonoma. He would have been ready to make tea there.

The way of tea is an essential road to travel to understand okuyukashii. It is also inextricably overlapped with the journey of the serious bugeisha. The link, on the surface, is an unlikely one, between the harsh, violent craft of the warrior and the serene contemplation of the *chajin*, the "tea person." It was welded during the despotic rule of Oda Nobunaga. Nobunaga, who introduced the deployment of musketry into warfare in sixteenth-century

Japan; Nobunaga, whose employment of commoners as foot soldiers in his army altered the course of mass combat during that period — Nobunaga was both a bugeisha and a chajin. A brilliant strategist in war as well as in peacetime, Nobunaga realized that if, in between campaigns, his samurai had nothing with which to occupy themselves, they might find mischief of a treacherous sort to get into. He cannily directed the bushi class towards other outlets besides combat for their energies. He brought connoisseurs of the various tea-related arts to his capital at Kyoto and he set an example he expected his samurai to follow by becoming an enthusiastic practitioner of chado.

Nobunaga's motivations for studying the rituals of tea may have been oblique, distracting his warriors or, as probable, striving to overcome his own peasant heritage by affecting chado the way newly wealthy young men and women posture today at playing polo or yachting. But he did infuse the samurai with an appreciation for chado and for other artistic pursuits, consistent with their ideal of the warrior/aesthete. Some, including contemporary daimyo of his who were both allies and foes, were at least as seriously devoted to chado as Nobunaga. After his death at his own hand in 1582, his successor, Toyotomi Hideyoshi, retained the chado masters Nobunaga had brought to Kyoto. Hideyoshi became an accomplished chajin in his own right. (Oda Nobunaga, incidentally, committed suicide after he was trapped in a Kyoto temple, where he'd stopped to sleep for the evening, by one of his own generals, Akechi Mitsuhide. Akechi had been a frequent guest at Nobunaga's tea ceremonies. The treacherous Akechi eventually died when his Sakamoto castle was besieged and razed by Hideyoshi. Before the fortress was put to the torch, Akechi had over sixty of his best chadogu, or tea utensils, lowered over the castle walls and delivered to the enemy for safekeeping, along with a message to Hideyoshi that read, "These treasures belong to the world.")

One of the chado masters retained by Nobunaga and then by Hideyoshi was Sen no Rikyu. Prior to Rikyu's time (his time was 1521-91), the performance of tea-making and drinking had frequently been the purview of the bon vivant in Japan. Effete aficionados delighted in one-upping each other with ever more extravagant tea bowls and other accouterments and with sumptuous banquets accompanying the ceremony. The way of tea was an exercise in egotism and Las Vegas-style gaudiness, an excuse to flaunt one's wealth and status. Rikyu loathed it. He equated ostentation with vulgarity. The chic he perceived for what it was and is: a boorish preoccupation with trendiness. He completely rejected the then-popular approach to tea. His teleology was a chado worthy of the appellation of a true form of the Do, the Way. In place of dilettantism, he advocated the virtue of an unpretentious connoisseurship dependent upon simple tastes. Instead of using the ceremony of tea to impress others, Rikyu pursued in chado a philosophy, a means to attain a moral and spiritual equilibrium that led in turn to a lifestyle as balanced, as imperturbable, as quietly beautiful as the movements of whisking a bowl of foaming green tea.

Rikyu was influenced in the development of his approach to tea by the poets of the mid-Muromachi era who had composed their verses a century before. One in particular, captured Rikyu's imagination, the eccentric poet Shinkei. Asked to explain the key to great verse, Shinkei advised, "Write of *susuki* reeds on a withered moor, or of the wan moon at dawn." When pressed to share the mentality necessary for writing his poetry, Shinkei replied with words that stirred Rikyu and which exemplify with succinct eloquence the attitude of okuyukashii. "Give your attention to that which is unsaid. Seek to understand the concept of cold melancholy." *Withered and chill...*

Rikyu replaced ornate and expensive tea bowls with ceramics that were rough, peasant-simple, glazed in gentle earthen tones of brown, beige, dark red, and black. Tea scoops, whisks, and water dippers were all plain as if they had been carved by the Shakers, and made of untreated bamboo. Under Rikyu's guidance, the surroundings of chado were modified and brought into alignment with his sense of aesthetics. To accommodate their many guests, previous tea practitioners held ceremonies in halls the size of banquet rooms. The most intimate gatherings were conducted in rooms the size of six or seven mats. Rikyu shocked the jaded establishment when he supervised the construction of a tea room that was inspired by a farmer's hut, four and one-half mats in size. In such close quarters, the number of guests a host might serve was limited to about four. All of the guests, from the lowest commoner to the warlord Hideyoshi himself when Rikyu performed the tea ceremony for him, entered the master's hut by crawling on hands and knees through the *nijiriguchi*. It was a doorway with a low transom, like a ship's cockpit hatch that forced their heads down as guests came through, a symbolic and literal prelude to the air of humility that, for Rikyu, was mandatory to experience real chado.

Sen no Rikyu is also responsible for the gardens surrounding the tea hut and for the *roji*, the "dew-sprinkled path" through them. For the chajin walking the roji, matters of everyday life, the concerns of business and war, the hustle and bustle of making a living, all were left momentarily behind. This is still the case. A tea garden and path properly constructed is almost a self-guided therapy session in this regard. In the outer garden, pathways will tend to be straight or broadly curved, with wide, flat stepping stones. As one comes closer to the tea hut, the path narrows. The stones are irregularly shaped, and they wind back and forth. The path through the outer garden is often called a *gankake*, a reference to the way a skein of geese fly across the sky, with regular, steady wing beats. The inner path is nicknamed the *chidorikake*. A *chidori* is a plover, one of the shorebirds that winds back and forth along the beach, avoiding the waves in an erratic walk searching for food. On the path of the outer garden, little is required of the visitor; his mind is expected to be occupied with all sorts of distractions. When he reaches the "plover's walk," he begins to slow down, physically, in order to stay on the path, and psychologically as well, putting him more in tune with the spirit of the tea ceremony that awaits.

If Rikyu's contributions to the maturation of the tea ceremony (and to the concept of okuyukashii) could be summed up in two words, they would undoubtedly be these: *wabi* and sabi. The first, wabi, meant originally in Japanese, "poverty." Its connotation was as negative as the English translation implies. Rikyu imbued the term with a wholly different flavor. He used wabi to mean a poverty of materialism, of superficial appearances. Wabi he defined as the minimizing of things, the better to gain a spiritual insight into oneself and the world around. Three hundreds years after he had died, a descendant of Rikyu's, Gengensai Seichu, a master of chado in his own right, composed a poem of protest when the Meiji government in Japan considered ranking chado officially as a form of "entertainment."

> *Not in clothing, food, or shelter,*
> *nor in utensils or gardens,*
> *no excess of any kind.*
> *So that by sincere practice*
> *the taste of tea shines through.*

The poem is a splendid example of the spirit of wabi. It explains too, why individuals devoted to okuyukashii like Rikyu so valued handthrown tea bowls that were rough glazed and textured. Rikyu's bowls were not magnificent works of art in the normal sense, not like the fine porcelain bowls imported from China that many tea exponents had used in the ceremony prior to Rikyu's time. They were modeled instead after the bowls from which Korean farmers ate their rice, thrown by craftsmen of humble potteries, bowls with their rims markedly uneven and often with pits and cracks in their sides. These bowls were beautiful to Rikyu because of their simplicity and because they had a feel of having been long used and cared for. A dilettante would commission a tea scoop to be hammered out of pure silver. Rikyu would carve his from a section of bamboo. The follower of okuyukashii today would barely notice the decorative filigree of the scoop made of precious metal. He will revere, though, the patina of the bamboo scoop. He will see beauty in the way the carver selected the bamboo so its node seems to balance the utensil and complement its clean, graceful lines.

That which is factory produced is sterile and anonymous, without wabi. Wabi is the quality of the natural and handmade; it reflects the personality and character of the maker. That which is fashionable or consciously current also lacks, by its nature, wabi. Wabi implies the timelessly stylish. It is the verdigris of moss cloaking the boulders of a tea garden, the sepia bleached thatch of the tea hut roof. Wabi is the worn braid of the bugeisha's sword handle, the frayed and patched indigo of his training jacket and hakama. (These are standard examples of wabi, but one must be careful lest the notion of wabi disintegrate into the sentimentally kitsch. Wabi, true wabi, enters everyday life. We can see it in the frayed leather of a salesman's sample bag that has been used for years, or in the well-worn hoe handle of the gardener who has been weeding the same patch summer after summer. Some will claim that in an age such as ours, where little is handmade and much is meant to be disposable, wabi can only be found in objects from the distant past. This reduces wabi to ordinary nostalgia. Wabi will always be present and it is the challenge for those of any age to find it.) Rikyu articulated wabi as an ideal. The person of okuyukashii inculcates it within his personality as the paragon of taste.

The earliest references in Japanese to sabi, the other of Sen no Rikyu's contributions to the way of tea, were, as with wabi, pejorative. Even today, when someone speaks in Japanese of *sabishii*, he is almost always indicating a kind of forlorn loneliness. On the surface, sabi seems unpleasant, a sensation to be avoided. Yet when the person of okuyukashii uses sabi as Rikyu used it, he speaks of matters far below the superficial.

In the melancholy
Of an autumn eve,
With its shrill-voiced insects
The only caller is the wind
Whistling over the reeds.

The poem is one by Fujiwara Ietaka, written four hundred years before the poet Shinkei, five hundred years before Rikyu. It is evidence of the enduring values of okuyukashii, for the melancholy of which Ietaka wrote was the same as Shinkei's "cold melancholy," which eventually became fundamental in Rikyu's conception of chado, as the element of sabi. Sabi is not just "aloneness." It is an acceptance of solitude, a resignation to it, even a calm and tranquil happiness in being by oneself. A winter's evening spent snowbound in a cabin in the country, enjoying a good book in front of the fireplace — that approaches the feeling of sabi. (One is tempted to add, for urban dwellers, that the book could be an old movie, the fireplace a hissing old radiator, the cabin an apartment on, say, the Lower East Side. Whether Rikyu would agree with this however, is questionable. Sabi, in its most authentic form, carries with it a notion of a comfortable proximity to nature. Will those of us in the next century who are pursuing an appreciation of sabi in particular and the spirit of okuyukashii in general be able to find these in the increasingly urban settings where most of us live most of the time?)

To appreciate sabi is to discover contentment in solitude. To integrate sabi into daily life is to recognize that all our relationships with others, even those we cherish and love most deeply, are limited and fleeting. Even the woman or man whose spouse has been at his or her side for fifty years feels it was but an instant when that partner dies. For Rikyu, this sensation of ephemerality was at the heart of the experience of chado. No matter how beautiful the flowers arranged at the tokonoma or how delightful the season of the tea garden surrounding the hut, these will pass in an eyeblink, as will the moments we share with others in the hut. The snow outside the cabin door will melt in the morning, the book we savored by the fireplace will be finished. We must leave the cabin, just like Thoreau left his beside Walden, and return to what he called "the wearisome and dissipating" company of society. (Rikyu would not have gotten along very well with Thoreau, I don't think, despite what seems to be a similarity in their thinking. The elements of sabi and wabi, and the whole notion of okuyukashii, cannot be dependent upon mere external circumstances. Thoreau used *his* hut as an escape from the world. The exponent of the tea ceremony uses the tea hut as a way of confronting the problems of life. Thoreau's appreciation of solitude seems to have been one of indulgence. His contentment in it is suspiciously like the calmness of the Zen devotee who is "centered" and at one with the universe when he is sitting quietly in meditation without distraction. The struggle for the exponent of tea and for all of those concerned with okuyukashii, is to take the lessons of chado and to apply them in that wearisome and dissipating company that is real life.)

Ichigo; ichi-e. "One encounter; one chance." Rikyu used this maxim to express the fragile transience of the tea ceremony: its sabi. The bugeisha uses the same expression to describe the desperate nature of encounters on the battlefield. A single strike determines life and death in a fight with a katana, since if an attack is missed, an enemy will almost certainly have the opening for a counter before there is any chance of recovery.

If there was one person or class of persons who understood Rikyu's concept of sabi, in fact, it was the bushi. The thread that connected him to his earthly existence, easily severed, was for that very reason, precious. He savored the moment fully. The here and now was what occupied him totally in the ritual of tea. And while he drew strength from his clan, from loyalty to his daimyo and from comrades, he was reliant ultimately, on himself. The deities might offer comfort, even protection in times of crisis. But it was in solitude that the samurai contemplated his fate and so he related to sabi. In the tea room, he was reminded constantly and powerfully of the ephemeral and the special beauty of the moment. He was reinforced there in his commitment to give up himself without hesitation when the time came.

The warrior may have gravitated towards sabi without any prompting, but it required the genius of Sen no Rikyu to teach the samurai class the worth of wabi aesthetics. Toyotomi Hideyoshi, a peasant by birth, was entranced by wabi's opposite. He craved extravagance with all the longing of the nouveau riche. In this way, he represented the majority of the military caste in Japan during his rule. Exposed to the pomp and grandiose nature of the court nobility above them in the feudal scale of things, the samurai aspired to similar airs. The task set by Rikyu, Hideyoshi's tea master, to hone Hideyoshi's sensibilities in accordance with the values of the tea ceremony, was no doubt a trying one. Their long relationship, master and disciple, lord and vassal, provides numerous anecdotes related to this.

One of Rikyu's tea gardens in Kyoto was famous for its trellises of split bamboo that supported magnificent growths of morning glories. In the mid-summer, the trellis hedge was a wall of blossoms, breathtakingly beautiful, and Hideyoshi had made arrangements to have tea performed in the hut of Rikyu's garden so that he could enjoy the flowers. When Hideyoshi arrived that morning though, he was puzzled to see that every one of the blooms had been removed from the bamboo trellises. Mystified, he entered the tea hut. There, in the alcove, arranged with exquisite simplicity, was a single morning glory...

Hideyoshi came to the garden eager to indulge in a superfluity of beauty. Rikyu's lesson for him, in the silent form of a solitary blossom, was that excess is vulgar; beauty, for the follower of okuyukashii, is abbreviated, not to be satisfied with or gorged upon, but to be glimpsed, enjoyed briefly, so that its taste lingers on.

On another occasion, Hideyoshi sought to challenge his teacher. Rikyu inevitably preferred natural and unpretentious objects for use as flower vases in the tokonoma of the tea hut. Some of his that still survive are nothing more than a tube of bamboo, or a fruit gatherer's basket, for instance—examples of the wabi that creates a sense of harmony with nature in chado. To test Rikyu, Hideyoshi met his master in the tea room one day with a bough of plum blossoms and an enormous bowl, its inside surface lacquered gold.

"Make an arrangement of this that is wabi," Hideyoshi demanded. And a demand is quite what it was. Rikyu may have been the chado master, but Hideyoshi was the ruler of most of the empire of Japan. Rikyu's position, his life, was at the whim of his sometimes obstreperous student. With another disciple, Rikyu might have clouted him for his effrontery. With Hideyoshi, the only way to chastise was indirectly. Rikyu did just that. He knelt and without the slightest hesitation, he filled the bowl with water. Then he stripped the branches of their blossoms, holding them above the bowl so the petals dropped randomly. The effect must have been stunning. The delicate pink petals of the plum, floating as if they had fluttered from the tree, settling onto the surface of a still pond. The lurid gaudiness of the lacquer was attenuated by this "arrangement." What remained was simple, poignant, suggestive: perfect wabi.

With Rikyu as his model, Hideyoshi could not help but attain some measure of insight into the way of okuyukashii. So what went wrong, I once asked Kaoru-san when we were talking about the death of Sen no Rikyu. She quoted a Japanese proverb. "If a swallow undertakes to give flying lessons to a badger, the swallow better be prepared for a resentful student." It is a proverb that combines the meanings of a couple of Western maxims: "You can't get blood from a turnip" (or a silk purse from a sow's ear) and "Biting the hand that feeds you." Kaoru was implying that breeding will tell. The warlord Hideyoshi was, in the end, simply not dispositionally sensitive to the nuances of okuyukashii. He was gifted enough, though, to see the qualities of the deep and broad in another, a person like Rikyu, yet not so much so that he could cultivate them within himself. To be able to acknowledge it, the way a badger can observe a swallow's airborne grace, and yet not to be able to emulate it, even with the vast resources, opportunity, and power of a Hideyoshi, must have been maddening to him.

So maybe that was it. The badger resented the swallow. Or maybe it was that Rikyu refused to allow his daughter to become a concubine of Hideyoshi's, despite his lord's request for the girl. (She committed suicide to take the blame from her father.) Some historians maintain that Hideyoshi feared Rikyu's growing reputation and the political influences that might arise from it as a threat to his own rule. Others dismiss such intrigue. It was, they say, nothing more complex than a case of a resentful badger. Whatever the cause, in 1591, accusing him of vaguely-defined offences, Hideyoshi ordered Rikyu to commit harakiri. On the final day of February, Rikyu complied with the order. He conducted a final ritual of chado in the Kanin tea room, legend has it, giving away some of his most cherished utensils. Rikyu left two schools devoted to the way of tea, the Omotesenke and the Urasenke, and he left two death poems as well, one in scholarly Chinese, the other written in colloquial Japanese. The latter read:

> *The sword that has been*
> *Close at hand so long.*
> *Now I toss into the sky.*

I was the only visitor at the Hall of Tranquil Living that day, and so I was free to meditate on the character of the original tea master of the room and upon the legacy that he left.

The dynamics between Sen no Rikyu and Hideyoshi Toyotomi are, in many ways, illustrative of the tensions within the samurai who aspired to become more than merely a proficient machine of killing. The average warrior's principal concern was in cutting or striking with his weapon, acquiring usable fighting skills, practicing and furthering them as far as possible. Military leaders like Hideyoshi were occupied with the control of lands, wealth, people. No matter what their level, the warrior was absorbed with power of one sort or another, power at the end of his katana or through political machinations that involved the entire country. Individuals like Rikyu, on the other hand, were devoted to matters in which power or domination or victory in battle had little value. Hideyoshi represented martial spirit, a kind of primal instinct for survival disciplined by valor, loyalty, and sacrifice. Rikyu represented the classical, the medieval moment in which Japan's culture blossomed, the shadow of enduring tradition against the brilliance of the Japanese renaissance over which men like Hideyoshi ruled. Rikyu's influence—and the influence of others of the okuyukashii spirit like him throughout Japan's long feudal epoch—is incalculable. It is because of their lessons and their lives that the warrior in Japan came to comprehend his profession not as one of military science, as in the West, but as martial *art*. In the Occident, the warrior can be also a scholar or a philosopher. Only in the East, with its institutions like the bujutsu, can the warrior be also an artist… or a person devoted to the ideals of okuyukashii.

I lingered at the Kanin tea room in the sub-temple at Daitokuji. Then I left to wander Kyoto, cutting off other slices of that wonderful old city, relishing them as broadly and deeply as I could.

Under foliage the color of lemons, which still clung to the branches of the giant ginkgo groves on the grounds of the Old Imperial Palace, families squatted and gathered stinky gingko nuts. The nuts, delicious when cleaned of their outer fruit and dried, are sheathed in a fleshy berry that reeks so malignantly the collectors plucked them up from among the fallen gold leaves with plastic bags pulled over their hands.

In an antique shop stall opened to Karasuma Street, the owner and I discussed the merits of a suit of Momoyama-era armor that was nicked and hatched with sword cuts from ancient fights.

On Ogawadori, the lane upon which both tea schools founded by Rikyu are still located, is a friendly little shop that has been selling tea utensils and other paraphernalia for chado since 1847. I bought incense there, wrapped by the proprietress for me, in five different papers that were colored and folded so they resembled the multilayered kimono of a court noblewoman.

Near the Kamo River, which bisects downtown Kyoto (the same river that flooded in 1519, keeping the allies of Miyoshi Nagateru from helping him in battle, the same Miyoshi who had owned the Bizen sword now resting in the tokonoma at Sensei's house), I ate at a restaurant specializing in grilled eel.

I spoke no more than was necessary to ask for directions. I just walked and stood and looked at Kyoto. In the midst of the city, while I was aware that my perceptions were still tending to drift in the shoals and the straits rather than steering into the deep and broad, I knew too, that my sensei had set me on the right course. I took with me from Kyoto images of the sort that have always inspired the okuyukashii: a bobbing spray of cobalt cosmos flowers blooming beside the river canal... a weathered wooden shop sign silvered by two centuries of exposure to the seasons, the kanji for "tofu" carved into it by a calligrapher monk... damp, dark stones like the footprints of a huge cat, stepping through the shadowed interior of a garden. I would take all of these images, and more from Kyoto. Yet more indelibly than any would be the patina of bare wood and bamboo, the plain, earthen-daubed walls, the restrained, subtle tranquility of the Kanin, where Rikyu had performed his last tea ceremony. The fragile essence of wabi. The fleeting atmosphere of sabi. The eternal spirit of the okuyukashii.

In the evening, the temperature dropped and the drizzle returned. I took a taxi to the Butokuden. The original Butokuden in Kyoto, the "Hall of Martial Virtue," is much older than the Budokan in Tokyo, the other grand palace meant for the practice and demonstration of the martial arts and ways. The Butokuden was built during the Meiji era, constructed by the government and through private donations, as a central training dojo for the entire Kyoto area. It has been the scene of many prefectural, regional, and national *shiai*, tournaments for kendo, judo, and karatedo.

Beside the old Butokuden is the new one, built recently, of the same ferroconcrete material that makes architectural warts of ugliness on the landscape of too much of Japan these days. The original, dwarfed behind the modern Butokuden, is—as originals tend to be—superior in aesthetic if not practical ways. It is unheated, cooled by opening the wooden sliding doors, and it looks small beside the newer version. But it is a splendid example of the architecture of a Japan poised between a feudal aristocracy and the triumph of industrialism. Its steep-hipped roof sheathed with curved tiles make it look like a temple. Inside, it is all wooden beams and floorboards and great grand pillars that support the immense roof above. Budo training of one sort or another goes on in both the old and new Butokuden on a nightly basis.

Naginata practice was under way in the old Butokuden. About thirty women and girls in hakama and white training jackets were armed with the long polearm, its scimitar blade nowadays replaced by a bent length of bamboo. *Atarashii naginata* is similar in many ways to modern kendo. The emphasis is on basic striking and blocking exercises and on competitive matches that are held regularly. Kata are taught at a more advanced level, a compilation of the kata of several classical naginata koryu. An obaasan, as frail as a twig of elm, was overseeing the action off to the side, as two young women went through the motions of a kata. She chattered out a verbal correction; the women did not seem to get her point. Shaking her head slightly, the obaasan tottered over to face one of them. She bowed curtly. Slash, click-click, slash. The fragility was gone. When the young woman's naginata came in at the teacher in a vertical, overhead stroke, the obaasan threw up the butt end of her weapon, using the bottom half of the shaft to parry the attack. It was not fast. It was not hard. Yet it was so exquisitely timed that the woman's naginata was knocked almost completely out of her grip.

"Understand?"

Both women snapped their heads in a joint bow. They returned to their kata. Their teacher toddled back to her seat on the floor and returned to being an obaasan.

After watching the naginata class, I took another taxi to the Inari Station, where an old friend was waiting for me. There are worse ways to finish a long day in Kyoto than to have a friend meeting you in the darkness and drizzle of late autumn. She braved the chilly mist from beneath a blue and white *noren* awning in front of a closed-up vegetable stall. She lifted a hand from her raincoat pocket to wave when I arrived. A pale hand and a round face against a black raincoat and blacker hair. Many ways worse to finish a day in Kyoto.

We took a taxi to the Fushimiku neighborhood in southern Kyoto. We were going to Tamaya, a ryokan inn that has hosted guests since the days when the Tokugawa shoguns ruled. Travelers on the highway from Osaka to Kyoto once lodged at Tamaya. So did pilgrims coming to worship Ukanomitama-no-Mikoto, the goddess of rice cultivation, at her shrine the Fushimi Inari, which was right beside the inn. Graceful Kyoto women of the upper classes met their lovers at Tamaya too, away from the inquisitive eyes of the city's more populous central district. Along the creaky plank hallways of the ryokan once

—and sometimes still—

carried the sounds of whispers, breathless mingled stanzas of "bed skill poetry."

The cool breeze

—is the opening line of a haiku by Issa, the avuncular poet of the fifteenth century. It is a kind of challenge, too, a verse recited to demonstrate a presence of mind under the most diverting of circumstances, posed by a partner when one was apt to be thoroughly involved in something else.

comes winding and wandering

—is the next line of Issa's poem. Any linked verse could be used in bed skill poetry, actually, so long as it made reference to nature or to the seasons, and so long as it was well-known enough to be familiar to both participants in the challenge.

At last it's here.

—is the final rejoinder. The skills of bed poetry were an exercise, erotic and esoteric, indulged in while making love. When one of the couple felt the other might be about to give in to the culminating spasms of passion, he or she would suddenly test the concentration of the pair, presenting a poem's opening verse. The partner had to recall and recite the next line. And it went, back and forth, now uttered through clenched teeth, now with a soft murmur or moan, until the final stanza come out inevitably as a *yonaki*, a cry of consummation in the black night air of the ancient city.

14
Harakiri

*Y*es, run the cord through there, so it wraps around and then the knot isn't going to be chafing against your ankle."

One of the more intriguing features of the bujutsu, and one which separates them from the modern budo, is that of the collective martial skills contained within the teachings of a typical koryu, there are a variety that are not precisely, directly, fighting skills. The popular image of the samurai is of a fierce combatant, animated in battle, resplendent in silk and lacquer armor. This is the stuff of Kuniyoshi's ukiyoe prints and Kurosawa movies. It is romantic when viewed from a certain, non-critical distance. Yet in his own time, the bushi had to deal with some decidedly prosaic matters to get him through a battle. He might be equipped with the finest of weaponry, for instance, protected in the most magnificent armor; however, if his shoes weren't tied, he'd have very quickly been flat on his face—or worse.

They were not exactly shoes that I was learning to tie; they were *waraji*, sandals woven out of plaited rice straw, the soles like the woven rope of a sisal doormat, the uppers a web that fastened around my foot. Waraji were once the preferred footgear of travelers in Japan. They are perfect for hiking the rough mountain trails there. The warrior adapted the waraji, putting them to use in combat. They were light, functional when wet or muddy or frozen, and waraji gave secure footing on all kinds of ground. The last factor was important. It wasn't just mountain trails that were rough in Japan. Nearly perpendicular ravines, rock strewn hillsides, swampy, marshy plains—most of Japan's feudal battlefields, the sites of epic clashes between the great contenders there, are to be found on the most rugged and difficult of terrain. The samurai's waraji had to remain securely fastened under extreme conditions. And so he devised methods of knotting and tying them on that met these needs. It was not long before such methods had been codified, incorporated into the curriculum of many koryu and of course, zealously guarded from those outside the ryu.

Tying on waraji so they would not slip during a fight is admittedly not so vital a bit of information needed by the bugeisha as, say, knowing how to swing a sword or thrust with a spear. That did not mean he could afford to treat it or other seemingly insignificant concerns lightly, or take them for granted. Mastering such abilities could provide the edge that kept him alive for the next encounter, leaving his opponent dead. These subordinate and accessory skills are sometimes referred to in the koryu as *fuzoku bugei,* or "auxiliary martial arts." Chikujojutsu, the art of constructing and penetrating castle fortifications, which I had been reminded of back in Suwa at the Takashima castle, was a fuzoku bugei. So was *karumijutsu,* the skill of quickly shedding elements of armor when the warrior had to swim, or climb, or move in some way that required speed and special agility. Riding a horse over varied terrain, signaling troops by blowing calls on a conch shell or setting signal fires, these are also fuzoku bugei. Many of the remaining koryu have lost some or most of their auxiliary arts, understandably. What is surprising is how much of this arcane knowledge is still retained within the organized traditions of the bujutsu. There are martial arts masters living in Japan who can tell you how to saddle a horse for riding into a battle so the animal can be steered with the knees and the stirrups can be used as striking weapons against an enemy encountered on foot. Others conduct special classes for senior disciples within their ryu in the details of wearing armor according to the teachings of the school—how it is put on, repaired, and cleaned. (One of the last pieces of written instruction that my sensei had given me before he returned to Japan was a small scroll that contained the recipe for a solution that would rid armor of lice, a real problem for samurai on long campaigns who had to wear their armor day after day, week after week.)

I began learning some of the ancillary technical details of the Shinkage-ryu almost from the moment I had begun my training. But there were too many fundamentals and kata for my sensei to spend too much time with the fuzoku bugei. Then too, since the minutiae of a koryu are as much a signature of its traditions as are its kata, instruction in these details is a process slowly measured out to the student. It is not usually done in any set way, either. Suddenly—or at least so it appears to the student—the master will mention some aspect of fuzoku bugei. It is up to the student to retain this information and to figure out how it may fit into the other teachings of the ryu.

Training with him in Japan, especially as the time for my departure grew near, Sensei started to instruct me more and more in the areas of the auxiliary arts. It seemed that in his and in the ryu's native environment, he was more eager to make my connection to the traditions of the Shinkage system more real. It was also easier. In America, the lesson of tying the waraji properly would have necessitated his sending back to Japan for the rice straw sandals to be bought and delivered by someone. With him in Japan, I could get a pair myself, as I did at a shop in Nara, and ask him for instruction when he brought up the subject…

—or when I brought up the subject. The means a student employs to gain initiation into matters like the fuzoku arts are as subtle and oblique as the master's teaching itself. The student may seek directly to be admitted to the sensei's tutelage. After that, it is blatant, gauche, to ask for anything straightforwardly.

"Sensei, at the Genyokan the other night, we were practicing the kata *junto,* from Omori-ryu."

"Hmm." Sensei took a sip of tea. Junto is a kata from iaido that teaches the movements used in assisting another in the ritual of harakiri, unsheathing the katana discreetly out of sight of the condemned and then cleanly severing his head from his body to end the suffering of his own, self-inflicted wound.

I sipped my own tea and paused. "I've been told, though, that the way it's done in junto is a modern interpretation, not exactly the way it really would have been done."

"Yes," Sensei said. "That's true. In the koryu, there are lots of different techniques for actually performing the role of *kaishaku*."

I sipped again. The kaishaku is the aide to the person committing the act of a formal disembowelment. The choice for the job was often left up to the person killing himself and it was common for him to choose a close friend to be his executioner. "Does the Shinkage-ryu have a special kata for it?" I asked.

"No, not a kata in the usual sense," Sensei said. "But there are some techniques that are taught to handle it correctly."

"Ah, that must be interesting."

"Yes, they are," Sensei said. "Remind me; tomorrow when we train, I'll show you some of them."

"Oh? Thank you," I said. "Would you like some more tea?"

It was that simple — or that complicated, depending upon how you look at it. Had I come out openly and asked for instruction in these teachings, I would have risked putting my teacher on the spot. He may have thought I was not ready yet to learn about these techniques and if so, he would have to have bluntly refused me. Not that refusing me would bother him to any great degree. That was part of his responsibility as my sensei. It was simply poor form to have to do it directly. On the other hand, I had to consider that he was assuming mistakenly that I wasn't interested. By coming at the matter from an angle, I introduced the subject, giving him plenty of opportunities to redirect the conversation. He provided me with enough to keep it going. As a form of communication, it is hardly the epitome of brevity. Or maybe it is, if brevity may be thought of as the most expeditious means to reach a mutual conclusion with a minimum of possible discomforts. No matter. In the relationship between sensei and deshi, in a discipline as venerable and thoroughly Japanese as the bujutsu, it works — remarkably well.

Sensei and I trained the following day in a flat clearing before a small, neighborhood Shinto shrine that was set into the hillside. The shrine was the size of a postbox and despite its being out in the woods, it was spotlessly clean, obviously well tended. An offering of sake in a porcelain cup was left on the shelf before the shrine. Neatly arranged beside the sake were three two-liter bottles of beer. Hard-drinking party gods in these parts. There was a wooden torii arch at the border of the clearing we'd passed under, where the local custom of decoration was still followed. Stones had been balanced along the torii lintel by those who came to pray there, a votive gesture of some kind so primeval its original meaning has been lost. After going through some of the points he wanted me to practice in the iaijutsu of the art, Sensei introduced me to a role I could never possibly have played for real, that of the kaishaku.

It is a rite that is bloody to the point of goriness, one of the most painful ways to die imaginable, as bizarre to us today as burning at the stake. But harakiri was an honored institution of the warrior culture of Japan. He might choose to perform it for a number of reasons; whatever the motivation, the bushi's grim immolation was an expression that commanded respect from his society. Harakiri, more politely termed seppuku, was also known by several other names. Sen no Rikyu's suicide, for instance, is an example of what was called *funshi,* the form of harakiri undertaken for reasons of outrage at a superior's behavior. Rikyu slit open his abdomen, then pulled out a section of his intestines, placing them on a tray used during the tea ceremony and asking that they be delivered to his lord, Hideyoshi. His intent was to demonstrate that his hara, the physical and spiritual center of his body, was pure. The ultimate "not guilty" plea, so to speak, and a wordlessly eloquent way of expressing contempt.

Oibara was seppuku performed to follow one's lord into death. Oibara came in and went out of fashion at different times in Japanese history. When it was in vogue among the samurai, imperial or shogunal officials had to issue severe edicts to curtail the practice, so great would be the loss in manpower when an important daimyo died and left many of his samurai eager to show their loyalty by joining him. Laws against the already dead warrior would obviously have had limited effect. Punishment was promised against the surviving families or, as important a deterrent, against the reputation of the samurai's name and heritage.

Kanshi was an act of self-disembowelment meant to remonstrate another. One of Oda Nobunaga's bushi committed kanshi early in Nobunaga's career, killing himself purely for the purpose of urging his lord to reconsider his reckless ways.

To open the belly to apologize for a crime or an insult was called *sokotsushi*. When a bushi named Taki Zensaburo, incensed over the presence of Western foreigners in Japan one year after the country admitted them for the first time, led an attack against a British outpost in Kobe, he was ordered to commit sokotsushi. His suicide, the first seppuku ever witnessed by a non-Japanese, was recorded by a Lord Redsdale, in 1868. Redsdale described the rite with a journalist's eye for accuracy, summing up his account with the succinct comment: "It was horrible."

No matter what form it took, assisting in the ritual of seppuku was a piece of tricky business, Sensei pointed out to me. Yes, the samurai lived for honor, revered duty, and all of that. But when a man, even a samurai, is sitting in front of a dagger, about to plunge it into his stomach, he is apt to consider options... like maybe sticking the knife into his kaishaku assistant and making a run for it.

"The first concern for the kaishaku is to make sure the job is done," Sensei noted. He was speaking in the present tense, as though the possibility I'd be called upon to assume the role might come up tomorrow. "So the kaishaku has to be sure he doesn't get killed by the fellow he is supposed to be helping." Sensei showed me how to crouch at an angle to where the seated victim would be, close enough to observe his shoulder, far enough to guard against an impulsive, last-second attack.

"You have to be able to see his shoulders at all times," my teacher said, because while a person might be able to conceal his intentions in his facial expressions, if he was considering a desperate move to evade fate, it would evidence itself in the minute movements of his shoulders. Then too, the kaishaku's crouch, slightly out of sight of the performer, allowed the latter not to have to be directly aware of his executioner and the sword. He was free to concentrate entirely on maintaining his own composure.

The knife or dagger in harakiri is inserted into the lower left abdomen and drawn across to the right side. "This almost always causes him to bend over backward from his position in seiza," Sensei told me. (There are techniques for the performer of seppuku, too, such as tucking the kimono sleeves under the knees to keep oneself from falling over backward.) As the body lowers, the kaishaku takes his aim. Sensei showed me a method for judging just where along the neck to make the beheading stroke. He taught me a trick, too, for twisting the blade as the cut is nearly completed. The result of the twist, he explained, would stop the head from being completely cut away from the body. The objective of the kaishaku was not to lop off the condemned man's head. He sought instead to go nearly through the neck, leaving just a strip of flesh from the throat still connected.

"Cut it all the way off, the head goes rolling around. Messy."

There was more I wanted to know about, even methods for removing the head from the body and preparing it in a special box for inspection by the authorities who may have ordered the suicide. Gruesome details to be sure, but engrossing in the insight they provided into the mentality of the bushi and into the world in which he lived. The lesson, though, was finished. Once again, I'd gotten more information than I could absorb. I hurried back to the house and added to a steadily growing collection of notes.

We bowed to the shrine before we left and put a *mikan* tangerine beside the sake and the beer to thank the kami for allowing us to make use of their precincts. We passed back under the torii arch, returning to a world where only those who are afraid to live take suicide as a course of action.

There is a very good question to be asked when considering the relevance or even the wisdom in keeping and passing along knowledge such as the skills of an executioner. It seems silly in a way. In others, it appears an almost adolescent preoccupation with the grotesque or macabre. There is a dark underside to the martial arts and ways of Japan, one that, in fact, surfaces wherever esoteric fighting arts are taught. Most practitioners of combative arts from all over Asia are as normal and well-adjusted as the rest of society, certainly. And a lot of them I have known are a lot more mentally healthy than the general population, it seems to me. Yet, there is no use denying that drawn to these arts are people who have their own psychological problems. It is an unfortunate truth that many martial arts teachers and practitioners in Japan, even those involved with the elite bujutsu, indulge in behavior that is sadistic and sociopathic. To my way of thinking, the skills learned in fighting arts feed and reinforce some rather disturbing fantasies and mentalities. Should the "gory details" (in this case, literally) be passed on? For what reason? Is it not enough to know that the kaishaku once existed? Do we really need to preserve the fine points of his task? It is one thing to claim, as I have, that learning these methods provides insight into the past. But is it not another to maintain that learning them, learning it all, is essential to the upkeep and continuation of the koryu?

There are no easy answers to questions like these. They are ones that, as with so much of the bujutsu, must be contemplated by the exponent. In the end, he must come to his own conclusions about his role in the legacy of the classical martial traditions of Japan and what it is he wishes to pass down when his turn comes to transmit the knowledge of the ryu.

One of the most veiled and obscure of the fuzoku bugei in many koryu is *shinobijutsu*. Shinobijutsu is better known in the West as *ninjutsu*, the art of espionage, stealth, and counter-intelligence. In Japan, the black-robed figure of the ninja populates folklore and TV and movie storylines. He is credited with mystic, supernatural powers, a stock character whenever some agent of perfidy is called for. In the West during the sixties, one of the James Bond movies, which was set in Japan, introduced an appropriately sensationalized version of ninjutsu. Enthusiastic, would-be devotees of this mysterious Oriental art of subterfuge were drawn to what they perceived as its more spectacular aspects. Not surprisingly, they tended to interpret ninjutsu according to their own cultural preconceptions, envisioning it as a macho mishmash of guerrilla warfare/secret agent derring-do/survivalism. "Ninjutsu" enjoyed the fleeting status of a faddish product in the West, commercialized and peddled in storefront "academies." (As an ironically amusing result of Occidental would-be ninja scurrying about in their black garb, ninja masters suddenly appeared in Japan for the first time in over a hundred years. Overlooking the obvious—that the essence of ninjutsu must be anonymity and secrecy—these "masters" opened their own, well-advertised ninjutsu schools that catered to the misconceptions of the foreigners who came there to study.)

The historical facts surrounding ninjutsu are at least as colorful as the myths. To begin, two nearly separate versions of ninjutsu existed in feudal Japan. One form of ninjutsu was practiced by some clans of lower-ranked samurai or commoners who had gained a measure of combative experience. These groups formed into bands of terrorists-for-hire. Their services could be rented by the daimyo or wealthy merchant in need of the odd assassination or bit of espionage, or the kind of politically motivated viciousness that today is the specialty of similar groups to be found in the Middle East and elsewhere. This diabolical form of ninjutsu was understandably vilified by most Japanese. If the ninja was caught, he could look forward to a humiliating execution after he was tortured for information.

The other form of ninjutsu (from which the first obviously borrowed in some of their strategies and techniques) was a true fuzoku bugei, one of the auxiliary martial arts found in several feudal era koryu. This was the bugeisha's ninjutsu. It was remarkably multifaceted in scope. In some ryu, ninjutsu teachings might include special methods of walking to allow the exponent to slip along an enemy fortress or position without being detected or to cross open ground without leaving traces of the passage. Ninjutsu techniques involved camouflage, smokescreen-type deceptions on the battlefield, even hypnosis to be used in extracting information from a captured foe. The warrior used ninjutsu to gather intelligence, to disrupt life for his enemy, to accomplish all the things with which military counter-insurgency units deal in our time.

The Shinkage-ryu contains a few techniques that are considered its ninjutsu. To my astonishment, the widow whose home was at the edge of the neighborhood where Sensei lived, one day told me that she knew something of the art.

"What?"

We were standing together at her gate. I had dropped by the obaasan's house to collect some *warabi* ferns she had offered to us, pickled earlier that summer according to her family recipe. I was taking with me a mesh bag full of persimmons for her from the old tree beside Sensei's house. Horiguchi obaasan was elfin; the top of her head barely reached my chest. Her shoulders were stooped severely from decades of work in the fields. She did not seem to have a neck at all, but she smiled constantly, giving her the appearance of a droll, incredibly aged turtle. Horiguchi obaasan had asked how my training was going, why I preferred something as obsolescent as the bujutsu rather than a more "exciting and youthful," as she put it, pastime like kendo. When I told her there were many aspects of the koryu I found interesting in a way that modern budo never could be, she nodded.

"Yes," she said. "I've had some experience with Shinkage-ryu ninjutsu."

"What?" I said again.

"Um hm," she said. "Do you know about *yobai?* No, of course, you're too young. But you should ask your grandmother about it. I bet she'd know."

Horiguchi obaasan had a tendency to meander in her conversations. As it turned out, my grandmother would likely have known more about pickling those Japanese ferns than she would have known about the custom of yobai.

The obaasan shifted her stance. She used a cane for longer walks; now she gripped the gatepost for support. When she was a girl, she explained, when a young man took an interest in a girl—and had established to his satisfaction that his interest might be reciprocated—he would make a midnight visit to her parents' house. Before proceeding, he would wrap his head in a cotton towel, leaving his eyes exposed but at least minimally concealing his features. Taro-san would sneak into the Suzuki house, for example, searching for the futon where the young and nubile Misako-san was sleeping, and finding it, he would try to awaken her as quietly as possible. If Taro's conclusions were correct, Misako would be ready to receive him for an amorous, if stifled, evening. (The term "paper-thin walls," it must be remembered, had a literal meaning in a traditional Japanese home.) If Taro had misjudged the affections of Misako, she would scream. Taro would take off like a frightened deer. Afterward, he could pretend, because of the towel, that wasn't him at all there in the Suzuki house that night. Nope, must've been some cad from the next village over that got into the place and caused such an uproar.

That was the custom of the premarital shenanigans called yobai, the obaasan explained to me. I nodded, still unsure of how Shinkage-ryu ninjutsu figured into her tale.

"Well, when the boy I eventually married and I were courting, he would visit me at night sometimes." The widow's perpetual smile blossomed into a devilish grin. "The *genkan* shutter that opened into the house was new then, and it squeaked like a wild cat when it was moved."

Her suitor countered this noisy barrier by relying on a trick, the obaasan told me, that was passed down from the espionage teachings of the Shinkage school, to be the shared knowledge of all the vigorous young men in Nara Prefecture. She grinned more broadly still.

"In the old days, when a samurai had to get into his enemy's house without being noticed, he had a way to get the genkan shutter open without making any sound. My boyfriend used the same technique," she said.

"Yes?"

Horiguchi obaasan's grin crackled into a giggle that broke away the years from her and made her sound as she must have when she was a girl and beautiful in a way different from now.

"Why," she said, "you pee into the track where the shutter slides. Works better than any oil, I can guarantee you that!"

15
Yagyu Village

*D*uring the Tokugawa era, young, cosmopolitan gadabouts who scaled to the heights of fashion in Nara and other cities were enamored of the concept of *iki*. Iki was a term that expressed all that was chic, sophisticated, and in vogue. Iki has been succeeded, at least in part during the time I was in Japan, by *hotto pinku*. Dunkin' Donuts is a very popular place in Nara, because its decor features a color scheme highlighted by lots of hotto pinku. It was crowded in the morning, with breakfasters and those like me, waiting for buses that arrived and departed from Nara Station across the street, happy for a dry spot while they waited, out of the sprinkling rain.

A paper cup of orange juice at hotto pinku central cost nearly three dollars in yen, still another touch of modern Japan. But I spent the money without grumbling, knowing that my bus ride would be taking me to another Japan, and I was too eager to be going there to be distracted by high prices. I had invited Chiyoko-san to go with me, and Sensei, too. But my teacher said no. "You need to go to Yagyu-zato by yourself," he said.

The drizzle was leaden. It stained dark the thatched roofs of farmhouses I glimpsed through breaks in the forest as the bus passed by them. Yagyu-zato, the ancestral village of the Yagyu family, is about twelve kilometers northeast of the city of Nara and for me, a couple of hundred years or so from it and from the rest of Japan, in time.

I hopped off the bus and ducked under the eaves of a little dry cleaning shop to get my bearings. I was promptly buttonholed by the obaasan owner of the shop who materialized apparently from nowhere. I never heard the shop door open. One minute I was alone, the next, she was beside me. In a rapid-fire rural dialect that was not rendered any more intelligible by her toothlessness, she launched energetically into an animated spiel, extolling the sights of this antique village. On down the road, she pointed, were the foundation stones, all that remained of the original Yagyu mansion. In the woods down and around that bend there, were the severed halves of the boulder, split, legend has it, when a master of the Shinkage-ryu crossed blades with a feisty mountain goblin. Along that very lane right there walked samurai of the Yagyu clan on their way to posts as teachers and confidants to the most powerful shogun in Japan's history. My self-appointed tour guide paused in her machine-gun monologue, seeming to notice for the first time that I was a gaijin, a foreigner in a backwoods of Japan where such outsiders might not appear five times in a decade.

Politely, but with bucolic bluntness, she asked, "What in the world are you *doing* here?"

It was a long story, I said. I explained that in America I had once trained in the Yagyu Shinkage-ryu style of swordsmanship. I had come now to see this place where the art began. She expressed no surprise at this tale, only invited me inside her shop to offer me a plastic raincoat against the weather while I explored. I tried to pay her for it. She refused. Think of it as a welcoming gift, she said, because, "After all, aren't we both Yagyu-*nin*?" Both of us, "people of Yagyu."

Yagyu-zato has not changed much in some ways, in the four centuries since Munenori and Munetoshi and the other famous masters of the Shinkage-ryu lived there. Now, as then, it is secluded, separated from Nara by dizzily pitched mountains and vertical ravines, accessible only by narrow roads that twist and switchback and meander—separated too, from the busy hustle of the big city. Yagyu-zato drowses, a hamlet of a few dozen houses, mom-and-pop stores, and a prefectural police box. A junior high school near the center of the village appears to be the only significant architectural addition to the town since the Tokugawa era. A woman and her daughter chatted in a doorway about the price of sweet potatoes. An old man pedaled past on his bicycle, fishing rod balanced on his shoulder. When Chiyo-san and I were touring the temples of Nara, we'd talked with a Buddhist priest and I mentioned to him that I wanted to go to the village of Yagyu—had he been there? "Yes," he said, a long time ago. On a school outing. An interesting place if you were interested in history, he said, but not terribly exciting otherwise. Then he added, "In Yagyu village, you'll find the people are outnumbered by the ghosts."

The priest's observation was true, perhaps. But he could not have known that as far as I was concerned, these were no common ghosts I'd come to visit. The present, in this distant section of Nara Prefecture on the rainy autumn morning I arrived, was quaint, somnolent. Yagyu-zato, though, was the setting for dramatic events in Japan's past, the neighborhood of illustrious characters. I waited under the eaves of the laundry shop for a gust of rain to pass, comfy in my new rainproof jacket. I breathed in deeply the atmosphere of my past.

For centuries, the village of Yagyu was remarkable for little besides the fragrant teas cultivated on the precipitous slopes around it. Stonecutters chiseled into granite cliffs nearby. Tax collectors made the long journey to the hamlet regularly to levy their due in rice. Otherwise, the modest fief of the Yagyu clan was ignored. It might have remained that way forever, like a thousand other rural burgs just like it in Japan, were it not for the ambitious plans of the daimyo, Tokugawa Ieyasu. Ieyasu was the third of Japan's three stellar military leaders of the medieval age, and the last. Oda Nobunaga tried to rule through cunning and ruthlessness. Hideyoshi was a despot; intimidation was the métier of his power. Ieyasu's chosen path to becoming shogun was through the strategy of the bugeisha. He employed heiho, using the elements of battlefield strategy in making war as well as in his negotiations for peace. Tokugawa was, by turns, flexible and obstinate. He perfected balance while adroitly tripping up those who opposed him. Ieyasu bided his time through the closing decades of the sixteenth century, losing some battles, winning more. Always he kept his goal, to rule all of Japan, at the forefront of his strategic aims. In 1600, he was ready to have a go at it. Never one to overlook an advantage, the canny Ieyasu schemed to enlist all manner of ninja, mercenaries, militant priests, and hermit warrior-farmers into his forces. He chose the best recruiter he could find, for to the woodsy hills around Yagyu-zato such reclusive types naturally gravitated—and the hamlet's baron, Yagyu Munetoshi, knew them all.

Through Munetoshi's efforts, Ieyasu got his partisan troops. With their aid, he defeated all comers at the Battle of Sekigahara. He emerged the primogenitor of the Tokugawa line of shoguns who would govern Japan for two hundred and fifty years, well into modern times. Yagyu Munetoshi was granted an increase in his stipend. He received too, an invitation to the new shogun's capital in Edo, to teach his martial skills.

Left to themselves in the countryside, the Yagyu clan had devoted themselves to the art of swordsmanship for many years, with an almost religious fervor. Munetoshi was the first of his family to rise above the ranks of the average in terms of his bujutsu prowess. By his mid-thirties, Munetoshi was widely regarded as the most accomplished martial artist in the whole region of Nara. In a challenge match with Kamiizumi Nobutsuna, though, Munetoshi was so convincingly beaten that he escaped with his life only because Nobutsuna was wielding a weapon of split bamboo encased in leather rather than a real sword or bokuto. Nobutsuna was a legendary master of the Kage-ryu; his inspirations into the craft of swordsmanship had, in part, led him to found a "new" or *shin*-Kage-ryu. Upon Munetoshi's defeat, he became Nobutsuna's disciple. Munetoshi was eventually initiated into the *okuden,* the deepest teachings of Nobutsuna's ryu. The Yagyu warrior in turn, devoted himself to the further development of the Shinkage tradition. He taught his own children, including a particularly adept son, Munenori.

The exact roles of both Munetoshi and Munenori in the battle at Sekigahara are still wrapped in secrecy. Both were alleged to have directed the activities of the partisans Munetoshi recruited into the service of the Tokugawa. Both were said to have directed efforts at intelligence-gathering and other activities that assisted Tokugawa behind the scenes. Did they actually do this, or were their cloak-and-dagger doings more in the realm of fiction that has grown up since the event? It is almost impossible to know for sure. Whatever the exact nature of the Yagyu family's contributions, they must have been significant enough to have caught the attention of Ieyasu once again. I say "again" because Sekigahara was not the first meeting of the Tokugawa lord and the Yagyu. Some years before, having heard of their swordsmanship, Ieyasu had invited both Munenori and Munetoshi to demonstrate before him and some of his officers. Munenori gave him more than he asked for, especially after Ieyasu, the man who would soon be the first Tokugawa shogun, asked for a match.

The salient characteristic of the Yagyu Shinkage-ryu is that it seeks to teach the bugeisha to attain victory by penetrating into the opponent's mind. Through various exercises that are an integral part of its curriculum and by constant training, the Shinkage-ryu swordsman learns to "read" the intentions of an adversary and to respond a split instant before those intentions are realized. In less philosophical, more practical terms, this means that it is not until the oncoming strike is unleashed or the opponent's evasion against him already committed that the Shinkage-ryu exponent acts. Timing is critical. Correct distancing is essential. A fraction too early or too late, a hairsbreadth too near or too far, and it is death for certain.

Munenori waited until Ieyasu's blade was a whisper from his forehead. Then he spun into the angle of the strike. He blended with its force, and snatched away the weapon. Ieyasu was sent stumbling, into a heap. The Tokugawa lord brushed himself off and there must have been a hush at the scene of the demonstration. It was not an everyday event, to say the least, for a lowly country vassal to seem to be making a fool of a leader of Ieyasu's standing. Ieyasu, however, was no fool. He recognized the worth of the art he had just seen. Once he became shogun, he immediately appointed Munenori as his personal fencing master. It was an extremely influential position, one that continued to be held by a headmaster of the Yagyu Shinkage-ryu throughout the reigns of every one of the Tokugawa shogun until the abolishment of their long regime in 1867.

As every fan of TV historical dramas and movies in Japan knows well, however, the swordsmen of the Yagyu clan were more than just martial arts instructors. Dozens of popular films and television series have recounted their exploits—with only occasional or tangential accuracy. Spymasters, adventurers, sword-slinging heroes in the intrepid service of their shogun, sometimes coming to the aid—à la Robin Hood—of the poor and oppressed, other times portrayed as the arch henchmen of a draconian Tokugawa government; the Yagyu bugeisha have played nearly every fictional role available. In truth, there were swordsmen of the Yagyu Shinkage tradition who were all of these and more. Their legacy, though, is best expressed in the accolade afforded them and their martial traditions by Tokugawa Ieyasu. Ieyasu, who was Japan's shogun during the longest period of unbroken peace and prosperity in the whole of the history of the empire, said of his own leadership and successes that, "I have based my policy and my administration on the principles of the Yagyu Shinkage school of martial strategy."

Extraordinary ghosts in Yagyu-zato, indeed.

The first stop for me in Yagyu village, so my obaasan guide had insisted, was at Hotokuji, the Hotoku Temple. She gave me directions to get there that I did not need. From my sensei I had heard stories about this place, had read about it, since I was a child. I could have gotten to Hotokuji blindfolded. I walked through the village and turned left at the sound of the gushing brook that ran through the middle of the village. A plank bridge led over the stream. The trail on the far side—as steep as the one that led up to the Genyokan Dojo and even older—looped up the mountain's shoulder. The path was cobblestone, the stones dark buns, polished slippery by the rain. They had been laid so many years ago it seemed the path was almost a part of the terrain. It led me through bamboo thickets with stalks two stories tall, and then into an evergreen forest, switchbacking upward, offering intermittent glimpses of the village below and of more mountains off in the distance, long beards of mist hanging like gauzy curtains between their peaks.

Hotokuji is a repository of the Yagyu past. I had it to myself, except for a couple of attendant priests who were content to sit in their office drinking tea and watching a sumo tournament on their little Sony. I strolled between glass-topped cases in one hall of the temple that had been converted into a museum. It is always nice to have such places to oneself, particularly so in Japan where museums, public gardens, and historical sites can often be found just by listening for the gabbling crowds and squawking informational recordings that play on endlessly. Armor was on display—helmets and lacquered breastplates, a saddle and stirrups, all heirlooms of the Yagyu family, all emblazoned with the distinctive crest of the family, a stylized depiction of a pair of *jingasa*, broad-brimmed woven reed hats. There were rows of *tsuba*, or handguards fitted atop the hilt of katana, forged by Yagyu Hyogonosuke Renya Taira no Toshikane, the fifth headmaster of the Yagyu school.

Toshikane was also a master craftsman and his tsuba are worth thousands of dollars to collectors, when a rare one comes up for sale. He is the subject of a number of legends. He was, for instance, believed to have been a man of considerable reserve and taciturnity, frosty of nerve. He trusted no one, the stories have it, except for a mistress he adored. He is largely responsible for the common portrayal of the Yagyu bugeisha as stoic and emotionally distant. Toshikane was supposedly the epitome of the warrior's igen, or impassivity. When his mistress fell ill with pneumonia, goes one tale about him, Toshikane left her deathbed to go back to his smithy. He was still close enough to hear, as his household servants did, the wracking of her cough. While the servants fretted, Toshikane took up a hammer to work on a tsuba he was finishing, the only sounds a dying woman's pathetic coughs and the tap-tap-tap of her master's hammer at the forge until, with a final gasp, his beloved was gone. In the dreadful silence that followed, the servants held their breath. They knew the vastness of Toshikane's loss. But his agony was hidden. The tapping of his hammer never faltered, never lost its rhythm.

It is easy to misinterpret the story (and that is all it is—a story. There is no concrete historical evidence to support it), Kaoru-san had explained to me. Toshikane did not abandon his mistress to let her die alone. She dismissed him, knowing that for Toshikane to stay with her in her final moments would be more than even he could bear without his stoic sense of igen being cracked in an undignified way. She granted him the last measure of her love. She allowed him to preserve his igen. He, in turn, honored her in a way equally oblique, by the unbroken tap-tap-tapping of his hammer.

Yagyu Toshikane was so fearsomely demanding of himself as a craftsman that he was rumored to have made a practice of tossing his newly forged guards into a cask and pounding them with a mallet. Those that came out of the cask unblemished were judged by him to be worthy for use. Today, the characteristic "wet copper" look of these tsuba are, as I said, considered gems among collectors of Japanese swords and sword furniture. To stand over a case with more than a dozen of them on display in one place, by far the largest example of Toshikane's oeuvre, was mind-boggling.

Inside the glass cases at Hotokuji, too, were examples of the *densho*, the handwritten scrolls containing the teachings and many of the secret principles of the Shinkage-ryu. Spidery, ink-brushed figures illustrated the scrolls, brandishing their swords in the various postures of the ryu. It occurred to me that they had been drawn by swordsmen to illustrate theories of combat that were weighted with the actual experience of dealing life and death with the sword. There were also careful diagrams instructing in the proper situating of a house or castle to protect it against attack from an enemy or from the elements, and arcane formulae of eso-teric mikkyo lore for predicting weather conditions that would be favorable to battle. Matters my sensei had mentioned only briefly or in passing, I could read about in these scrolls, and I shook my head in wonderment at the depths of the traditions that were still left for me to explore.

At the main altar of Hotokuji presided a wooden effigy of Yagyu Munenori, stern and severe in his expression. Munenori could stun sparrows in the hedges with his shout. He could slice solid oak tree limbs with the edge of a dull wooden practice blade more cleanly than other men could cut through those branches with a weapon of sharp steel. Less fabulously, Munenori is re-vered for his philosophical contributions to the way of the warrior, particularly for the flavor of Zen that he stirred into the pot of the Japanese martial arts.

Early on in his career Munenori, already a master bugeisha, came under the influence of one of Japan's true characters, the Zen Buddhist prelate, Takuan Soho. Takuan was an eccentric, an iconoclast of the first order. When he met Munenori in 1632, he was, primarily because of those very traits in his personality, in serious trouble with the second shogun of the Tokugawa line, Tokugawa Hidetada. Hidetada had banished Takuan (at that time an abbot of the Daitokuji Temple) for Takuan's complaints about what he considered meddling by the shogun and his of-ficials in temple affairs. Munenori used his status and position as Hidetada's fencing master to intervene in the matter. Eventually, Takuan's banishment was lifted. Under Hidetada's successor, Tokugawa Iemitsu, Takuan's star rose again and ascended even higher. The priest mingled with nobility, with daimyo and wealthy merchants, and the great scholars and artists of his age. He and Munenori developed a special relationship as Zen master and disciple.

The underpinnings of Munenori's devotion to Zen were fixed in the changed climate of the peaceful Tokugawa suzerainty. During the reign of the Tokugawa, massed warfare—previously a regular occurrence for the samurai—was rare. Combat for the bugeisha of the Tokugawa period consisted almost entirely of training and in duels resulting from challenges, vendettas, and inter-ryu rivalries. When he did engage in a serious exchange of arms, it was on an individual basis rather than as a part of a clan or an army. This kind of one-on-one match involved a somewhat different mental approach than was useful for the samurai going into large-scale battles. Under these conditions warriors had the opportunity to consider the philosophical ramifications of their profession, and the moral implications and dimensions of their bujutsu. In some cases, the uncompromising discipline of Zen provided him with an approach to meet these philosophical confrontations and bugeisha like Munenori took to it enthusiastically. The Yagyu master had his own master in Takuan. The correspondence Takuan wrote to his disciple as a guide to Zen training was naturally couched in the terms and analogies of swordsmanship. These writings have been published, translated into English even, and they are regarded by those in our time who take up the martial arts and ways of Japan as embodying some profound teachings and insights. In particular, Takuan's letters to Munenori express Zen as a means of going beyond the particular—swordsmanship in this instance—to the general: life itself.

"The accomplished man uses the sword but does not kill others," Takuan wrote in describing the enlightened bugeisha. "He uses the sword and gives life to others. When it is necessary to kill, he kills. When it is necessary to give life, he gives life. When killing, he kills in complete concentration. When giving life, he gives life in complete concentration. Without looking at right and wrong, he perceives them. If he is able to gain this freedom, he will not be confounded by anyone on earth. In all things, he will be beyond companions."

Takuan's ideas were not lost upon Munenori. Along with the mikkyo ritual and Shinto lore handed down within the Shinkage-ryu from the older traditions of the Kage school of fencing, Munenori incorporated some of the concepts of Zen philosophy into his family's martial ryu. "The welfare of the populace is an art identical to the art of strategy." "The sword that promotes life and the sword that destroys life." The notion of responding to an attack in a way as instantaneous as the "spark struck off from flint and steel." All of these are maxims of the Shinkage-ryu. All reflect Takuan's perspective on Zen. Once he began to absorb Takuan's teachings, the katana for Munenori could never be simply a weapon. He saw the sword as a key for unlocking the most basic mysteries of life.

Yagyu Munenori's grave is secluded on a knoll behind the Hotoku Temple. The stone marking it is carved in the shape of a memorial tablet resting atop a turtle's shell. It is in the center of a diminutive walled plot, one crowded with the headstones of other members of the Yagyu clan. All around the cemetery, towering stalks of green bamboo rustled and dripped; cryptomeria boughs creaked in the wind like rusted hinges. The grave markers were all encrusted with lichens. The flat surfaces of Munenori's stone were dappled with copper coins left as offerings, donations that were used in the upkeep of the grounds. I added my own and bowed. This was the abode of those ghosts the priest in Nara had mentioned to me. But there was no sense of the eerie. Only a kind of awe for me. I had called upon revenants before during my time in Japan. My teacher's teacher at the cemetery in Nara. Sensei's brother at the Yasukuni Shrine in Tokyo. I felt a kinship with those ghosts, ties and connections. In the presence of the spirits of Yagyu, I was humbled. I'd come a long way to get to this place, I'd told myself on the bus ride out from Nara, and again on the trail up to the temple here in Yagyu-zato. Before the grave of Yagyu Munenori, I could only think of how very far it was I still had to go.

A covey of curious private school girls surrounded me as I was leaving the grounds of Hotokuji. They were off on one of those innumerable school trips that Japanese students seem to be taking all over the country, all year long. We posed for pictures of each other at the temple gate, then walked together the short distance down the slope to the Masakisaka kendo dojo. The practice hall was empty. In the evening, its walls would resound with the war cries of young kendoka and with the racketing clatter of their bamboo weapons. Kendo is a frightfully rigorous form of budo, what with the perspiring under the heavy mask and armor, accepting without complaint the full force strikes that accidentally yet regularly find unprotected areas. Still, if one is going to follow it as a budo, could there be a more satisfying place in which to train? I was envious of the members of the Masakisaka dojo, practicing on this mountainside above the village of Yagyu, so close to the resting place of the most famous swordsmen of old Japan.

The schoolgirls were impressed when I identified the scroll painting of the guardian mikkyo deity Fudo Myo-o that was hanging in the alcove of the training hall. I slipped a few notches in their collective estimation, though, when they found I was not a personal acquaintance of any members of an American rock band with whom some of their group were currently enthralled.

The rugged hills around Yagyu-zato are crisscrossed by narrow footpaths that ribbon into the woods, traversed once by farmers and—maybe, if the stories are true—by some of those sinister types who pledged their clandestine services to the shogun at Munetoshi's bidding, at the battle of Sekigahara. The schoolgirls and I parted company, they back to the main part of the village while I turned up one of the woodsy trails, one marked by a weathered, hand-lettered sign. It led me out past terraces of tea bushes and through the portals of a Shinto torii. The tea bushes gave way to more forest. The trees closed in all around, became deeper and denser the further I walked. The green canopy had not yet lost its thick foliage to the season. The only other place I have ever been in a darker forest was in the coniferous woods of Maine. The quality of the shade was adumbral—heavy. Sounds were muffled. There was a brief gap in the denseness as I came around a corner and there, sitting in a clearing, was a boulder shaped like an egg, a few feet taller than me and twice as long. It was granite, split neatly in halves. Myth has it that one moonless night Yagyu Munetoshi was strolling along the very path I'd taken, his way lit only by the lightning from a storm. He was blocked by a tengu that flew down with a wild rustling of wings, spoiling for a fight.

Tengu are Japanese goblins. They have played a significant role in the traditions of many of the schools of classical martial arts, including the Shinkage-ryu. Tengu have wings and clawed feet and in that sense, they are portrayed as birdlike. Some have enormous, phallic noses; others have sharp hooked beaks. Tengu, though, are supposed to have the arms and bodies of men, and the capacity for speech, if they feel like talking. They do not always. They are said to be a cantankerous lot, and changeable in their nature. They invariably haunt the most inaccessible reaches of the mountains, far from human habitation... not too far, however, because according to the country folk of old Japan, tengu were often to blame for rock slides that came tumbling down without warning, for torrents that washed away rice paddies, for all sorts of mischief. And many a farmer or woodcutter caught out late on the mountain trails would later swear he'd been stalked by a tengu, flitting silently in the black branches above him, frightening him into running for his very life.

Tengu are feisty demons, yet as I said, they are of a capricious nature. Sometimes they seem to take a benign interest in humans, especially in ascetic bugeisha who secluded themselves in alpine tengu territory in order to perfect their art. Yoshitsune, the boy-general of the Minamoto clan, was taught the art of fencing by tengu when he was living in a Shinto shrine atop Mount Koya.

Several koryu credit the supernatural intercession of tengu as the source of their school's martial principles. Bugeisha of both the Kage and the Shinkage traditions once encountered these goblins, their lore has it, and in both cases miraculous techniques were imparted, methods with the sword that had never been seen before. One whole section of the kata of the Shinkage-ryu are called the tengusho. The tengu who drew his blade against Munetoshi that stormy night was no goblinish sensei, though. Not according to the story that has grown up to explain the split boulder. He wanted a fight. Munetoshi gave it to him. The tale has it that villagers down the mountain in Yagyu-zato could hear the clashing of the katana of the two fighters, the roar of the beaked tengu mixed with the gunshot bark of Munetoshi's kiai. The duel was an epic one, a Japanese Beowulf and Grendel. At its climax, Munetoshi uncorked a ferocious whack that would have sent his weapon right through the tengu—had not the crafty goblin executed a nimble dodge. The swordsman struck instead the boulder that has been called ever afterward, the *itto seki,* the "single stroke sword rock," cleaved by a force so enormous that the explosion it made that night, if you stand alone in the clearing where the rock is, seems still to echo along the valleys and gorges all around.

There are other places around Yagyu-zato that have their own particular resonances. Another trail I took goes across the old Yagyu highway to another hilltop on the outskirts of the village proper. From the crest at the ridge of the hill a tall cedar spikes up. Its crown is gray and lifeless, but nevertheless, the size of the tree would lord it over the surrounding forest even if it were planted on level ground. It was planted on the hill, if the folklore is correct, as a puny seedling by another headmaster of the Yagyu Shinkage-ryu, Yagyu Jubei Mitsuyoshi.

Yagyu Toshikane, the smith who forged handguards for swords, was the essence of the ryu's frigid stoicism. Jubei was its fire. If popular legends are again consulted and believed, Jubei was blinded in one eye when his father Munenori hurled a stone at the young Jubei when the boy's antics had finally exasperated him. If that's true (and no reliable records or portraits of Jubei verify that it is), the cruel punishment failed to dampen Jubei's spirit. Nor did it seem to compromise his skills with a katana. Jubei took to swordsmanship with a passion. One of his first training partners was a young noble of the Tokugawa clan near Jubei's age, one who grew up to be the third of the line of Tokugawa shoguns, Iemitsu. Jubei was a servant and companion to Iemitsu, just as Jubei's father at the same time was the fencing teacher and confidant to Iemitsu's father, Tokugawa Hidetada. The official and personal relationship between the boys continued smoothly until both were young men. It continued on for three years after Iemitsu assumed the role of shogun, in fact. Exactly what happened between them is unknown. Most historians who have researched the lives of the Yagyu swordsmen suspect that Jubei, as dedicated to hard drinking as he was to the bujutsu, became drunk—*chidori ashi* or "plover legs" drunk—at a celebration thrown by the shogun. Supposedly, Jubei made some grossly inappropriate remarks to his friend Iemitsu, in front of others. Whatever it was that happened, it was bad enough so that Iemitsu banished Jubei from the capital as punishment.

More fanciful explanations of the rupture in the friendship between Iemitsu and Jubei include one version that maintains the entire incident was nothing but a clever ruse. The two concocted the drunken insult scene, so the story goes, so that Jubei would have a cover for leaving the capital and roaming the countryside as a spy for Iemitsu's Tokugawa government. As improbably espionage-novel-intriguing as this explanation sounds, the loyal Yagyu swordsman willing to take on the cloak of shame as a subterfuge in serving his lord, it does make some sense. Iemitsu was cognizant of the Japanese adage that "in the third generation comes dissolution." His grandfather Ieyasu constructed the Tokugawa regime. His father Hidetada molded it into an efficient system of government for the entire country of Japan. Iemitsu was determined that the Tokugawa dynasty would not crumble under his administration. To keep it healthy he imposed numerous laws and other restrictive measures to strengthen his control. Not all of these were appreciated by the many daimyo, some of whom were already chafing under Tokugawa rule. Iemitsu needed all the political information he could gather to stay atop those who might be plotting his downfall. Who better for the job of chief intelligence operative than a master swordsman with family connections to various ninja groups and other denizens of the Japanese underworld?

However he spent the period of exile, Jubei's "mystery years" lasted more than a decade. It was time enough for him to later be placed at the center of all kinds of sword-slinging adventures that form the basis of novels, movies, and TV dramas. Jubei himself only hinted once at how he passed the years. In his writing, he mentioned that he returned to Yagyu-zato and devoted himself to both the martial arts and to meditating upon his future and the refining of his character. The latter stuff, about his future and character might have been written by Jubei to serve as a kind of document of his penitence. But the explanation that he spent a lot of his time practicing swordsmanship while he was gone from the capital must have been quite accurate. If Jubei Mitsuyoshi was an expert martial artist before his banishment, he was hell with a katana when he returned to Edo in 1639. Not long after he came back into the service of the shogun, Jubei wrote *Tsuki no sho,* a text on the art of martial strategy. The book compiled the techniques and teachings of the Shinkage-ryu into catalog form and it traced the technical development of the ryu from the time of Kamiizumi Nobutsuna. In addition to his writing, Jubei also refined several of the kata of the ryu. He was as well, as his father had been, appointed as the official martial arts teacher of the Tokugawa family. Despite these accomplishments, Jubei remains famous, however, for his derring-do in personal combat.

By the first part of the 1640s, when Jubei had assumed the role of headmaster of the Yagyu Shinkage-ryu (his father, Munenori, died in 1646, a few years after having passed the title of headmaster to his son), the opportunity for military engagements on the battlefield where the sword was used were long past. The pax Tokugawa eliminated warfare on this scale. And as all martial arts are apt to in periods of peace, battlefield empiricism was largely supplanted by abstract theory. Fencing "masters" who had never risked a drop of their blood were soon as common in Japan as the mushrooms that pop up after a warm spring rain. Some of these martial philosophers could back up their theories with impressive physical prowess and did so, in grueling training sessions where all comers were enthusiastically taken on. Yet there were many that would today be called "dojo bushi." They were warriors only in the safety of light practice and were at their best during long lecture sessions about the bujutsu where their ideas and musings about the art of the sword could develop comfortably, never tested by actual combat. Jubei hated these types. He suffered their prattle and restrained from criticizing in public the tracts they published on the subject. But finally, he'd had enough.

Jubei was particularly incensed by a theorist style of swordsmanship that had emerged in Edo. It was referred to as "passive swordsmanship." Waiting with drawn sword for an opponent to make a mistake, holding back to look for an opportunity; these were the characteristic techniques proposed by advocates of this style. To Jubei, such an approach was a corruption, an insulting bastardization of the Shinkage-ryu's principle of tai. Tai, or "waiting," was the concept of drawing an enemy into an attack so that an effective response could be used to cut him down. There are several methods of the ryu that exploit this kind of timing. Jubei was especially adept at adopting the strategy of tai and while the theorists claimed their passive fencing was an improvement on the principle of the Shinkage tradition, Jubei knew better. He applied to his student, the shogun Iemitsu, for permission to engage in a duel. Fighting of this nature was strictly forbidden without written approval from the government (although of course it flourished, carried out secretly at night or in remote locations), and Jubei was able to secure a go-ahead only after he reminded the shogun that such frippery as the passive art of fencing was being touted as a development inspired by the techniques of the Shinkage-ryu. The reputation of the Tokugawa's own martial ryu was being besmirched. That was all it took. Jubei got his permission to engage in a duel.

Jubei picked a gathering of swordsmen, seven of them, who were standing on a street corner in Edo. He launched a few insults to stir them up, then, when the group failed to be roused to a killing mood by his words, Jubei began spitting on them. It did the trick. The seven drew their katana *en masse*. Jubei responded. While they were settling into the waiting mode they had advocated, looking for an opportunity, Jubei slashed through the upraised arms of one, reversed his sword and chopped deeply into the shoulder of another. He severed the arm of one more of the group before the rest decided that an opening in Jubei's attacks was not likely in the immediate future. They ended the encounter by scrambling for their lives. Jubei had, in his own inimitable way, proven his point.

It would be a mistake to assume, based upon this incident, that Yagyu Jubei was entirely reckless or that he lacked a sense of morality. The tale of his challenge and lethal response to the "passive" swordsmen is recounted often as an example of his coolness in the face of danger and his swashbuckling character. But another episode in Jubei's colorful life is illustrative of a different, more sober aspect of his personality.

Jubei was paying a visit to an Edo daimyo at the same time another swordsman was at the daimyo's home as a guest. Naturally, the conversation turned to the art of strategy. The daimyo solicited the views of each of his visitors on the subject. And not unexpectedly, it was the daimyo who eventually suggested a match between the two so that they could demonstrate their arguments. Such friendly contests, conducted with bokuto, did have an element of danger about them. Sometimes participants would be killed, usually accidentally. If the fencers were competent and careful though, the results were usually not terribly unhealthy for either contestant. (Bruises and other contusions were as expected for the bugeisha as calluses on his writing hand were for the accountant. A good many of the top ranks of the warriors during the era of Yagyu Jubei were disfigured, afflicted with the problems caused by improperly set broken bones and other chronic injuries.)

The two crossed bokuto in the courtyard of the daimyo. Stillness, then motion, as both struck. Their wooden blades cracked together, startling the doves nesting in the topmost eaves of the daimyo's mansion. Both stepped back to readjust their distancing. They closed, and once again the courtyard resounded as their bokuto met, each cutting with what appeared to be equal speed and force.

Observing their match, that is what the daimyo thought. "A mutual strike," he announced.

Ai-uchi, attacks landed simultaneously, occurred frequently in duels. About one third of the time a bugeisha took up his sword to fight, he could expect to be hit just as his blow hit its target. Another third of such matches he fought he would be defeated cleanly, outclassed, having met an opponent who was simply better or luckier. Another third of his encounters would be an unscathed victory for him, according to the odds. All told then, a warrior had only one chance in three of surviving a fight to the death. One in three. These odds explained why the practice of dueling with bokuto instead of live blades became more popular during the Tokugawa era.

Jubei waved his hand. He turned to the swordsman. "How did these matches end?" he asked.

"They were draws," his opponent confirmed.

Jubei nodded his head. "I see," he said.

"Are you suggesting they were not draws?" the swordsman asked him sharply.

Jubei tried to mollify the man, but he was bluntly honest enough to say that he believed the swordsman still had some lessons to learn about his craft.

The daimyo and his guest took exception to Jubei's remark, naturally. They accused him of trying to talk his way out of face lost over the inconclusive matches. Jubei was indeed trying to talk his way out. But not out of losing face. He sought to avoid the inevitable, a demand for a real duel with katana. Such a duel, though, was inevitable, as such confrontations always are when men of lesser qualities respond with angry bravado instead of thoughtfulness and prudence in the face of a difficult situation. Jubei's opponent was furious. He insisted on a match that would end with an outcome that was beyond dispute.

With reluctance, Jubei agreed to the contest. He drew his sword. The fight was exactly like the two previous ones. The tips of two blades clicked together, a step here, there; searching for the kill spot, and then what appeared to be perfectly simultaneous overhead strikes... except this time there was no backing away after the blows had landed. The swordsman facing Jubei froze, his eyes wide, and then he stumbled back and fell, a bright freshet of crimson already staining the lapels of his outer kimono.

"In the true art of swordsmanship," Jubei said solemnly, "the distinction between life and death is measured in fractions." Then he showed the daimyo his own kimono. While his opponent had been cut with Jubei's sword penetrating about an inch into his chest, Jubei had only the outer fold of his kimono breast sliced open. The margin between victory and defeat, between life and the inert heap on the daimyo's courtyard, had been that close.

In his recollections, the third headmaster of the Yagyu Shinkage-ryu would regret the incident in the courtyard (unlike the duel he fought with the street-corner warriors who trusted in their passive swordsmanship, an encounter he deemed necessary for the benefit of the martial arts in general and the good name of the Shinkage-ryu in particular). Life was taken; Jubei mourned because his opponent was not skilled enough in his profession to recognize the subtle lesson Jubei was trying to impart in their first two contests.

A man who regretted a duel he could not really have avoided and who took pride in one he went out of his way to provoke—I was thinking of this, standing by Jubei's cedar, when a gust of wind hit. All day the breeze had been manic, unsteady and damp. It scraped through the dead white limbs at the top of the cedar, murmuring something I could not quite catch. There is a scattering of gravestones below the branches of the tree and there is a phalanx of stone statues of Jizo, the Buddhist guardian of farmers and children. Yagyu Jubei died in 1650, not far from this tree that, legend has it, he planted. He was on a hawking expedition outside Yagyu village when he suddenly took ill. He died not long after. Even in his death, mystery surrounds Jubei. He was only 43 at the time, and speculation that he was poisoned by rivals was immediately rumored. About much of his life historians have really nothing more than those kinds of rumors, vague clues that are subject to a variety of interpretations. Even senior members of the main lineage of the Shinkage-ryu, among them his descendants who have access to private sources regarding the clan, diaries and personal letters, have made little progress in uncovering the truth. They speculate, just I did on the hilltop across from the village that was Jubei's home. Flamboyant and secretive, bold to the point of impetuosity and dispassionately contemplative, Jubei was, above all else, an enigma.

The wind gusted again. The statues of Jizo were adorned with little red knit hats and bibs, gifts from mothers who had lost or aborted their babies. The bibs were ruffled by the gust. Suddenly, I wanted to be in the company of more recognizable companionship and among noises less ethereal. So I descended back down into Yagyu-zato to slurp a bowl of soba at a noodle shop, sharing a table with a crew of local highway maintenance workers.

Fortified by lunch and the colloquial conversation of the workers, I had time before my bus to walk down the central road through Yagyu-zato a ways, past the junior high school, to wander among the remnants of the once-fortified residence that had been home to the Yagyu family. Some of the living quarters of the mansion are still there, restored and kept as a museum. There was enough of the original inner architecture to see how rural gentility like the Yagyu barons lived, very similar to the manner in which their English equivalents lived on country estates in Essex, say, or Dover. Interesting. But there was a tale for me, one to be told where the main part of the mansion had originally stood. Of it and the battlements that once surrounded it, only the foundations remain. The mansion foundation is on a man-made plateau, grass covered earth, not so tall as the mountains encircling the village but well up above everything else in it. The fortified home—it could hardly have qualified as a castle, even when the Yagyu were in their glory—was built according to the principles of Shinkage-ryu heiho, situated to offer maximum protection from anyone seeking to attack it. It had withstood some minor assaults over the centuries. But it succumbed finally not to the ravages of war. It toppled from the inside, from decay and neglect, and that was the tale for me, the reason Sensei had me come alone here, and why I came last, after touring the rest of Yagyu-zato, to the ruins.

The Yagyu Shinkage-ryu is dated in origin from the time Yagyu Munetoshi attained complete mastery in the Shinkage tradition and was so certified by his teacher, Kamiizumi Nobutsuna, around 1570. Munetoshi fathered five sons (along with six daughters) and while normally the eldest of these, Yoshikatsu, stood to inherit the ryu after his father, Yoshikatsu was wounded in a battle while he was still young. Crippled, he was unable to take on the important position of headmaster. Another son was deemed unacceptable for the role for some reason; the next two in line chose the profession not of warrior but of priest. That left Munenori to assume the title of the second headmaster of the ryu. Under Munenori, of course, the Shinkage-ryu became favored by the Tokugawa shogun and so the focal point of instruction in the school shifted, from Yagyu village to the capital of Edo. That's where matters concerning the Yagyu Shinkage-ryu begin to get complicated. For while the ryu thrived in the capital, it was also still alive and well back in the hamlet of the clan outside Nara where it began.

Two centers of instruction; a single ryu. The prediction of an eventual schism would not require a psychic to make. Munenori's son Jubei became the third headmaster (around 1643) of what could be thought of as the Edo Yagyu Shinkage tradition. Yet while Munenori took the reins of the school from his father and passed them on to his son, Munenori's eldest brother, the crippled Yoshikatsu was, by law, the inheritor of the Yagyu lands and the rights of lineage. Yoshikatsu's son, Yagyu Hyogonosuke Toshitoshi, displayed a flair for the martial arts while still in his childhood. Taught by his father and his grandfather, Munenori, the young Toshitoshi mastered the techniques, the strategies, and the deepest secrets of the Shinkage-ryu. In 1615, armed with his katana and armor and a license of full mastery, Toshitoshi became a retainer of a cousin of the Tokugawa shogun, Tokugawa Yoshinao. Yoshinao was the daimyo of Owari, a province north of Nara and Yagyu-zato, and far south of, and away from, the influences of Edo. Toshitoshi instructed his lord in the martial disciplines and so began another line of the ryu, one that is called the Owari Yagyu Shinkage-ryu.

(This is even more complicated than it sounds. The original, main trunk of the Shinkage-ryu has an enormous number of branches and has provided the seeds for even more martial traditions that have germinated and matured under its canopy. Virtually every major classical martial art of Japan has experienced this sort of evolution and factionalization, with eventual distinctions in technique and strategy that are so subtle they are invisible to all but the expert. But probably no major combative ryu has provided a wider impetus for such growth than the Shinkage tradition.)

It is natural that a certain rivalry would be fostered between the big-city Edo Shinkage school and its country brother, the Owari faction. While technical distinctions between them were minor, not so their sensibilities. Separated by geography, the two were also different in their outlook on politics. That a martial arts ryu would have a political outlook may surprise those not familiar with Japanese history, those who suppose that the schools of fencing, spearmanship, and so on, were merely centers for instruction in these arts and nothing more. Not so. The martial ryu, while it was of course a means of preserving and passing on combative skills, was as well a political unit. Different ryu vied for the attention and patronage of powerful daimyo. The ryu were, in turn, used by military and political leaders. In the case of the Shinkage-ryu, political connections were obvious. It was the official school of strategy of the Tokugawa. Such a position was a powerful one and brought great status to the ryu. Still, it was not without pitfalls and dangers.

Despite the steel grip in which the Tokugawa government had clenched most of Japan for so long, its control was never complete or absolute. There were always daimyo, some of them quite influential, who supported a return of the rule of the emperor to Japan. Under the Tokugawa system, the emperor was mainly a figurehead, chosen from one of about five families by the shogun and his cabal. Emperors "ruled" only under the influence of the shogun and lived for the most part in seclusion and royal splendor that kept them away from the affairs of state. Encouraged by Confucian scholars and intellectuals who had always been a thorn in the Tokugawa side in their urging for a restoration of imperial government, there were always some dissident daimyo in Japan. From the 1700s onward, these daimyo became an increasing threat to Tokugawa hegemony.

Struggle between those daimyo in favor of retaining the order of the Tokugawa and those seeking a return of the emperor's leadership finally came to a head in the latter half of the nineteenth century. This was the period of the *bakumatsu* (the "end of the era of military government" is an awkward translation). After more than a dozen of its family leaders had ruled for a span of over two hundred years, the reign of the Tokugawa clan was dying. It was an agonizing period for Japan, broken once again by civil war. No one in the country felt the pain and anguish of the period more keenly than those of the Yagyu clan and many of the members of their ryu. The Edo and Owari branches of the ryu were splintered by their respective politics. Those in Edo, government officials and teachers of the shogun, were, not surprisingly, loyal to the

Tokugawa house. The Shinkage-ryu members in Owari Province, although they were also employed by cousins of the Tokugawa, were among the advocates demanding an overthrow of the regime and a restoration of some kind of government under imperial rule. Not all of the Tokugawa family favored the continuation of the shogun's power. One of them, Tokugawa Nariaki, was so outspoken in his opposition to it that he was finally arrested, in fact. Another opponent was the Tokugawa family daimyo of Owari, who became a prominent figure in the dissent against the shogun.

Always there had been an undercurrent of a feud lurking between the Edo and Owari factions of the ryu. Each could make claims that they were the "legitimate" Yagyu Shinkage-ryu and the other was only a branch from the trunk. The question of rule that divided Japan was a friction that ignited a kind of war between the factions. Duels were waged by swordsmen from Edo and Owari and other places. The results were deadly.

In short, the Yagyu Shinkage-ryu did to itself what no rival martial arts school had been able to accomplish. The ranks of the members of both the Edo and Owari schools were decimated. Some parts of the curriculum of the tradition, brought down largely intact since the fourteenth century, were lost entirely during the hostilities. Those who knew all of the methods and techniques died without passing them on. The prominence of the Yagyu Shinkage-ryu was ended.

The government of the Tokugawa shogun collapsed quietly. In 1867, the country became a constitutional monarchy. The emperor's power was restored, in a very limited way. It was the Meiji emperor, the grandfather of the late Hirohito, who led Japan in the period from 1867 to 1912. Some researchers of Japan's martial history have suggested that the Yagyu Shinkage-ryu, denied its patronage by the Tokugawa, was unable to maintain its martial vitality. This is an overstatement. The ryu continues today, as do many of its branches and offshoots, one of which was my own teacher's lineage. None of the three hundred or so classical ryu still practiced in Japan has the status they once did. Still, there is no denying that the Shinkage-ryu met with a precipitous decline. A reason for the decline was to be found, perhaps, in the ruins of the mansion in Yagyu village. The obaasan, the woman from the dry cleaning shop I'd met when I arrived in Yagyu-zato, had provided a clue for me, in a way, as she stood with me at the bus stop that afternoon as I was waiting for my ride back to Nara.

"Terrible thing about the mansion," she said. "It must've been beautiful once."

"What happened?" I asked her.

"Oh, back in samurai days, the mansion was quite grand," the obaasan said. "I wasn't there, you know. I'm not *that* old." And she gave me a toothless smile. "But I remember my grandmother talking about it. Anyway, once the samurai were gone, Japan got all caught up in becoming modern. Seems a lot of the old Japan was neglected until it just decayed away."

She was right, up to a point. The classical beauty of medieval Japan blooms tentatively in the soil of the present age. The mansion at Yagyu-zato did not crumble with the fall of feudalism, though. Not entirely. Its stone and mortar and beams tumbled down because its inheritors occupied themselves with matters of the moment, with politics and fame and other transitories that distract from the qualities of the timeless: courage, sincerity, gracefulness. Koyagyu, the mansion of the Yagyu, was destroyed not from forces without, but from within its walls. Those responsible for it disregarded the importance of kodomo tame ni. Their actions were not for the sake of generations to come, not for their children. They were selfish and shortsighted and it cost them dearly.

It was a tragedy, a shame I did not comprehend except in the most academic way, not until I was confronted with the remains of the Yagyu mansion.

"You look sad," the obaasan said.

"No, no, just thinking," I said. "I saw a lot here today."

And ghosts, the obaasan said. "That priest in Nara you mentioned this morning, the one who said there were so many ghosts here. Was he right?" Had I seen any ghosts in Yagyu-zato on this gloomy autumn day?

No, none, I told her. But I told the obaasan too, that I believed I'd felt the presence of one or two.

"They have anything to say to you?"

"Kodomo tame ni," I said.

"That's good," she said. Then the drizzle resumed and the ragged clouds dragged tattered curtains of mist over the mountain peaks around Yagyu-zato. The obaasan spread her umbrella above us until my bus came.

16
A Persimmon Wind

*H*ey!"

I hurried into the house. Sensei was jotting a shopping list at the table. Kaoru-san was reading the paper. Chiyoko, home early from work, was coming down from upstairs.

"How come you guys didn't bother to mention anything to me about the hurricane?" I asked.

"Typhoon," Sensei said.

"What?"

"In this part of the world, they're called typhoons," he said laconically.

"Whatever," I said.

I'd discovered that a typhoon was bearing down on the coast of Honshu, the main island of Japan where we were, as I was on the bus coming back from Yagyu-zato. A few stops after I got on the bus to take me back into Nara, a swarm of primary school children chattered aboard. It was way too early in the day for them to be out of class, but I knew it was hopeless to ask them why. They stared at me and gave me all the room they could, sitting as far from my seat as was possible. One intrepid young scholar finally crept to the seat ahead of me and proceeded to fix me with a gaze that lasted for several kilometers, the kind of look he would have given me if I had been the Elephant Man, until he finally got off at his stop. At last, a brazenly courageous girl ventured close enough to perch on the same seat with me, responding to the dares of some of her comrades. They hooted at her. One of them predicted, "He'll grab you!" So actually speaking to her, I knew, was not part of the program. A while later some high school students got on with us.

"How come you're out of classes so early in the day?" I asked one of them. He was as tall as I am, wearing the dark blue, stiff-collared Prussian uniform of a high school student. His black hair was studded up on his head, cut short.

"Because of the *taifu*," he said.

Tai fu, tai fu, I kept repeating the word in my head, trying to make sense of it. I was so accustomed to picturing unfamiliar Japanese words in the possible kanji used to write them that it took a moment for me to realize this was not entirely a foreign word.

Ohhh. Typhoon.

I grew up in the American Midwest. Dorothy Gale and Toto country. Tornadoes, violent thunderstorms: I knew these. My acquaintance with hurricanes — typhoons — was limited to the tales my father and his side of the family told of the epochal New England hurricane of 1938. Damage beyond calculation, entire towns swept clean of trees and roofs, ocean-going boats washed ashore and miles inland.

"I didn't think it was important enough to worry you with when you left this morning," Kaoru-san said casually. She turned a page of the newspaper.

Sensei grunted. "Most of the time these storms veer off before they get to us."

They were nonchalant. Sensei referred to it as a "storm." Nothing more. So I calmed down and even took a nap. Later, as the afternoon waned, he and I returned to the clearing by the Shinto shrine to train.

There were no new lessons for me. I had now to refine what I had learned and to demonstrate that I had learned it. It is a hallmark of the bujutsu that they are communicated, in their essence at least, at a level that is beyond words. A technique as simple as knocking away an opponent's sword, for instance, can be explained in a full hour's worth of lecture, dealing with the nuances of contacting the weapon at the critical moment when the opponent's hands are furthest from his body, applying a jolt of force at the right time to slam the sword down so viciously it can break the wrist of the man holding it. No matter how many words are spoken or written about it, though, the technique cannot be learned, truly learned, until it has been practiced, again and again, feeling the shock in one's arms when it is performed against you, and reproducing that same energy correctly when you are the performer. When you have done it ten thousand times, knocked away the sword in summer's heat and the bitterness of winter, when you have done it perfectly and feel you could do another hundred just as well, and when you have done the technique so poorly you despair of ever getting it right, then perhaps, if your training was good, you will have begun to learn it.

The world is full of experts in the analytical or theoretical sense of that word. They are authorities on military tactics although they have never had a shot fired at them. Childless psychologists speak endlessly and write books on the art of raising youngsters. The bugeisha respects analysis, values theory. But he recognizes that such knowledge is etic in nature, knowledge outside and untempered by actual physical experience. He knows too, that a culture (or a person), if it is to have complete balance and diversity, must be complemented by a dose of the emic, the sweat, the pain, the pure expression of energy and motion.

Sensei and I were joined in communication of a kind that was not verbal. We expressed a language that did not deal in the abstract of words or symbols. Learning, in the scholarly sense, was secondary in our practice. Absorption at the visceral level was the primary goal. Maybe later we would discuss what we had done. For now, what mattered was to *do*, to experience directly — action unencumbered, undistilled. It is important for modern man and vital to the maturation of the martial artist to immerse himself periodically in this kind of activity. He needs to put aside temporarily the concepts and words and ideas, to act instead from the core of the physical self. True, a society without concepts and abstract ideas and the means of expressing them symbolically is no society at all, or at least not a civilized one. But what can we say of a society that disdains the immediate physical exertions that once occupied our ancestors through much of their waking hours? When we relegate those activities to the status of "fun" what do we lose?

Our practice went on, working our way again through the sets of kata that comprise the teachings of the ryu. There was no need to speak. Finally, when Sensei did give voice, it was in the form of the roaring "Haaaaahhhh!" that is the kiai specific to the Shinkage-ryu, unleashed only in some of the advanced kata. When he shouted, as if in echo came a reply. It was the rumbling of thunder, tumbling and tolling on the other side of the furthest mountains that we could see, distant, from a storm still a hundred miles offshore that had begun to roll long breakers against the shore at the port city of Osaka, to our south.

"What are you *doing?*"

"Falling off the roof," I answered Sensei. That was very nearly true. It was the next morning, after stories of the typhoon were starting to dominate news broadcasts, and he and I were teetering up on the house roof, fitting heavy storm shutters over the windows on the second story. It was a moderately tricky business. The pitch of the roof was serious. Hard gusts of wind punched unexpectedly and crazily, from different directions. The curved blue tiles were rain-slick. The shutters were unwieldy, wooden rectangles with grooved tops and bottoms, and which was which was far from clear to me. We took them from their storage bin in a shed by the house and Sensei, from the top rung of a ladder leaned against the eaves, passed them up to me on the roof. He went back inside when we'd gotten them all stacked above a hipped gable and then came out through a window to join me. While I waited for him, I realized I had a rare opportunity before me… or to be more exact, an opportunity *above* me. I hoisted one of the larger shutters and climbed higher, to the ridgeline of the main roof.

In his autobiography, Gichin Funakoshi, the Okinawan karate master who introduced his art to Japan in the 1920s, wrote of an incident from his early years, while he was still living on Okinawa. A typhoon bore down on the island and Funakoshi, always alert for a chance to train his body, decided to crawl up on the roof of his home, carrying a tatami floor mat with him to face the raging storm. Holding the tatami before him like a shield, Funakoshi took a strong stance, braced against the gale, to test the strength and tenacity of his posture.

Well, how many times does a fellow have a chance to be atop a roof in the preliminary blows of a typhoon, with a tatami-sized piece of wood handy? I only hesitated a couple of seconds before giving it a try—and I lasted roughly twice that long against the first blast of wind. For an awful second I had the sensation of being lifted up, the image of the shutter transformed into a giant kite that would take me flying right down the valley. Then I was skidding down the slope of the roof, trying to hold on to the shutter with one hand and grabbing at the wet tiles with the other. My slide didn't take me very far before I stopped myself. But the clatter I'd made did not go unnoticed. Kaoru-san stuck her head out from a window in the kitchen below me.

"*Ara!*" she yelled. "We've got some crazy monkey running around on the roof!"

Without further incident, Sensei and I fixed the shutters into place. Finished with the chore and with my stance practice for the time being, we took a break. We were roosted on the ridgeline of the roof's peak. The whole of the narrow valley stretched out below us. Amidst the canopy of golden maple and the rich, blue-green of the pines, I could pick out the houses of the neighbors. The Suzuki, the Okawara, and down at the foot of the hill where the asphalt lane curved off towards the city of Nara, was Hori-guchi obaasan's place. I saw her bent figure, shuffling back and forth in her yard, directing the efforts of a couple of the Suzuki's five sons who had come over to shutter her house against the storm. Behind us, Ito-san had closed over his windows the same way and was moving grids of bamboo lattices that had supported his gourd vines all summer, getting them into the lee of his house where they would be out of the wind. The neighborhood was battening down, tucking things away, securing their property against what was to come. Getting ready.

Past Horiguchi-san's house another hill pushed up abruptly against the horizon. It wore a furry coat of pines that were almost black underneath the reflection of what had become a gauzy gray sky that shifted with a restless, erratic motion. The clouds lumbered and bulged in places, drooping as if the whole sky was becoming too heavy to bear its own weight.

The wind went on, ripping about sporadically. But the periods of calm were, for the moment, longer. A soft thin little breeze funneled up through the mountainsides. It came on like the scent of a wine wafting from the lip of the glass and it brought with it aromas that were at once mingled and yet distinct enough I could sort out some of them: the moist, fertile bouquet of pine needle mulch and leaf mold; the smoky, pungent prick of rice straw stubble being burned somewhere; the cider tang of apples just past full ripe and mellowing now, their skins turning leathery, their juice frothy and amber. It was the smell of autumn. Of nature and man poised at the axis point of another season's cycle. All the smells of October in that part of Japan were blended together and then chilled as the earth cooled and the breeze carried them up to me. Along with the smell of wet humus and dry, dusty grasses gone to seed, the wind brought pensive thoughts, tinged with shibui, of the possibilities of life that were lost to time, of paths not taken, and of those I had taken that were all too soon coming to an end. I was filled with the "melancholy of an autumn even" of which the poet Ietaka had written, the sense of poignancy that has inspired the poets of haiku for generations.

"A persimmon wind," Sensei said. A wind bittersweet.

When visitors had dropped by a few evenings earlier, I'd gone without being told to into the kitchen to boil water for tea. That was one of the chores of the deshi, the student in the home of any Japanese teacher, and that is how I would see myself always in relation to the man who sat on the cold wet roof beside me, no matter what else in life I did. A wind seasoned with the tannin fruit of persimmon reminded me that I was other things as well now though, had responsibilities elsewhere. I would be leaving soon to take them up again. But the scent of autumn's "cold melancholy" drifting on the breeze brought an infusion of sights and smells and sensations that were all the more precious because they were so ephemeral. They made me yearn to hold on to a moment, to do nothing more than to sit here with my sensei, for just a little while longer.

The weather reports monitored the eye, now well-developed, of the typhoon. It was sitting and staring, almost stationary, off the southeast coast of Honshu, right beside the island of Shikoku. To me, it looked on the radar screen on the TV news like the eye of a malevolent water beast that was prowling offshore and searching unblinkingly for a weakness of the land to rush against and attack. That night was to be my last opportunity to train in iaido at the Genyokan Dojo. So, betting we would be home again before the main body of the storm hit, if it was going to hit us, we left for the dojo, Chiyoko-san and I, and Sensei accompanied us. I was mildly surprised. Sensei practiced iaido occasionally, but the bulk of his training was devoted to the older forms of the Shinkage-ryu.

The pavement was glistening, slippery from another shower that burst hard and quick and then was gone and once, as we came around a bend exposed to the wind, a blow snatched at the Nissan. We shimmied, skating over the asphalt until the tires bit for purchase into the road surface. If the typhoon strikes here, I asked, will the wind get worse than that? From the back seat, Chiyoko-san made a sound between a laugh and a groan. She had been through typhoons before. Sensei, driving, just said, "Yes."

"No, no, nooohhh!"

Koyomi-san was again demonstrating her command of English for me. Her verbosity was occasioned by my *tatehiza*. Tatehiza is a way of sitting, the "standing knee" squat. It calls for the swordsman to sit with his left leg tucked beneath him so the side of his heel is squarely below the crease of his buttocks. The right leg he bends fully with the knee pointing up, nearly vertical. Tatehiza was a method the warrior could use to sit while wearing armor. Maybe in the full-throttle release of adrenaline that war calls for, the samurai didn't notice it, but while tatehiza is practical, allowing rapid movement in every direction and lets him use his sword quickly at the same time to attack or defend, it is a remarkably uncomfortable position to take for any period longer than a couple of seconds. Left alone, the iaido practitioner will adopt all kinds of bad habits related to his practice of tatehiza. Koyomi-san was determined to correct mine. So she was being particularly critical of the section of iaido kata I was working on, the movements of the Eishin-ryu. The Eishin-ryu is one of the schools of iaido that has been collected under the larger Muso Shinden-ryu, the style of iaido practiced at the Genyokan. The kata of the Eishin-ryu are all performed beginning in the tatehiza position.

"This is the wrong angle for my knee to be raised, isn't it?" I asked, when there was a pause in her string of corrections.

"Yes," she said. "How did you know?"

"It was too comfortable."

Koyomi-san gave me half of a smile. I was half serious. After two decades of involvement in the traditional Japanese arts and ways, I was still a beginner. I was, however, far enough along to recognize that of all of them, from the budo and bujutsu to chado to *shodo* calligraphy, all of them place an emphasis on sitting correctly.

To "sit squarely" or *zashikko*, was an admonition from the old days in Japan, a time when daily life there was lived, for the most part, directly on the ground or very near it. The Japanese slept with only a thin futon between themselves and the tatami floor. They spent their waking hours, when sitting, on the same surface. If he was a craftsman, then in all likelihood most of his work, carpentry, weaving, pottery, was accomplished in a crouching or sitting position. Even today, a great many artisans in Japan ply their trades in the same way. Swordsmiths, kite-makers, bamboo carvers, tatami weavers—all work seated on the floors of their shops.

The ramifications of sitting on the floor as a daily habit are much wider than might be immediately apparent. The Japanese, spending so much time close to the ground, evolved a sense of balance and of strength that was distinct from those concepts as they are understood in the West. To the Westerner, balance is centered in the chest and shoulders; strength emanates from the same place. His sports, boxing, baseball, and the like, tend to emphasize upper body mechanics. When he makes an all-out effort, he "puts his shoulder to the wheel." His work is on a bench or a table and he tackles it sitting on a chair or standing. The Japanese pictures his balance centered in his hips and belly. Historically, he prefers sumo and its wrestlers with their massive waists and loins. When an extra umph is needed, he will *tanden ni chikara wo ireru*, or "put his strength in his hips." Put another way, the Westerner tends to idealize physical power as broad shoulders and narrow hips, an inverted triangle. The Japanese is apt to personify the same attribute with narrow, sloping shoulders and a thick, muscular middle: a pyramid. Rodin's *The Thinker* sits on a pillar to think, head resting on his fist. The great Buddha of Kamakura meditates cross-legged on the ground, hands low in front of his abdomen.

Tatehiza, sitting with one leg tucked and the other poised to push up; the method of seiza with both legs under the hips; *kyoshi* or *iaigoshi*, the combative crouch of the classical bugeisha: these are the ways of seating oneself in iaido. None are comfortable until after many years of practicing them. And even a master cannot assume tatehiza for very long before his legs begin to throb and ache. Each of these ways of sitting, though, allows the practitioner a balance and power that comes directly from the ground below him, which is uniquely Japanese, I think. I suspect as well that the very effort and suffering required to take these seated postures is a salient feature of the arts and ways of Japan. The pain of tatehiza, like seiza and the other forms, must be borne in absolute stillness and with a calm sense of zanshin. It builds a particular form of toughness. It is not the kinetic stamina of action. It is placid endurance. To be able to sit with balance and more, with dignity, is perhaps not the goal of the iaido adept, yet it distinguishes the skilled among his ranks as certainly as it does the expert craftsman or the artist of Japan who labors constantly in intimate contact with the earth.

Koyomi-san and I were resting along the side of the dojo practice floor, while some of the other members took their turns. Among them was my sensei, who was practicing the *oku-iai*, the deepest level of the Eishin-ryu of iaido. These kata are devoted to techniques for unsheathing and using the katana under difficult or unusual circumstances. Hemmed in from above by a low ceiling or some other hindrance overhead, the kata *tanashita* teaches a way to get the blade out and to strike effectively from a position where it is poised, laid resting right along the spine of the crouching swordsman. *Moniri* deals with the problem of enemies rushing to attack through a narrow door where a wide, horizontal cut would be useless. The oku-iai are as complex and demanding as iaido gets. Their timing must be flawless. Watching Sensei go through them was a lesson I would remember long after his katana had clicked home into his saya for the last time that evening. Koyomi-san nudged me.

"You see, timing is everything," she said. "Do it correctly and it is never slapdash, but also never too slow."

I translated, as best I could, Goethe: "Do not hurry, do not rest."

Koyomi-san's eyes brightened. "How do you say *hai* in English?" she asked me.

"Yes."

"Yes, yes, yes!"

My senior at the Genyokan had just doubled her command of English. But before I could congratulate her, the lights of the dojo blinked, flickered, then died. In the sudden shadowy silence I heard the wind coming again. I had forgotten all about it during the training session, concentrating on my practice. It was a wailing sound now, a keening that seemed pitched just this side of the human range of hearing. Candles were produced from somewhere, and a couple of flashlights. By the makeshift illumination we hastily closed the session and mopped the dojo floor.

On a clear, quiet night, the walk back down the mountainside upon which the Genyokan sat was something of a feat if one did not know the path well. It ran over mossy stones and steep steps, the trail zigzagging without warning. In the spiraling edges of a typhoon, the walk was like taking a stroll off the lip of the world. The boughs of cryptomeria above the footpath had lost their soughing. They hissed now and whipped frantically overhead, as if that far-off wailing was a sound terrifying even to the trees of the forest here. The sky was ripped and manic. Except for the *fzzzt* of lightning that twisted out of it, we were surrounded in a blackness so intense that when I paused for a moment and Sakunami-san in front of me got a few paces ahead, he simply disappeared. I looked down. It was so dark I could not see the path at all. I couldn't even see my *feet*. Gingerly, I ventured a step. Then another, trying to feel through the soft rubber soles of my zori where the natural paving stones gave way to the cleanly cut slabs of granite that indicated we had reached another section of steps. A stumble on those stone stairs, I knew, could mean more than a skinned knee. The incline on the outside borders of parts of the trail, had a skier been poised on them, would have deserved the black diamond of the expert's slopes. When I finally caught up with Sakunami-san, he turned around. I could tell he had, not because I saw him do it, but because his voice was closer now than if he had been speaking over his shoulder.

"Not a good idea to be wandering around by yourself up here," he said. "After all, there is a typhoon on the way."

"Okay," I replied with as much élan as I could muster. But I accepted his offer to grab on and for the rest of the hike down to the road I held onto the end of his sword bag, which he had tipped over his shoulder to me.

A compact truck outfitted with revolving lights and the insignia of the Nara prefectural civil defense was waiting for us by the cars we had parked by the roadside earlier in the evening. I wondered if they'd just happened to arrive when we got there, but when one of the men got out and came over I saw he was dressed in the uniform of a police officer and I knew it was no coincidence. There is not much the police in Japan do not know about the comings and goings of a community or the neighborhood where they are assigned. I was sure the training schedule at the Genyokan was available to them. The officer bowed his head with a quick snap. He had some bad news, he was sorry to say. The road going to the left was closed a few kilometers down.

"A rock fall," he said. "The road is covered with some rather large boulders."

Tengu, I thought. The shrieking we'd heard earlier, up on the mountain. The cliff above the highway didn't give way because the soil was saturated with all the rain we'd had. The rocks were spilled down the cliff by the same devious winged goblins that had once tumbled boulders into the rice fields around here. It was a conclusion not so difficult to come by, not with the treetops tossing and the swirling, furious skies and all that blackness.

"Do any of you need to be going that way?" the officer asked.

Some of us did, but all could manage to find suitable detours except two. Sakunami-san and Koyomi-san were both stranded. The road they both lived on was in between the closed section. The officer sucked in his breath. A crew with heavy equipment would be brought up from Nara as soon as the danger of the typhoon had passed. Until then...

"You both should stay with us," Sensei said.

I leaned against the car. This would take a while, I knew. In the country, visitors invited over just for tea would accept only after a series of elaborate refusals and counter-invitations. There was really nothing else either Sakunami-san or Koyomi-san could do other than to spend the night with us, as everyone concerned understood. But both had to go through the motions, motions that could not and would not be suspended, even in the face of a typhoon that could, for all we knew be readying to flatten the house where they were being invited to stay.

Sensei's house was still standing when we finally arrived, all five of us, and as we did, I saw the structure as it must have looked a generation ago. A lantern glowed, left on a landing halfway up the steps, to illuminate them. The genkan door was cracked open, beckoning with a skinny shaft of yellow light.

Kaoru-san had switched the radio's power source over to its batteries and we all trooped inside, shaking off the wet, in time to hear reports of a cargo ship driven ashore by the storm at Osaka. Trains all over the southern half of the country were idle, the radio said; stranded passengers were interviewed as they prepared to bed down in stations. Sleeping arrangements at our household were more commodious. There were plenty of futons and more than enough floor space. Our immediate problem was informing Sakunami-san's brother and sister-in-law with whom he lived, and Koyomi-san's husband that they were safe and with us for the night. The nearest telephone still operating was probably at a local police box. It was two miles away. Driving there was out of the question. The car, boxed about by the wind, had slewed danger-ously on the way home from the dojo, and interspersed in the radio accounts of the typhoon's fury were warnings, among them strict admonitions to stay off the roads.

"It'll be quicker to walk anyway," Sensei said. He told us to cut through the rice fields and the forest behind the house on a trail that led past the site of the Shinto shrine where he and I had been training. The trail emerged onto the highway near the police box. We would be protected from the brunt of the storm most of the way, Sakunami-san and I reasoned, by the shoulders of the hills. And we were; protected from the brunt, that is. But the winds of a typhoon, as I discovered about four steps from the door, churn and whirl and seem to come from every direction at once. Even baffled by the hillsides, the punching of the wind was literally staggering. A fast crack caught us from behind, a big slapping hand that shoved me hard between my shoulders. I stumbled forward, feet dragging behind me. It was like walking in a riptide surf. In the dark.

"You have to crouch when the big blows hit," Sakunami-san advised. So we made our way, walking and crouching, and while I thought this job of just moving forward was really quite enough to keep me occupied, Sakunami-san unloosed a narrative of local ghost stories. Over beyond those ridges there was a farmhouse where a case of fox spirit possession had occurred just before the war. The spirit of a demonic fox entered into the body of a farmer and had to be exorcised by a priest. Right up here where the trail crosses the road at the bend lurked a specter on certain dark summer nights, a woman who in her natural life was jilted by a married lover and then murdered by him right on the spot. Japanese ghosts run toward the hideous and malevolent, the doings of their demons and ghouls ghastly and grisly. "Chicken skin," the Hawaiians call tales of things that go *butsukaru* in the night—a good description. The flesh on my arms pimpled as much from the stories as from the rain that soaked through my sweater and jeans.

Our flashlights beamed punily against the vast darkness and once our eyes adjusted, we clicked them off. Black as the sky was, it pulsed with an eerie light that we could see well enough by, but which also turned the landscape into a series of grotesque shapes, made grasping bony fingers of the bamboo and shadowy shuffling creatures of the trees that lurched and danced.

"What about the deserted temple over by the dojo?" I asked. "Chiyoko-san said you knew how it became abandoned." Sakunami-san said he did and he told me the story, punctuated by the clap and rumble of thunder and the brilliant strobes of lightning.

Now it is long ago, Sakunami-san began, but there was a time when the temple, small as it was, he said, flourished. For longer than anyone could remember, an order of monks of the Tendai sect of Buddhism had lived and worshipped at the temple. It had been longer ago than anyone could remember too, when the devout monks had a more devout leader than their abbot. Pious and devoted to his calling, the abbot never missed a service, never failed to have an academic answer for the thorniest question regarding the laws of the Buddha.

Had it been any priest other than the abbot then, eyebrows would not have been raised when he began to consort with a young and beautiful girl. Not exactly consorting, it was. The girl appeared mysteriously one late winter morning, seeking religious instruction. The abbot obliged her. A week later she returned with more questions. The week after that she was back again. Her visits became regular and no one thought it odd that she and the abbot spent afternoons strolling in the woods, discussing spiritual matters.

In their talks, the girl learned much of the Tendai faith, for no one knew it better than the abbot. He, on the other hand, learned very little about his beautiful student except that she was the daughter, she said, of a wealthy baron who lived beyond that mountain over there. It was off in that direction that she would depart at dusk each time she said good-bye, and watching her slim form disappear into the evening mists, the abbot felt a stirring within that he had not experienced for many a year. The relationship between the young girl and the pious abbot continued through the spring, into the heat of midsummer. And as sometimes happens despite a man's devotion to the Buddha, the abbot became a bit less pious, the girl a bit more comely to him. They fell in love — or at least into a serious case of lust. The abbot and the girl slipped into one another's arms on an afternoon walk and despite her youth, the girl was energetic and inventive. Despite his piety, before they'd left the forest that day, the abbot was already longing for another encounter. He had it with her the next week and then the week after and then the girl was in his embrace again, except this time her passion was anguish. She was pregnant. Worse, her father knew, and knew the abbot was responsible. Worse still, he was threatening to expose the sordid liaison and reveal the abbot as a letch.

Frantic, the abbot sought a way to keep his transgression a secret. Her father was a greedy man, the girl suggested. If there was something of value with which to buy his silence, she hinted, something like that silver statue of the Buddha in the abbot's quarters… Take it, the abbot said immediately. It is too small to be missed by anyone else at the temple, he said, but its silver might placate her father. The statue was not missed. Neither was a chalice or a scroll that left under the girl's kimono on her next two visits. But her father's avarice seemed endless, she told the abbot, and so by summer's end the treasures of the temple were all gone, carried off by the beautiful girl to her home over the mountain.

The abbot, as men are wont to do when they have been led gradually down a road that reaches its destination only with the total destruction of their soul, realized all of a sudden what he had done to himself and his temple. When the girl next appeared, he took her to his quarters to show her that nothing of the temple's wealth remained. Nonsense, she insisted. There must be more. She jumped about the room, peering into closets, climbing to look in the space above the ceiling. In her exertions, the abbot noticed what had until then escaped his attention entirely. Despite her claim to be pregnant, she was as slim and agile as she had been when he'd first seen her last winter. Where was the swelling of her belly? As the answer dawned, the abbot was horrified. The pregnancy, the greedy father—it was all a swindle, all a lie. At that moment, consumed by rage and by guilt, the abbot seized his duplicitous lover by her slender throat and he strangled her. His own throat he then slashed, a murder-suicide. That is the way the two would be found was his last thought… almost his last thought, that is. For in his dying, the abbot rolled his head to gaze a last time at the woman who had brought such pleasure and misery into his life, and he saw that she was changing. Even in death, she was transmogrifying into something that magnified his horror a thousand times over...

In Japan there is an animal of the deep forests. It looks like a cross between a raccoon and a dog, called a *tanuki,* and today, most Japanese and nearly all visitors are most likely to see only taxidermy specimens that, wearing the straw hat and carrying the staff of the traveler, seem to decorate noodle restaurants and other such businesses all over the country. The tanuki is a mysterious beast. Many of the biological details of its natural life are still unknown. The tanuki is most famous in folklore for his inordinate fondness for sake and for his legendary ability to play his roly-poly stomach like a drum. (Well, the truth is, it's his large testicles he supposedly plays. Some Japanese legends, like some of our own, have been cleaned up some for modern consumption.) Myth also credits the tanuki with an ability to assume the shapes and identities of humans. In a famous Kabuki play, a tanuki transforms into a handsome young man and his true identity is revealed only when sake is served and in his excitement, the tanuki's tail begins wagging vigorously, coming out from beneath the folds of his kimono. In a children's tale, a tanuki shifts into the form of an obaasan whom he has killed. Then he feeds her for dinner to her unsuspecting husband.

An acolyte at the temple came to summon the abbot to evening vespers and that is when the abbot was discovered, sprawled lifeless on the tatami of his room. Beside him was a dead tanuki, wrapped in the scarlet and blue kimono of a young girl.

The wealth of the temple was gone. The bizarre suicide of its abbot frightened off parishioners. Before long, the monks abandoned the place too, muttering as they left about the wraith they'd glimpsed in the still hours of darkness, wandering about the temple searching — searching, it seemed, for something that was missing.

I started to ask why the tanuki, if he could turn himself into a girl, couldn't turn himself just as easily into a pregnant girl, but Sakunami-san concluded his story before I could get out my question. "I asked my grandfather—he's the one who told me that tale—if he thought it was true about the tanuki and the abbot."

"What'd he say?"

"He said no, he didn't. But he also told me that when he was cutting wood up on that mountain over there he never went by a tanuki den without looking to see if there was a temple's treasures hidden away inside it."

While we were gone to make the phone calls, Kaoru and Chiyoko put together a meal of rice and pickled vegetables to stretch the dinner of *oden* stew to feed the two extra mouths. The radio announced that the eye of the typhoon had curved away from the southern shore of Honshu. The full force of the storm would only nick us, striking a glancing blow. If we were getting an indirect hit that night, I thought, I'd hate like hell to be on the receiving end of its fully concentrated force. An hour earlier, the bullying of the wind had been enough to shove Sakunami-san and me around on our walk to the phone. Now the gusts were jarring the whole house. The beams complained, groaning, the walls shuddering periodically as if trying to shrug off the onslaught of the storm. But the typhoon was relentless. The rain had come, raking in horizontal volleys against the windward side of the house, penetrating the outer and then the inner shutters, seeping in through cracks where I would not have thought a razor blade could have been pushed through. We took turns stuffing towels along the edges of the wooden hallway floors to sop up the water that was rapidly pooling there.

When we weren't tending to the house, Sensei climbing up to peer into the attic to check for water there, the rest of us searching for and stanching new streams and rivulets that sprung up all over, we sat around the table in the kitchen and drank barley tea. We were in candlelight. Chiyoko-san and I listened to the conversation for the most part. The conversation tacked in one direction and then another. The really *big* storm they had, what was it now, twenty years ago? The one where the Suzukis lost half their roof. The intertwined economic future of Japan and the rest of Asia. The technical details of fox spirit possession. A written transcript of the talk would have been insufficient. To truly get a sense of it would require a recording. The words and sentences on paper could not capture the fluid idioms, the fluid homey phrases of the rural Japanese dialect that was being spoken. It has to be heard to be fully appreciated. When I first arrived at Sensei's home, I had gulped it in long draughts and swallows. Now, satiated, I rolled the language around on my tongue, relished its vintage on my ear the way a wine lover does with a splash of old Burgundy in his mouth. And just as the wine bottle is emptied in lingering sips, slowly we all fell silent, fell under the spell that is woven by a candle's flicker in a big, dark house. It was, as the novelist Tanizaki put it, "the wavering candlelight, announcing the drafts that find their way from time to time into the room, luring one into a state of reverie." And so we finally blew out the twitching flames and all trooped upstairs to sleep.

Even if Sakunami-san's gentle snores did not drone intermittently, I would not have slept well in my room, which I was sharing with him. The sounds of the typhoon were varied, sometimes a roar, other times almost a screeching howl, but they never stopped. There was never anything that could be called a lull, only a change in the pitch or frequency of the unbelievable wind. It screamed about outside, prying and uncovering a chink in the shutters. Then it would slither in and all the shoji screens on that side of the house would be set rattling madly. The whole skeleton of the house creaked. Lightning whickered. Something, a branch perhaps, slapped with a wet smack against the roof and skittered across it. Sakunami-san's breathing jumped at the sound. He rolled over and flung his arm over his head. No one could have slept very deeply. I recognized the pad of Kaoru-san's footsteps along the hallway. Then unfamiliar ones that must have belonged to Koyomi-san. Then, a moment later, Sensei's. The sounds of tea being made came up to me from downstairs. I dozed, then woke later on at a knock. The inside shoji to my room slid open a sliver.

"I'm going downstairs for some tea." Chiyoko-san. "Want some?"

Chiyo-san and I made a potful of *genmaicha* that smelled of sweet new tatami mats and tasted musty and country-plain. It was late, well past midnight. We'd been in the dark, without electricity so long now that we could see our way around the kitchen easily. We took our cups of tea into the room at the rear of the house and sat side by side on the mats at the table. This room, the first I'd entered when I came to Sensei's house, held the family Shinto kamiza on a shelf on the wall. The zigzag paper *gohei* streamers that hung from the bottom of the altar shelf were rustling and swaying in the drafts. The house was chilly. Chiyoko-san pulled her yukata closer around her.

Chiyoko fascinated me. She was very different from most Japanese girls her age. She had taken up kendo when she was in high school, a rare choice of hobby for a girl. The art must have triggered some martial chromosome handed down by her Matsunaga ancestors. The typical female college graduate in Japan takes some kind of secretarial or clerical job and then begins scouting for a husband. Most young women in Japan are noted for their perfection of *kawaii*—"cuteness." Chiyoko was cute, but when a lot of those other women had traded their kawaii for a middle-aged dreariness, I suspected she would become beautiful. She was saving her money in the hopes of one day going into business for herself, owning her own silk fabric shop. One of her grandfathers had been a silk merchant and she wanted to revive the family tradition. Chiyoko-san had chosen too, to pursue the path of the classical bugeisha, which set her apart not just from the average woman her age but from the majority of modern Japanese as well. I wondered where this path would lead her.

"You know, Sensei went with us to the dojo tonight..." She paused. "It was because he is proud of you, and because he is going to miss you when you leave us."

"I know that. You know I know that."

Chiyoko nodded.

"If I had been Japanese, you would never have told me that. You would have assumed I knew it without having to talk about it."

She nodded again. "But you're not Japanese."

"No, I'm not."

"But you are not American, either," she added.

"Yes, I am, Chiyo-chan. I am completely American."

"At your home, you told me that you and your wife sleep on a futon, on tatami," she said. "You write, you do your work every day at a *tsukue* desk, sitting on the floor. You go to a dojo every morning. Tell me, how many Americans live like that?"

"You might be surprised," I said. "But that's all beside the point, isn't it? Those are not the things that make anyone Japanese. Eating with chopsticks, wearing a hakama; that doesn't make you Japanese. You know that."

"No, of course not. But there's more to you than just that," she replied. "We've talked about sabi and wabi. You understand shibui. Could I have conversations about things like that with the average American?"

"No," I admitted, "not using those words. But there are more Americans than you might think who are sensitive to the concepts behind those words, even if they don't know the terms themselves. Sabi, wabi, shibui: those are Japanese words but the concepts they describe are not some kind of exclusive property of your country."

Chiyoko pressed the spigot of the thermos to add hot water to the tea pot, then she poured some of the fresh brew into my cup. "Okay," she said, "then what is it that brought you to Japan?"

To see our teacher, and Kaoru-san, and to meet her, I said.

"But even if we hadn't been here," she pressed, "you would have come, wouldn't you?"

Yes, I said. I told her about walking past the house on the quiet street where Sensei and Kaoru had lived when I learned under his instruction, about the old gymnasium floor where he and I had practiced together, which was now splintered and gone; about the changes in the millrace where I'd undergone the Shinto ritual of misogi beneath the waterfall. I told her about all the memories of those places that were lost now. I told Chiyoko too about the sounds I'd imagined that seemed to be urging me to come to Japan, the clatter of bamboo, the crack of the Noh chanter's clappers, the click of my Sensei's bokuto against my own. And the rattle of ancient bones… "I needed to hear those sounds in Japan," I finished.

"*Wakatta*," Chiyo-san murmured. "I understand." There was more that could be said between us, yet nothing more needed to be said. Not right then. We listened to the rain, still hammering, though without such dreadful velocity, and to the wind, which chattered in the shoji upstairs and down but which no longer jolted the house. The typhoon was blowing itself out somewhere off to the west, out over the Sea of Japan. When we got up to go back to sleep, our legs stiff, our teacups cold, Chiyoko said quietly, "I think the sound you needed to hear in Japan was the beating of your own heart."

I slipped under the fat fluffy *kakebuton* counterpane. The futon still held a lingering outline of my body heat. The typhoon mumbled and thrashed, growing more and more impotent as the night went on. The sky must have already been clearing, in fact, because later, around four in the morning—the Hour of the Tiger by the old way of reckoning—I heard a hooting, just as I fell asleep. It was the cry of the gray owl that I'd first heard in the woods going up to the Genyokan Dojo. He must have been flying over the house, from the sound of his call. I went to sleep with an image of the view I knew he had, flapping silently over the houses in our valley, pines and bamboo groves and the bare autumn fields below.

17
A Fall of Golden Leaves

$\mathcal{W}$e trained together again before I left, Sensei and I, in the clearing in the woods in front of the community Shinto shrine. The sky was scrubbed clean by winds gone high aloft in the wake of the departed typhoon; it was wide and flawless, a deep bright azure. The ground, against my bare feet, was cold and springy with a carpeted litter of pine needles and mounds of damp, fallen leaves.

We went over the most basic and some of the middle level kata. Sensei challenged with his bokuto; I responded until he was satisfied enough with my answers to call a halt to the practice. We bowed to one another and to the kami of the shrine. The kami had no more to say than did my sensei. He offered no parting profundities, no encouragement towards "graduating" from the ryu. The way of the bugeisha culminates only at the conclusion of his life. All else is a journey to ever-receding destinations. There can be no final lesson, no ultimate secret to reveal. While one might master the technical range that comprises a martial koryu, there is always more to learn, more broadly and deeply to go. There is for the bugeisha, only more practice, and a steady refining of the spirit. For now, however, we had finished. Our more immediate destination was the rice and pickled vegetables and grilled trout that Kaoru-san was setting out for dinner.

Sensei led the way home, climbing up the path. The sunlight was dappled and muted where the foliage closed in over us. I followed. I paused at a bend in the path to turn back for a last glimpse of the shrine and the torii arch in front of it and I saw them for an instant, against the backdrop of the mountains and hills of Nara Prefecture. And then a breeze, a persimmon wind, quivered the big birches on either side of the trail, shaking loose their splendid cloaks. And all I saw of the valley and of Japan was a fluttering shower-fall of bright, golden leaves.